Tangl

English for Lawyers and Law Students

English for Lawyers and Law Students

With a Short Introduction to the US Legal System

Mag. Dr. Astrid Tangl

3., aktualisierte und erweiterte Auflage 2014

Zitiervorschlag: *Tangl*, English for Lawyers and Law Students³ (2014), Seite.

Bibliografische Information der Deutschen Nationalbibliothek

Die Deutsche Nationalbibliothek verzeichnet diese Publikation in der Deutschen Nationalbibliografie; detaillierte bibliografische Daten sind im Internet über http://dnb.d-nb.de abrufbar.

Das Werk ist urheberrechtlich geschützt. Alle Rechte, insbesondere die Rechte der Verbreitung, der Vervielfältigung, der Übersetzung, des Nachdrucks und der Wiedergabe auf fotomechanischem oder ähnlichem Wege, durch Fotokopie, Mikrofilm oder andere elektronische Verfahren sowie der Speicherung in Datenverarbeitungsanlagen, bleiben, auch bei nur auszugweiser Verwertung, dem Verlag vorbehalten.

Es wird darauf verwiesen, dass alle Angaben in diesem Fachbuch trotz sorgfältiger Bearbeitung ohne Gewähr erfolgen und eine Haftung der Autorin oder des Verlages ausgeschlossen ist.

ISBN 978-3-7143-0260-8

© LINDE VERLAG Ges.m.b.H., Wien 2014
1210 Wien, Scheydgasse 24, Tel.: 01/24 630
www.lindeverlag.at

Druck: Hans Jentzsch u Co. Ges.m.b.H.
1210 Wien, Scheydgasse 31

Preface to the Third Edition

When writing a textbook on a general subject such as the US legal system, the temptation to include additional topics and aspects in each new edition is large. I have tried hard to resist this temptation and to focus instead on rewriting and expanding the already existing chapters and adding a few selected subchapters. In doing so, I have updated and increased a large part of the book and have added a variety of new terms and concepts. Carrying out the express wish of my students, a complete German-English vocabulary list has been added to the already existing English-German one.

Students as well as teachers who have been using the book in class should find the revised edition more readable and more focused. Naturally, my main audience remains law students. I hope that they will find this new edition both inspirational and user-friendly.

Let me thank them for having provided me with suggestions and corrections over the past seven years.

Preface to the Second Edition

After just one year, the helpful comments of my students have induced me to revise and enlarge the first edition. Modifications and updates were specifically made to chapters VIII (Legal Profession), IX (Jury System) and X (Case Flow). New chapters have been added on legal assistance and arbitration. I wish to thank my students for their useful suggestions and encourage them and all readers to again critically review the second edition so that I can incorporate further comments in yet another edition. Once again, I would like to express my gratitude to Monique for her valuable assistance at short notice.

Preface

The goal of this book is to familiarize lawyers and law students whose native language is not English with legal texts and legal language and to introduce them to basic American legal terminology and concepts. Since legal language can neither be taught nor understood without context, the book provides a brief overview of the US legal system, particularly its court structure, legal education scheme, law school teaching methods, case citation and briefing, various legal professions, court and litigation procedures and jury matters as well as selected civil and criminal law issues. Readers with legal knowledge will find it easier to study and work with this book; however, it is also a meaningful tool for readers who are not yet familiar with the law and should enable them to grasp the fundamental differences between continental European and US legal (both state and federal) systems and court procedures. The book's contents are selective rather than comprehensive and only give a short summary of the individual issues since the focus lies on legal terminology rather than content. Thus, each chapter is followed by a list of related legal terms and concepts, whereby the bulk of legal terminolgy is defined and explained in English rather than forced into a German corset. Due to the differences between the US and the continental European legal systems, a word-by-word translation of US legal concepts would – for the most part – be misleading and confusing. Therefore, the book tries to acquaint the reader with legal terminology by contextualising it first and then defining or translating related legal terms and concepts at the end of each chapter.

Very special thanks go to my friend Monique Ferguson who proofread the entire manuscript.

Contents

Preface to the Third Edition		V
Preface to the Second Edition		VI
Preface		VI
I.	**Important Differentiations**	1
	Civil Law versus Common Law (Legal Systems)	1
	Concepts	2
	Vocabulary	4
	Substantive Law versus Procedural Law	4
	Vocabulary	5
	Private Law versus Public Law	5
	Concepts	6
	Vocabulary	7
	Civil Law versus Criminal Law	7
	Criminal Law Concepts	12
	Civil Law Concepts	13
	General Concepts	13
	Vocabulary	15
II.	**The Adversarial (Adversary) System of Trial**	19
	Concepts	21
	Vocabulary	22
III.	**The Actors in a Courtroom**	23
	Concepts	25
	Vocabulary	25
IV.	**US Court Structure**	28
	General System	28
	State System	31
	Federal System	33
	Concepts	36
	Vocabulary	39
V.	**Case Citation**	42
	Concepts	44
	Vocabulary	45

Contents

VI.	**Briefing Cases**	46
	Background Information on *Hopwood v. State of Texas*	48
	Hopwood et al. versus State of Texas et al.	50
	Concepts	54
	Vocabulary	55
VII.	**US Legal Education**	57
	General	57
	Law School Admission	58
	JD Program	59
	Financing Legal Education	60
	Law School Accreditation	61
	Master's Degree in Law and other Postgraduate Degrees	62
	Teaching Methods	62
	Pro Bono Opportunities	63
	Bar Exam	63
	Law School Admission and Affirmative Action	64
	Grutter v. Bollinger et al.	65
	Concepts	69
	Vocabulary	72
VIII.	**The US Legal Profession**	76
	Legal Jobs	76
	Stratification of the Legal Profession	78
	Partnership Track	80
	Billable Hours	81
	Legal Ethics	82
	Concepts	84
	Vocabulary	86
IX.	**The US Jury System**	90
	General	90
	Grand Jury	91
	Excuse / Exemption from Jury Duty	92
	Voir Dire	94
	Jury and Trial Consultants	96
	Jury Deliberation	97
	Jury Nullification	98
	Concepts	101
	Vocabulary	103
X.	**Case Flow**	106
	General	106
	Criminal Pre-Trial Activities	106

	Civil Pre-Trial Activities	109
	Trial	111
	Post-Trial Procedures	112
	Concepts	114
	Vocabulary	122
XI.	**Mutual Legal Assistance**	125
	Letters Rogatory	125
	Mutual Legal Assistance in Criminal Matters	127
	Extradition and Rendition	128
	Concepts	131
	Vocabulary	131
XII.	**Alternative Dispute Resolution**	134
	General	134
	Arbitration	134
	Mediation	136
	Concepts	137
	Vocabulary	137
XIII.	**Selected Issues**	139
	Property Law	139
	Family Law	139
	Equity	140
	Contract Law	141
	Tort Law	141
	Corporate Law	142
	Concepts	143
	Vocabulary	146
	Crimes	148
	Vocabulary	150
	Elements of Crimes	151
	Concepts	153
	Asset Forfeiture	154
	Concepts	155
	Vocabulary	157
Index Concepts		159
Vocabulary (Eng–Ger)		163
Vokabular (Ger–Eng)		189

I. Important Differentiations

Civil Law versus Common Law (Legal Systems)

Civil or civilian law (as opposed to Common Law) is based on Roman law, especially the *Corpus Juris Civilis* of Emperor *Justinian*, as later developed through the Middle Ages by medieval legal scholars. Modern systems are descendants of the 19th century codification movement, during which the most important codes came into existence. The **Austrian Civil Code** was completed in 1811. Around this time civil law incorporated many ideas associated with the Enlightenment.

Today people use the term "Common Law" to denote the system of law that developed in England and was imported into countries influenced by the English. Civil law, on the other hand, is also sometimes known as "Continental European Law" although it is practiced around the world, such as in Latin America, Japan and most former colonies of continental European countries, but also in Quebec (Canada) and Louisiana (USA).

In the civil law system the primary source of law is a **code**, whereas Common Law rules are developed based on **court rulings**, (thereby also referred to as **case law**. The general principle of a case law system is that similar cases with similar facts should be solved by using the rules created in former similar (so called **precedent**) cases.

Still, the difference between civil law and Common Law lies less in the mere fact of **codification** than in the **methodological approach** to codes and statutes. Since **legislation** is seen as the primary source of law in civil law countries, courts base their judgments on statutes from which solutions in particular cases are derived. Therefore, courts reason extensively on the basis of general legal principles or draw analogies from statutory provisions to fill gaps. By contrast, in the **Common Law** system **cases** are the primary source of law, while statutes are interpreted narrowly. Consequently, judges have an enormous role in shaping the law.

It is often said that Common Law opinions are much longer and contain elaborate reasoning, whereas legal opinions in civil law countries are usually very short and formal in nature. But this is not the case in all civil law countries, since there are notable differences between the various **legal methodologies** used. In fact, in German-speaking countries court opinions are sometimes as long as American ones and often discuss prior cases and academic writing extensively. There are, however, certain **sociological differences**: civil law **judges** are usually trained and promoted separately from attorneys, whereas Common Law judges are regularly selected from accomplished and reputable attorneys. Also, the influence of academic writing by **law professors** on case law tends to be much greater in civil law countries. Civil and Common Law systems also differ considerably in courtroom procedure. While Common law functions as an adversarial system (contest

I. Important Differentiations

between two opposing parties before a **judge who moderates**), the civil law judge plays a **more active role** in determining the facts of the case. Also, civil law systems rely much more on written than on oral argument.

SIMPLY
Civil law is primarily contrasted against Common Law, which is the legal system in England, the US and other countries influenced by the English. The **distinguishing characteristics of the civil and Common Law systems** lie in the **sources of law** and the **procedure used in courts:** civil law is a law enacted by a nation or state for its own jurisdiction; it is a codified system of law setting out a comprehensive system of rules that are applied and interpreted by judges. In the Common Law system the primary sources of law are **judicial decisions**. These opinions contain legal principles that can be applied to solve future cases.

Discuss

Which other meaning of civil law do you know?

Explain the main differences between civil and Common Law!

How do the careers of civil law judges differ from their Common Law counterparts?

Is the role of a civil law judge different from the role of the Common Law judge?

Are there any advantages / disadvantages of the civil law judicial design?

Concepts

branches of government

most governments (such as the US government) can be devided into three separate branches: legislative, executive and judicial branch, whereby each branch has its own responsibilities (making, executing and interpreting the law).

case law

in Common Law systems, higher court decisions are binding on lower courts in cases with similar facts and similar legal issues. This concept of *stare decisis* (see below) means that lower courts are bound to appellate cases. The law based on judicial decision and precedent rather than on statutes (case law) is distinguished from "statutory law," which is the statutes and codes (laws) enacted by legislative bodies.

civil law

as opposed to Common Law: body of laws and legal concepts derived from old Roman laws which differ from (Angloamerican) Common Law; *also:* generic term for non-criminal law.

code

systematic and comprehensive (written) compilation of laws, rules or regulations, which are classified according to subject matter. The process of collecting and restating the law is known as "codification".

I. Important Differentiations

Common Law

the system of deciding cases referring to former (precedent) cases, which originated in England and was later adopted in the US. Today, many Common Law principles have been transformed into statutes with modern variations.

Court of Equity

originally, in English Common Law and in several states there were separate courts (some called "chancery courts") which handled lawsuits and petitions dealing with various non-monetary claims. The judicial remedies ("equitable remedies") developed by these courts provided flexible responses to changing social conditions allowing courts to use their discretion. Nowadays, most Courts of Equity have merged with courts of law.

judiciary

the judicial branch of government.

legal methodology

the system of methods followed in a particular (*here:* legal) discipline; an organized set of procedures and guidelines (method, *modus operandi*, approach). Sometimes, methodologies include a step-by-step "cookbook"-approach for carrying out the procedure.

legislative act

an act passed by a legislative body.

legislative enactment / legislation

lawmaking; the preparation and enactment of laws by a legislative body.

precedent

an appellate court decision which establishes a legal rule (authority) and is therefore cited as an example to resolve similar questions of law in later cases. The principle that a lower court must follow a precedent is called *stare decisis* (see below).

provision (of law)

a statute often has various provisions (articles, clauses).

stare decisis [ster-ē-di-sī-səs]

Latin for "to stand by a decision"; it expresses the (Common Law) doctrine that lower courts are bound by higher court decisions (precedents) on a legal question which was raised by the lower court. A trial court judge must not ignore the precedent until the appellate court changes the rule.

statute

written law enacted by state legislature; local statutes or laws are usually called "ordinances." Regulations, rulings, opinions, executive orders and proclamations are not statutes.

I. Important Differentiations

NOTE THE DIFFERENCE

justice:	1. justness, fairness	2. judge
judiciary:	1. judicial system	2. the bench (= all judges)
jurisprudence:	1. legal philosophy	2. decisions of the courts
jurisdiction:	legal authority/power	

Vocabulary

article	Paragraph
binding precedent	bindender Präzedenzfall
codification	Kodifizierung
to enact a law, to pass a law	ein Gesetz erlassen, verordnen
equitable	billig, billigkeitsgerichtlich
to establish a precedent	einen Präzedenzfall schaffen
executive order	Durchführungsverordnung
to follow a precedent	einem Präzedenzfall folgen
judiciary	Justiz, Justizgewalt, Rechtssystem
jurisdiction	Zuständigkeit, Gerichtsbarkeit, auch: Rechtsprechung
jurisprudence	Rechtswissenschaft, Jurisprudenz, Rechtslehre
ordinance	Anordnung, Verordnung
to overrule a precedent	einen Präzedenfall außer Kraft setzen, aufheben
precedent (case)	Präzedenzfall
provision	*here:* Klausel
remedy	Abhilfe, Mittel, Rechtsmittel
to resolve	lösen, beseitigen, aufklären
sources of law	Rechtsquellen
stare decisis	Grundsatz der Bindung an Vorentscheidungen
using equitable discretion	nach billigem Ermessen

Substantive Law versus Procedural Law

The question of whether a law is procedural or substantive is often a difficult one to answer. In the criminal context one could say that substantive laws define which acts are criminal and the punishment for violating them, whereas procedural laws regulate the steps by which the guilt or innocence of someone who is accused of a crime is determined.

In general, procedural law comprises the rules by which a court operates and in doing so determines what happens in legal proceedings. The rules are designed to ensure a fair and consistent application of *due process*/fundamental justice to all cases that come before a court. Substantive law, on the other hand, is the statutory or written law that governs the rights and obligations of those who are subject to it. Lawyers often **distinguish procedural law from substantive law** by referring the latter to the actual claims and defenses, whose validity is tested through the former, namely through the procedures set forth by procedural law.

> **SIMPLY**
> Substantive law is that part of the law which creates, defines, and regulates rights as opposed to procedural law which prescribes the methods of enforcing these rights or obtaining reimbursement for their violation.

Discuss

Which substantive laws do you know?

What is the purpose of the prescription of procedural rules?

Do you think one of the two types of law is more important? If so, why?

Vocabulary

procedural law	Verfahrensrecht, Prozessrecht
substantive law	materielles Recht
validity	Aussagekraft, Echtheit, Gültigkeit

Private Law versus Public Law

Private or civil law is that part of a legal system which involves the regulation of interactions between individuals, such as the **law of contracts and torts** in Common Law systems and the **law of obligations** in civilian legal systems. Private law can clearly be distinguished from **public law**, which deals with relationships between natural or legal ("artificial") persons, such as business entities, corporate bodies, non-profit organizations etc., and the state. The most well known subdivisions of public law are **constitutional law**, **administrative law** and (in most instances) **criminal law.** Statutes imposing criminal penalties are usually considered to be public law, since they intend to protect all members of society and not just the areas of interaction between individuals. In general terms, public law involves **interrelations between the state and the general population**, whereas private law involves interactions between private citizens. This distinction is sometimes a hazy one, though. For example, many **consumer protection laws** are of a public law nature.

In German-language legal literature the distinction between public and private law is discussed extensively. Among the various theories, the "subjection theory" focuses on explaining the distinction by emphasizing the **subordination** of private persons to the state whereas the "subject theory" considers public law to regulate the conduct of **public authorities**. Hence, there are areas of law which are mixed under these definitions, such as **employment law**, parts of which are public law (such as the activities of an employment inspectorate when investigating workplace safety) and parts of which are private law (eg closing an employment contract). Under the Austrian Constitution the distinction between private and public law is of considerable importance, as private law is

I. Important Differentiations

among the exclusive competences of federal legislation, whereas public law is partly a matter of state (provincial) legislation.

SIMPLY
Private law is that part of a legal system involving relationships between individuals, such as the law of contracts or torts, as it is called in Common Law systems, and the law of obligations, as it is called in civilian legal systems. Public law, on the other hand, is the law governing the relationship between individuals and the state.

Discuss

Distinguish the scope of private law as opposed to public law!

Why is the distinction between public and private sometimes "hazy"?

Which theories dealing with the public- and private law definition in German-language legal literature are mentioned in the text?

Concepts

administrative law

refers to the body of law that defines the powers of administrative agencies and public institutions. It is administered by the executive branch of a government.

consumer protection law

(or consumer law) is considered an area of public law that regulates private law relationships between individual consumers and the businesses that sell those goods and services. Consumer protection covers a wide range of topics including product liability, privacy rights, unfair business practices, fraud, misrepresentation and other consumer/business interactions.

due process of law

fundamental principle of fairness in all legal matters. The universal guarantee of due process is set down in the Fifth Amendment to the US Constitution. Various legal procedures are set by statute and court practice in order to safeguard both private and public rights against unfairness.

employment law

broad legal area that controls how employers have to treat their employees, former employees and/or applicants for employment. Employment law encompasses a wide variety of issues like pension plans, retirement, occupational safety and health regulations, affirmative action, discrimination in the workplace and sexual harassment.

(legal) procedure

here: the methods and mechanics of the legal process. In the US, every state has its own set of procedural statutes (such as the the state codes of civil and criminal procedure). In

I. Important Differentiations

addition, courts have so-called "local rules," which govern times for filing documents, the conduct of the courts and other technicalities.

Vocabulary

administrative law	Verwaltungsrecht
consumer protection	Konsumentenschutz
contract law	Vertragsrecht
due process of law	faires / ordentliches Verfahren, Rechtsstaatsprinzip
employment law	Arbeitsrecht
to encompass	umfassen; *also:* umgeben, umschließen
hazy	unscharf, undeutlich, verschwommen, vage, unklar
law of obligation	Schuldrecht
legal procedure	Gerichtsverfahren
private law	Privatrecht
public international law	Völkerrecht
public law	öffentliches Recht
subordination	Unterordnung, Subordnination
(law of) torts, torts law	Deliktsrecht, Recht der unerlaubten Handlungen

Civil Law versus Criminal Law

General

Since crimes are considered to disturb the social order, sovereign government officials (such as the police, prosecutors and criminal judges) are responsible for the pursuit and punishment of offenders. Therefore, the criminal law "plaintiff" is the state which (in court) is represented by a **public prosecutor**.

Criminal law (also known as penal law) is the body of law dealing with the accusation and punishment of offenders for having broken certain (criminal) laws. A crime has to be clearly distinguished from a civil wrong (such as tort or breach of contract). A person that has committed a crime ("a criminal") shall be found and punished in order to achieve criminal justice. Criminal law neither requires a victim nor a victim's consent to prosecute the offender. Rather, the prosecutor's office investigates *ex officio* (without the need of specific authorization) and even over the objections of the victim.

Punishment

One of the most fundamental distinctions between civil and criminal law is in the notion of **punishment**. In criminal law, a guilty defendant is punished by either

- **incarceration**,
- a **fine** paid to the government,

or (in the US):

- the **death penalty** (in exceptional cases and not in all US states).

I. Important Differentiations

Crimes are divided into two broad classes:

- **felonies** (serious crimes) are punishable by death or imprisonment in excess of one year.
- **misdemeanors** have a maximum possible sentence of less than one year incarceration.

In a criminal case, the verdict is either an **acquittal** ("not guilty") or a **conviction** ("guilty") which is followed by sentencing. Thus, the final act of a criminal process that ends with a conviction is the **sentence.**

A criminal sentence can take many forms, the best known of which involve a **fine** or **imprisonment**. A sentence may also include the revocation of certain privileges, house arrest or community service. Beyond these primary terms of a criminal punishment, a defendant can experience further, far-reaching and unexpected effects: For example, a person convicted of a felony may (in addition to social stigma) experience a loss of federal loans for education (for drug charges) or eviction from public housing. Such consequences – which are not intended by the judge and are mostly far beyond the terms of a sentence itself – are known as **collateral consequences.**

A civil defendant is certainly never incarcerated and never executed. Basically, a losing defendant in civil litigation has to do or pay what the plaintiff asked for (eg reimburse the plaintiff for the loss caused by the defendant's behavior). In a civil case under tort law, there is a possibility of so called **punitive damages** if the defendant's conduct is egregious and had either a malicious intent (i.e. a desire to cause harm), gross negligence (i.e. conscious indifference) or a willful disregard for the rights of others. Unlike most compensatory damages for civil suits, the purpose of punitive damages is not to reimburse the plaintiff but to **punish the civil defendant**. Punitive damages are awarded only in special cases (usually under tort law) in order to deter future wrongful conduct by others.

Standard of Proof and Burden of Proof

The standard of proof expresses the **degree of satisfaction** that the plaintiff must – through the evidence and materials presented to the court – create in the mind of the judge or each individual juror. This standard is **very high in criminal cases**, where the prosecutor has to prove that each element of the statutory definition of the alleged crime is satisfied "**beyond a reasonable doubt**" (which is a certainty of at least 98% or 99%). Meanwhile, the defendant is considered to be innocent (**presumption of innocence**). In civil cases the plaintiff succeeds "**on the balance of probabilities**", meaning (s)he wins the lawsuit if the **preponderance** of the evidence is in his/her favor, which – compared to criminal law – is a rather low standard. In percentage terms this means that if the jury (or the judge) believes that there is more than a 50% probability that what the plaintiff claims is true, the plaintiff wins. A few tort claims (such as fraud) require the plaintiff to prove his/her case at a level of "**clear and convincing evidence**" which is a standard higher than preponderance, but still less than beyond a reasonable doubt.

While the standard of proof expresses the degree of conviction of each juror (or the judge) in order to find for the plaintiff, the **burden of proof** refers to **the party who has** the **task of proving** the alleged facts. In criminal litigation, the **burden of proof** is always on the state, which must prove that the defendant is guilty. In some civil issues the burden of proof may shift to the defendant, eg if (s)he raises a certain factual issue in defense.

Legal Aid and Legal Representation

According to the 6th Amendment of the US Constitution criminal defendants are entitled to have a **legal counsel**. If they are financially unable to obtain adequate representation by private counsel a **public defender** is appointed for their representation **at government expense**. By contrast, in (US) civil proceedings there is **no general right** to have **free legal assistance**. In civil cases some litigants obtain free or low-cost representation through so a so called "**lawyer referral service**" usually offered by state and local bar associations as a public service. The purpose of such a service is to increase access to justice by referring members of the general public to lawyers in private practice or to **legal aid organizations** or agencies for a nominal fee.

Litigants may also proceed *pro se* ("**pro se representation**"), that is, they may represent themselves without the assistance of a lawyer. Sometimes lawyers or law students perform legal work without receiving payment to help indigent people with legal problems ("**pro bono work**"). Aside from that, people who cannot afford hiring a private attorney are practically unable to obtain access to the courts in civil cases. The one notable exception is again in tort law (mostly in the context of personal injury law) where attorneys often take cases on a **contingency** (contingent) **fee agreement**: Instead of billing the plaintiff on an hourly basis, the attorney is entitled to a percentage of the **trial award** or of the settlement, usually in the amount of one-third. If the plaintiff does not receive any compensation for damages because he loses the lawsuit, the attorney receives nothing. Contingent fees are not allowed in criminal matters and are rarely permitted in family law cases. Not only the attorney who agrees to work on a contingency fee basis takes a risk. It is still the plaintiff who has to pay for expert witnesses, depositions and other expenses, which can – just during discovery – be rather high.

Insurance

In civil cases under tort law it is possible to purchase **insurance** that will pay damages (**liability insurance**) and attorneys' fees for tort claims (**legal costs insurance**). In contrast, it is certainly not possible for a criminal defendant to purchase insurance to pay for his/her criminal acts.

Plea Bargain(ing)

Plea bargaining can conclude a criminal case without a trial. When it is successful, plea bargaining results in a **plea agreement** between the prosecutor and defendant (see also page 108). In this agreement, the defendant agrees to plead guilty without a trial, and, in return, the prosecutor agrees to dismiss certain charges or **make favorable sentence recommendations** to the court. In the US, plea bargaining is expressly authorized in statutes and in court rules. In fact, most felony cases are handled through plea bargains – meaning without trial.

I. Important Differentiations

Constitutional Rights of the Accused

The first ten amendments to the U.S. Constitution are collectively known as the **Bill of Rights.** They protect basic liberties (such as freedom of speech) and officially became part of the Constitution in 1791. The 4th, 5th, 6th, and 8th Amendments provide much of the constitutional basis of the rights of persons accused of having committed a crime.

Fourth Amendment (Search and Seizure)
The right of the people to be secure in their persons, houses, papers, and effects, against unreasonable searches and seizures, shall not be violated, and no Warrants shall issue, but upon probable cause, supported by Oath or affirmation, and particularly describing the place to be searched, and the persons or things to be seized.

Fifth Amendment (Rights of Persons)
No person shall be held to answer for a capital, or otherwise infamous crime, unless on a presentment or indictment of a Grand Jury, except in cases arising in the land or naval forces, or in the Militia, when in actual service in time of War or public danger; nor shall any person be subject for the same offense to be twice put in jeopardy of life or limb; nor shall be compelled in any criminal case to be a witness against himself, nor be deprived of life, liberty, or property, without due process of law; nor shall private property be taken for public use, without just compensation.

Sixth Amendment (Rights of Accused in Criminal Prosecutions)
In all criminal prosecutions, the accused shall enjoy the right to a speedy and public trial, by an impartial jury of the State and district wherein the crime shall have been committed, which district shall have been previously ascertained by law, and to be informed of the nature and cause of the accusation; to be confronted with the witnesses against him; to have compulsory process for obtaining witnesses in his favor, and to have the Assistance of Counsel for his defense.

Eighth Amendment (Further Guarantees in Criminal Cases)
Excessive bail shall not be required, nor excessive fines imposed, nor cruel and unusual punishments inflicted.

Fourteenth Amendment
Section 1. All persons born or naturalized in the United States and subject to the jurisdiction thereof, are citizens of the United States and of the State wherein they reside. No State shall make or enforce any law which shall abridge the privileges or immunities of citizens of the United States; nor shall any State deprive any person of life, liberty, or property, without due process of law; nor deny to any person within its jurisdiction the equal protection of the laws.

The **Fourth Amendment** to the US Constitution places limits on the power of the police to make arrests, search people and their property, and seize objects and contraband (such as illegal drugs or weapons). The basic question is whether the search and seizure was "unreasonable" or not.

The **Fifth Amendment's prohibition against double jeopardy** also applies only to criminal cases. The corresponding concept in civil litigation is *res judicata:* one can have only one trial for claims arising from one transaction or occurrence. The double jeopardy clause protects criminal defendants against various abuses, such as a second prosecution for the same offense after an acquittal or a conviction and multiple punishments for the same offense. Furthermore, the prosecution cannot appeal a "not guilty" verdict. It is possible, though, to try a defendant in criminal court and then try him/her again in civil court for the same action. The most common example of this is a criminal prosecution for **homicide** and then a second trial for the same occurence based on the tort of **wrongful death** (such as in the O.J. Simpson case).

According to the Fifth Amendment a criminal suspect or defendant has the **right to remain silent** during questioning by police and prosecuting officials. Thus, the criminal defendant may choose to refuse to testify and the jury may infer nothing from the defendant's silence. A civil defendant, on the other hand, must be available and cooperative for depositions and testimony during the proceedings.

The **Sixth Amendment** establishes **seven rights** applicable in criminal prosecutions: (1) speedy trial, (2) public trial, (3) trial by jury (see chapter IX), (4) notice of the accusation, (5) confrontation of opposing witnesses, (6) compulsory process for obtaining favorable witnesses and (7) the assistance of counsel.

Originally, the Bill of Rights, including the 6th Amendment, was intended to apply only to the federal government. In *Barron v. Baltimore* (1833) the Supreme Court explicitly held that the 5th Amendment, like the rest of the Bill of Rights, simply did not apply to the states. The adoption of the **Fourteenth Amendment**, which was one of three Amendments added to the Constitution in the immediate aftermath of the civil war, set a process in motion, during which the US Constitution's basic rights where being extended to state and local governments. Originally, the Amendment was expressly targeted at state governments and was intended to protect the rights of former slaves. Until today Supreme Court decisions have made nearly all of the protections of the Bill of Rights applicable to state and local governments. The process of **nationalization of the Bill of Rights** is also known as **selective incorporation doctrine**. Today, even the 6th Amendment rights are applicable to the states.

> **SIMPLY**
>
> The English term "civil law" stands for two quite completely different things, which can be rather confusing at first. If the term is used in contrast to Common Law (such as in chapter I) it refers to a legal system that is based on a civil code, such as the Austrian ABGB or the German BGB. In its other sense, civil law refers to matters of private law as opposed to public law, and particularly criminal law, which is concerned with the prevention of harm to society at large by regulating the behavior of individuals and groups in relation to societal norms. The major objectives of criminal law are deterrence and punishment, while the main goal of civil law (in contrast to criminal law) is to regulate the relationships between individuals. Civil law remedies vary (eg damages or order to stop/ to perform a task) and it is usually clear from the context which type is meant.

Discuss

What is the purpose of criminal law as opposed to civil law?

Who is the criminal law plaintiff?

What is the outcome of a criminal case as opposed to a civil case?

I. Important Differentiations

What are the differences between criminal and civil law/ litigation regarding:
- *purpose / idea behind*
- *persons involved*
- *outcome*
- *rights / protections of the persons involved*
- *burden of proof*
- *standard of proof*
- *free legal assistance*
- *insurance*

What is a contingent fee agreement?

Which rights are provided to criminal defendants in the 4th, 5th and 6th Amendment?

Explain the doctrine of selective incorporation!

Criminal Law Concepts

arrest warrant
a judge's order to law enforcement officers to arrest a person charged with a crime, also called a warrant of arrest.

beyond a reasonable doubt
the highest level of proof which is necessary to get a guilty verdict in criminal cases. It means that the accusation must be proven to the extent that there is no "reasonable doubt" in the mind of a rational person (judge or jury).

(criminal) charge
the specific statement what crime the party is accused of (charged with) that is contained in the criminal complaint.

(criminal) complaint
the document that sets forth the basis upon which a person is to be charged with an offense.

double jeopardy
being tried twice for the same offense; prohibited by the 5th Amendment to the US Constitution.

felony
serious crime carrying a penalty of more than a year in prison.

misdemeanor
an offense punishable by one year of imprisonment or less.

plea bargaining

process whereby a criminal defendant and prosecutor try to reach a mutually satisfactory disposition of a criminal case, the outcome of which is called "plea bargain" and is subject to court approval.

Civil Law Concepts

(civil) complaint

the pleading that initiates a civil lawsuit by setting forth a claim for relief by the defendant. The complaint outlines all of the plaintiff's causes of action (eg negligence or assault) and the respective allegations (see also chapter X).

clear and convincing evidence

the level of proof sometimes required in a civil case for the plaintiff to prevail. It means the trier of fact (judge/jury) must be persuaded that it is highly probable that the claim / defense are true. The "clear and convincing evidence" standard is a heavier burden than the "preponderance of the evidence" standard but less than the criminal standard (which is "beyond a reasonable doubt").

liability insurance

insurance against claims of damage for which a policyholder has to compensate another party. The policy commonly covers losses resulting from acts or omissions that result in damage to the person, property, or legitimate interests of others.

pain and suffering

compensation for personal suffering.

punitive damages

a way of "punishment" in civil lawsuits – to set a public example to others for malicious, evil or particularly fraudulent acts – which can be awarded by a civil trial jury.

General Concepts

count

each separate statement in a complaint which states a cause of action which, standing alone, would give rise to a lawsuit; or: each separate charge in a criminal action. For example, the complaint in a civil lawsuit might state: first count (or cause of action) for negligence, and then state the detailed allegations; second count for breach of contract; third count for debt and so forth. In a criminal case each count would be a statement of a different alleged crime.

indigent party

a party that is financially unable to afford an attorney.

I. Important Differentiations

legal aid organization / agency

in the US numerous legal aid agencies provide legal representation without cost or for a nominal fee to people who are unable to pay the usual amount for a lawyer's services. These agencies are sponsored by charitable organizations, lawyers' associations, law schools and also by federal, state, and local governments.

litigation

judicial "contest" between private parties to determine and enforce their legal rights. Litigation lawyers / attorneys ("litigators") specialize in representing private parties in court (see chapter VIII).

preliminary injunction

a court order made in the early stages of a lawsuit or petition which prohibits the parties from doing an act which is in dispute, thereby maintaining the *status quo* until there is a final judgment.

preponderance

more probable than not.

prima facie [pry-mah fay-shah]

Latin for "at first look," or "on its face," referring to a civil lawsuit or criminal prosecution in which the evidence before trial is sufficient to prove the case unless there is substantial contradictory evidence presented at trial. A *prima facie* case has sufficient evidence to be presented to a jury. A *prima facie* case that is presented to a grand jury (see page 91) by the prosecution will usually result in an indictment.

pro bono

short for *pro bono publico* (Latin for "for the public good"); legal work performed by lawyers without pay to help people with legal problems and with limited or no funds or to provide legal assistance to organizations involved in social causes.

pro se (representation)

Latin for "for himself;" a party to a lawsuit who represents himself (acting *in propria persona*) is appearing in the case "pro se."

relief

generic term for all types of benefits which a court order or judgment can give a party to a lawsuit, including money award, injunction, return of property, property title, alimony and dozens of other possibilities.

selective incorporation doctrine

in the early part of the twentieth century the Supreme Court began to extend the application of the first ten Amendments to the Constitution, known as the Bill of Rights, against the states. This process became known collectively as the "doctrine of selective incorporation."

I. Important Differentiations

temporary (interlocutory) injunction

a court order prohibiting an action by a party to a lawsuit until there has been a trial or other court action. The purpose of a temporary injunction is to maintain the *status quo* and prevent irreparable damage or change before the legal questions are determined. After the trial the court may issue a "permanent injunction" (making the temporary injunction a lasting rule) or "dissolve" (cancel) the temporary injunction.

Vocabulary
Criminal Context

to abet	beitragen
accused	beschuldigt, Beschuldigter
to acquit / acquittal	freisprechen
acquittal	Freispruch
charge	*here:* Anklage(punkt), Beschuldigung, Belastung
to charge (with)	beschuldigen, anschuldigen, belasten, bezichtigen
to commit a crime	eine Straftat begehen
confession	Geständnis
to convict /conviction	verurteilen / Verurteilung
count	*here:* Einzeltatbestand, Anklagepunkt
criminal defendant	Angeklagter, Beschuldigter
death penalty	Todesstrafe
denial	Bestreitung, Leugnung, Verweigerung
detention	Festnahme, Arrest
to deter (sb from doing sth)	abhalten, abschrecken
deterrence	Abschreckung
to dismiss a case / lawsuit	eine Klage zurückweisen oder abweisen
to dismiss an appeal	eine Berufung zurückweisen, verwerfen
disregard (of rules)	Nichtbeachtung (von Regeln)
double jeopardy	Doppelbestrafung
egregious	ungeheuerlich, unerhört, entsetzlich
ex officio [ex oh-fish-ee-oh]	adj. Latin for "from the office," in der österr. Rechtssprache: Amtswegigkeit
felony	Verbrechen
fine	Geldstrafe, Geldbuße
forensic	gerichtsmedizinisch, forensisch
forensic expert	Spurensicherungsexperte
forensic medicine	Gerichtsmedizin
to incarcerate / incarceration	einkerkern / Einkerkerung
indictment	Anklageschrift
inmate	(Gefängnis)Insasse, Häftling
investigate	ermitteln

I. Important Differentiations

jail / prison	Gefängnis
jeopardy	Gefahr
malicious	mutwillig, böswillig, niederträchtig
medical examiner	Gerichtsmediziner
misdemeanor	Vergehen
offender	Gesetzesbrecher
penal law	Strafrecht
petty offense / petty crime	kleines Vergehen, Kleinkriminalität
plea	*here:* "Antwort" des Angeklagten auf die Anklage
plea agreement, plea deal	"Deal" im Strafverfahren
guilty plea	Schuldeingeständnis des Angeklagten
to press charges	gegen jm Anzeige erstatten / Anklage erheben
presumption of innocence	Unschuldsvermutung
prisoner	Gefangener, Häftling
punishment / penalty / sentence	Strafe
referral	Empfehlung, Verweis, Überweisung
to refute, to rebut	widerlegen, anfechten, entkräften
to release	entlassen, freilassen
to remain silent	schweigen, stumm bleiben
silent, mute	stumm, still, sprachlos
stigma	Brandmal, Schandfleck, Stigma
suspect	Verdächtige(r), vermutliche(r) Täter(in)
victim	Opfer, Betroffene(r), Verunglückte(r)
to violate a law	gegen ein Gesetz verstoßen
warrant	richterliche Anordnung
willful disregard	vorsätzliche Missachtung

Civil Context

amount in controversy	Streitwert
at government expense	auf Staatskosten
to award damages	Schadenersatz zusprechen
breach of contract / to breach a contract	Vertragsbruch, gegen eine vertragliche Verpflichtung verstoßen
civil action / civil complaint /civil (law)suit	Klagsschrift, zivilrechtliche Klage
civil law remedy	zivilrechtliche(r) Rechtsbehelf / Sanktion
claim	Forderung, Anspruch, Behauptung
to claim	geltend machen, fordern, verlangen
to close a contract	einen Vertrag abschließen
(compensatory) damages	Schadenersatz, Wiedergutmachung
damage / harm / loss	Schaden, Nachteil
damage mitigation	Schadensbegrenzung, Schadensminderung(spflicht)

I. Important Differentiations

indigent	bedürftig, mittellos, notleidend
lawyer referral service	*here:* Anwalts-Empfehlungsdienst
legal costs (expense/s) insurance	Rechtsschutzversicherung
liability insurance	Haftpflichtversicherung
pain and suffering	Schmerzen(s)geld
to practice (Br. practise) law	als Anwalt / Anwältin tätig sein, praktizieren
punitive damages	Strafschadenersatz
referral	Empfehlung, Verweisung
to reimburse	entschädigen, rückerstatten, rückvergüten
reimbursement	Entschädigung, Ersatz, Rückvergütung
relief	*here:* Rechtsbehelf, Rechtsmittel
remedy / compensation	Wiedergutmachung
settlement	Vergleich
to sue	klagen
to suffer a harm / loss	einen Schaden erleiden
tort (claim)	delikt. Schadenersatz(anspruch)
trial award	Zuspruch, Zuerkennung, Zahlungsverpflichtung des Beklagten
unjust enrichment	ungerechtfertigte Bereicherung

General

to afford	*here:* sich leisten können
approach	Annäherung, Ansatz, Methode
(local) bar association	(örtliche) Rechtsanwaltskammer
burden of proof	Beweislast
consent	Einwilligung, Zustimmung, Erlaubnis
defendant	Beklagter, Angeklagter
degree of satisfaction	Maß an Zufriedenheit; *here:* Überzeugungsgrad
to distinguish	unterscheiden, auseinanderhalten
elaborate	ausgearbeitet, durchdacht, aufwändig
to engage in	*here:* betreiben
to be entitled (to have..)	Anspruch auf etw haben
extensively	ausgiebig, flächendeckend
free legal assistance	kostenlose rechtliche Unterstützung
incorporation	Angliederung, Aufnahme
lawsuit	Rechtsstreit, Prozess, *also:* (An)Klage
legal counsel / representative	Rechtsbeistand, Rechtsberater, rechtl. Vertreter
multiple	mehrfach, vielfach, multipel
nationalization	Nationalisierung
negligence	Fahrlässigkeit
nominal	symbolisch, äußerst gering

I. Important Differentiations

nominal fee	Anerkennungsgebühr
notable	beachtenswert, bemerkenswert
notion	Gedanke, Idee, Vorstellung
(court) opinion	schriftliche Urteilsausfertigung
to outlaw	verbieten
plaintiff	Kläger
preponderance	Übergewicht, Überwiegen, Aufwendung, Ausgabe, Kosten
proceeding	Verfahren, (Prozess)Verlauf, Vorgehen
to promote	(be)fördern, unterstützen, voranbringen
to pursue an offender	einen Gesetzesbrecher verfolgen
reasonable	plausibel, vernünftig, verständlich
to receive	erhalten, bekommen, empfangen
to rely on	sich auf etw stützen, sich auf etw verlassen
sociological differences	soziologische Unterschiede
sociology	Soziologie
subordination	Unterordnung
transaction	Abwicklung, Durchführung, Transaktion
trial	*here:* Gerichtsverhandlung
underlying	darunterliegend, zugrundeliegend
wrongful	unrechtmäßig

II. The Adversarial (Adversary) System of Trial

The **system of trial** employed in most continental European courts is referred to as **inquisitorial,** investigative or interrogative. In Common Law countries the method of conducting a trial is known as **adversarial**, accusatorial or **adversary system** of trial. As the term "adversary" suggests, this trial system relies on the **skills of the different advocates** representing their party's positions and not so much on some neutral party (the judge) trying to find out the truth by asking questions and in doing so establish justice, as it is the case in the inquisitorial system.

In the adversarial system each party is permitted to portray the story behind the dispute as he or she sees it, with the jury left to determine the real facts of the case, which ideally is the **truth**. Thus, the primary role of the jury in the adversary system is that of an independent **factfinder**. In trials where there is no jury this "fact-finding-role" is taken over by the judge. Procedural rules are supposed to give each party an **equal opportunity** to present their side of the case to the jury and it is the judge's responsibility to make sure that the process is conducted fairly – as defined by these rules. Therefore, the **primary role of the judge** in a US courtroom is to **ensure** the fair play of **due process** and in doing so to guarantee a just outcome based on the truth.

Watching US courtroom dramas on TV one will notice that the judge usually only gets involved when called upon by counsel. Most disputes between counsels before and during a trial occur when they disagree on what evidence the jury should be allowed to see or listen to. The **rules of evidence** govern whether, when, how and for what purpose certain pieces of evidence may be placed before the jury for consideration. Some important rules of evidence involve expert testimony, hearsay and rules of physical evidence. Because evidence is to be presented to laymen (the jury) rather than to a legal expert (the judge) the rules of evidence (such as the rules on hearsay) are **considerably stricter** in Common Law countries than in civil law (continental European) systems. However, some lower level courts – such as domestic relations courts or small claims courts – are allowed some flexibility in applying the strict rules of Common Law evidence. Individuals who appear in these courts are often not represented by lawyers. Furthermore, in family courts, the judge has to protect the interests of children rather than be a neutral arbiter of justice. While most US states have adopted their own rules of evidence for use in their respective courts, the rules that govern the admissibility of evidence in the US federal court system are collected in the Federal Rules of Evidence (FRE).

Proponents of the adversarial system often argue that the system is fairer and less inclined to abuse than the inquisitional approach, because it allows less room for the state to be biased against the defendant. The Common Law trial lawyer has more opportunities to settle the dispute in an amicable manner before the case goes to trial and to un-

II. The Adversarial (Adversary) System of Trial

cover the truth in the courtroom. Most cases that are tried in a Common Law court are carefully prepared through a lengthy preparatory stage, the so-called **pre-trial discovery** (see page 109), before it is presented to the jury. When the trial starts the parties' legal representatives have a very good idea of the relevant issues and pieces of evidence to present in the courtroom. Their role during discovery is similar to the role played by investigative judges in investigative trial systems. Another argument in favor of the adversary system is that a trial by a **jury of one's peers** is far more **impartial** than any government-paid inquisitor, even if (s)he is aided by a panel of the defendant's peers.

Critics of the adversary system suggest that the ability of a party to obtain a favorable result primarily depends on the **quality of his or her lawyers** and not so much on the facts of the case. An uncharismatic lawyer may fail to convince the jury even with a good case whereas a highly charismatic lawyer may win over the jury by telling them a convincing story. The US system is also criticized for the lucrative advantages it appears to present to the lawyer (see: contingency fee). Although both civil and criminal defendants are generally permitted to represent themselves *pro se*, the complexity of the legal system often forces a civil defendant to either pay whatever it takes for legal representation or enter into a settlement with the opposing party.

> **SIMPLY**
> The adversary system is the system of conducting a trial used in Common Law courts. It can be characterized as a **system of procedural justice,** which is a system guaranteeing justice as the result of a process that runs fairly. The interrogative system is used in civil law (most continental European) courts. It relies on the skills of a neutral, highly trained expert in the person of the judge, who is in charge of the trial and who decides on the facts and on the law **(system of substantive justice)**. The goal of both the adversarial system and the inquisitorial system is to **find the truth**. But the adversarial system seeks to reveal the truth by having the parties "combat" each other whereas the inquisitorial system seeks the truth by having an expert question the witnesses und analyze all the evidence. Another difference lies in the **rules of evidence**. Because the adversarial system assumes that the evidence is to be presented to laymen rather than to legal experts, its rules of evidence are considerably stricter. The civil law judge, on the other hand, does not have to be concerned about undue influence, because even when laypersons take part in the decision making process (s)he will have some control over them during deliberation.

Discuss the pros and cons of the adversary system using the following phrases:

- *procedural justice: fair trial as the quest for truth*
- *substantive justice: professional expert finds the truth*
- *division of power in the courtroom*
- *combat of two equally skilled lawyers presenting their perspectives on the truth*
- *legal representatives / counsel / advocates as instruments for developing the proofs*
- *impartial third party / referee / neutral judge presides over the battle / directs the trial process / has control over what evidence is presented*
- *determination of the real facts of a case / factfinder / ultimate authority on the facts*
- *ultimate tribunal on truth and justice*
- *opinion of a highly trained expert*
- *undue influence on a jury of laypersons*

Concepts

admission of evidence

a judge's acceptance of evidence into trial; if evidence is admitted into trial the jury is allowed to see/hear it and consider it during deliberation.

deliberation

the act of considering, discussing and, hopefully, reaching a conclusion, such as a jury's discussions, voting and decisionmaking.

expert testimony

opinion stated during the trial or a deposition (=testimony under oath before trial) by a specialist qualified as an expert.

Federal Rules of Evidence (FRE)

a federal code of procedural rules that are applied in federal courts (see page 33–35) and govern the admission of evidence into (civil and criminal) trial. The Rules were enacted in 1975, with subsequent amendments. The jury is only allowed to see/hear evidence "admitted" by the judge according to these rules.

hearsay

(1) "secondhand" evidence in which the witness is not telling what (s)he knows personally, but what others have said to him/her; (2) a common objection made by the opposing lawyer to testimony when it appears the witness has violated the hearsay rule.

hearsay rule

the basic rule that testimony or documents which quote persons that are not in court are not admissible. Because the person who supposedly knew the facts is not in court to state his/her exact words, the trier of fact cannot judge the credibility of the alleged firsthand witness and the other party's lawyer has no opportunity to cross-examine him/her.

inquisitorial system

the system of trial used in civil law countries. In this system the presiding judge is not a passive recipient of information such as in the adversary system. Rather, (s)he is primarily responsible for gathering the evidence necessary to resolve a case. Therefore, the judge actively questions the witnesses. Attorneys play a more passive role and follow the judge's questioning with questioning of their own. Attorney questioning is often brief because the judge tries to ask all relevant questions.

objection

a lawyer's protest about the legitimacy of a question addressed to a witness by the opposing attorney with the purpose of making the trial judge decide if the question may be asked. A proper objection must be based on one of the specific reasons for not allowing a question (such as relevancy, hearsay, leading etc). An objection must be made quickly and loudly to halt the witness before (s)he answers.

II. The Adversarial (Adversary) System of Trial

physical evidence
evidence involving material things as distinguished from the mind or spirit.

Vocabulary

arbiter	Schlichter, Vermittler, Schiedsmann
authentication	Echtheitsprüfung, Beglaubigung, Beurkundung
bargain	Abmachung; *also:* (gutes) Geschäft, Schnäppchen
counsel	*here*: Vertreter, Rechtsfreund, Anwalt
critic	Kritiker, Bewerter
domestic relations court / family court	Familiengericht
to ensure	absichern, garantieren, sicherstellen
false confession	falsches Geständnis
to govern	regulieren, steuern, leiten
impartial, neutral, fair	unbefangen, neutral, objektiv
to incline	tendieren, neigen
to interrogate	befragen, vernehmen verhören
investigative judge	Untersuchungsrichter, Ermittlungsrichter
lay judge	Laienrichter, Schöffe
lucrative	lohnend, rentabel, lukrativ
outcome	Ergebnis, Folge, Auswirkung
peer	Gleichrangiger, adj: seinesgleichen
peer pressure	Gruppendruck
prejudiced	befangen, voreingenommen
privilege	Sonderrecht, Begünstigung
proponent	Befürworter, Verfechter, Vertreter
relevancy	Sachbezogenheit, Erheblichkeit
relevant	bedeutsam, wichtig, relevant
rules of evidence	Beweisregeln
scope	(Anwendungs)Bereich, Umfang, Reichweite
significant	bedeutsam, erheblich, maßgeblich
to steer	steuern, lenken, führen
to be supposed to do sth	etwas tun müssen / vorgesehen sein zu, sollen
trier	Prüfer, Prüfgerät

III. The Actors in a Courtroom

Plaintiff

The plaintiff is the party who initiates a lawsuit by filing a complaint (legal action) with the clerk of the court against the defendant(s), demanding damages, performance and/or court determination of rights. The criminal plaintiff is the **state** or the **federal government** represented by the **prosecutor** (state attorney or district attorney [D.A.] in state courts and federal prosecutor in federal courts).

Defendant

The defendant is the party sued in a civil lawsuit or the party charged with a crime in a criminal prosecution. In some types of cases (such as divorce) a defendant may be called a "respondent".

Judge

The judge is an official with the authority and responsibility to preside in a court and enter judgments. In the US there is no specific judge-training-program; rather, most judges used to be attorneys. In phrases such as "the court found the defendant at fault" or "may it please the court" the word "court" refers to the judge. Sometimes the word "bench" also refers to the judge or judges in general. State court trial judges usually gain office by election, by appointment or by some judicial selection process in case of a vacancy. Federal judges are appointed for life by the US President with confirmation by the US Senate.

Justice

Judges on appeals courts are often referred to as "justices."

Counsel

The term "counsel" is generally used for a lawyer, attorney, attorney-at-law, counselor, counselor-at-law or advocate (in England solicitor or barrister) licensed to practice law and to represent clients in court.

Public Defender

A public defender (P.D.) is an elected or appointed public official who represents people accused of a crime that cannot afford a criminal defense attorney in private practice. Public defenders are either employed by the government (at the federal, state or county level) or they work for non-profit entities funded by the government.

Court Reporter

A court reporter is a person whose occupation it is to transcribe spoken or recorded speech into written form, typically using stenography equipment to produce official

III. The Actors in a Courtroom

transcripts of court hearings, depositions and other official proceedings (stenotype reporter or stenographer).

Juror

A person who actually serves on a jury is called a juror. Lists of potential jurors are chosen from various sources such as registered voters, automobile registration lists or telephone directories. The names are drawn by computerized random selection and requested to appear in court for possible service. A member of a Grand Jury (see page 91) is called a grand juror. The sworn body of persons convened to render an impartial verdict is the jury. The jury's task is to find the facts of a case, apply the law to those facts as instructed by the judge and in doing so reach a verdict.

Jury Consultant

See pages 96 and 102.

Witness

A witness is a person who testifies under oath in a trial (or a deposition – see page 115); *also:* a person who observes the signing of a document (like a will or a contract) and signs as a witness on the document attesting that the document was signed in his/her presence.

Expert Witness

An expert witness is a specialist in a certain field that is asked to present his/her expert opinion in court without having been a witness to any occurrence relating to the case. Expert testimonies are an exception to the rule against giving a personal opinion in trial, provided that the expert is qualified by evidence of his/her expertise, training and special knowledge.

Bailiff

A bailiff is a court official, usually a deputy sheriff, who keeps order in the courtroom and handles various errands for the judge and clerk. He calls the witnesses and usually administers the oath to prospective jurors and witnesses. The term "Bailiff" has its origin in Old French *(baillier,* to take charge of) and Middle English *(bailif)* for "custodian". In some US jurisdictions the term bailiff also stands for a person appointed by the court to handle the affairs of an incompetent person or to be a "keeper" of goods or money pending further order of the court.

Court Clerk

A court clerk (not to be confused with **law clerk** – see page 77) is an official or an employee who handles the business of a court, maintains files of each case, issues routine documents, keeps the records and assists the judge in courtroom management. Traditionally, the clerk was also the custodian of the court's seal, which is used to authenticate copies of the court's orders, judgments and other records. Sometimes he also fulfills the duties of a bailiff (and eg swears in witnesses, jurors, and grand jurors).

Discuss

Are there similar / different / more courtroom actors in your legal system?

Concepts

approaching the bench

an attorney's movement from the counsel table to the front of the bench in order to speak to the judge off the record and/or out of earshot of the jury. Since the bench area is the "sacred territory" of the judge the attorney must ask permission to approach the bench.

bar

(1) all attorneys are collectively referred to as "the Bar;" this denotation comes from the bar or railing which separates the general spectator area of the courtroom from the area reserved for judges, attorneys, parties and court officials. A party to a case or criminal defendant is "before the bar" when (s)he is inside the railing; (2) to prevent some legal maneuver, as in "barring" a lawsuit due to the running out of the time to file; (3) to prohibit and keep someone from entering a room, building, or real property.

bench

the large (usually long and wide) desk raised above the level of the rest of the courtroom, at which the judge or panel of judges sit; also used as a general term for all judges, as in "the bench."

bench trial

trial without a jury (*also:* court trial). It is basically identical to a jury trial, except the judge decides both the facts and the law applicable to solve the questions in dispute.

Vocabulary

attorney	Rechtsanwalt
automobile registration	Automobilzulassung
bailiff	Gerichtsdiener, Gerichtsvollzieher, Verwalter
to chair a panel	*here:* den Vorsitz (eines) Rechtsmittelsenates führen
(legal) counsel	(rechtl.) Vertreter / Rechtsberater
court clerk	nichtrichterlicher Gerichtsbediensteter
court reporter	Schriftführer(in)
(criminal) defendant	Beschuldigter, Angeklagter
deposition	eidesstattliche Aussage (außerhalb der Gerichtsverhandlung)
earshot	Hörweite
expert witness	Sachverständiger
foreperson	(gewählter) Obmann der Geschworenen
juror	Geschworene(r)

III. The Actors in a Courtroom

jury	Geschworene(nbank)
lawyer	Jurist
litigation team	Verhandlungsteam
paralegal	juristische Hilfskraft
party	*here:* Partei
pending	*here:* vorbehaltlich, anstehend
performance	*here:* Erfüllung einer Verpflichtung
plaintiff	Kläger
to preside	den Vorsitz führen, leiten
presiding judge	vorsitzender Richter
prosecutor	Staatsanwalt
public defender	staatl. finanzierter Verfahrenshelfer im Strafverfahren
railing	Geländer, Barriere
random selection	Zufallsauswahl
referee	Schiedsrichter
seal	*here:* Siegel, Stempel; *also:* Verschluss, Dichtung
(assistant) state attorney (ASA), (deputy) district attorney (DDA)	Staatsanwalt (in the state system)
trial attorney, litigator	Prozessanwalt
(friendly/hostile) witness	Zeuge der eigenen / gegnerischen Partei

What's going on in the courtroom

admissible / inadmissible	(un)zulässig
to admit evidence	Beweise zulassen
to be admitted to the bar	als Anwalt zugelassen werden
allegation / contention	(Parteien)Vorbringen, Behauptung
to allege	vorbringen, behaupten
to approach the bench	sich der Richterbank nähern
bar	*here:* Balken / Barren (im Gerichtssaal)
the Bar	*here:* Anwaltschaft
bench, the Bench	Gerichtsbank, *also:* Richter
to be on the Bench	Richter sein
to challenge evidence	die Beweisführung anfechten
code of evidence	Gesetzbuch, das die Zulässigkeit von Beweisen regelt
to conduct a trial	eine Gerichtsverhandlung leiten, führen
cross examination	Kreuzverhör
direct examination	direkte Befragung
documentary evidence	dokumentarische Beweisführung
evidence	Beweismittel
(physical) exhibit	Beweisstück
hearsay	Hörensagen

instruction of the jury	Belehrung der Geschworenen
interrogation	Befragung
leading	Suggestivfrage
litigation	Prozess, Rechtsstreit
litigator, trial attorney	Prozessanwalt
objection	Einspruch
to overrule an objection	einen Einspruch abweisen
to rest one's case	seine Beweisführung abschließen
to sustain an objection	einem Einspruch stattgeben
to swear in	beeiden
to take the stand	den Zeugenstand betreten
testimony	Zeugenaussage
under oath	unter Eid
verdict	Urteilsspruch der Geschworenen
witness stand	Zeugenstand

IV. US Court Structure

General System

Very generally stated the US court system is a **three-tiered system**, comprising trial courts, (intermediate) appellate courts and courts of last resort. This organization of the courts serves two purposes:

- first, the courts of appeals can **correct errors** that have occurred during trial court procedure,
- secondly, the highest court (court of last resort) can ensure the uniformity of decisions by reviewing cases in which important legal issues have been decided or in which two or more lower courts have reached different results.

Trial Court

Trial courts or courts of first instance are the courts where a case starts and where trials (if any) take place. The party filing the lawsuit on this (first) level is – in the civil context – the **plaintiff** who initiates the lawsuit against a **defendant**. In the criminal context it is the state (in the state system) represented by the **state/district attorney** or the federal government (in the federal system) represented by the federal prosecutor who charges the **(criminal) defendant** with a crime. Many trial courts hear cases regardless of the money involved or the issue raised. Such courts are referred to as **courts of general jurisdiction**. On the trial court level there are, however, also courts of **limited jurisdiction**, which hear only specific cases, such as cases in which the **amount in controversy** is rather low or cases involving a certain subject matter, such as **traffic courts, juvenile courts, labor courts or probate courts**. These courts of limited jurisdiction do not fit within the major three-tiered hierarchy but are an addition to it. They also form an exception to the general rule that only the courts of first instance deal with factual issues. That is to say that a party dissatisfied with the final decision a trial court of limited jurisdiction has reached may turn to the trial court of general jurisdiction and ask for a completely new trial (a "**trial de novo**") with a new determination of the issues of fact raised in the case. Apart from that, factual issues are never raised on appeal since appellate courts only deal with **issues of law**.

Trial courts are considered to be courts of **original jurisdiction** meaning that they hear a case for the first time, whereas appellate courts have **appellate jurisdiction**, which means they hear a case after it has already been decided by a lower court.

Trial courts are also referred to as **courts of record**, which underlines their task to keep a detailed record of their proceedings so that higher courts (which do not conduct trials) are able to **review a case**. The most informative part of the record is the **transcript** (minute, protocol), a verbatim documentation of every word uttered during the trial. In addition, the record includes the **preliminary pleadings**, which are the formal initial documents filed by each party, such as the complaint, the answer, the reply and the rejoinder (see page 109). Also, each **motion** filed before (**pre-trial**), during and after trial (**post-trial**) is part of the record and kept in the court file. Furthermore, the (physical) exhibits introduced into evidence by the parties, as well as the jury's verdict and the judge's final judgment, are part of the record, since only a comprehensive documentation of all the trial court proceedings enables an appellate court to fulfil its main task, namely to **find and correct legal errors** that may have occurred during the trial court's proceedings.

Trial courts are also called **courts of first impression**, because these courts hear the cases for the first time and in doing so get a first impression of the issues involved. A trial court is headed by one judge and usually convenes with a jury, unless both parties waive their right to have the case heard by a jury (in the criminal context it is the defendant who may waive this right). **On the trial court level** issues of fact and issues of law are raised for judicial determination, whereby **the focus lies on finding the facts**. Thus, a trial court's main task is to determine what actually happened in a case, because justice can only be administered if the trial unveils the **truth**. Applying the right law to the wrong facts leads just as well to a wrong (unjust) outcome as applying the law incorrectly based on a true factual situation.

The **factfinder** is either **the jury** or (in a bench trial) the trial court judge. After having observed all the evidence that was admitted into trial the jurors have to decide what they think really happened in a particular case. As the **final authority on the law it is the judge** who has to instruct the jury on the law at the end of the trial. After that it is up to the jury to apply the law to those facts they believe to be true from the evidence presented. Still, it is the judge who is responsible for determining what rules of law to apply to the particular case, how to interpret those rules and how to instruct the jury on them.

The Appeals Process

A party dissatisfied with the trial court decision has **a general right to go on appeal** once and ask the intermediate appellate court (2nd instance court) to review the case. An appeal is not a retrial of the case. Rather, the appellate court **reviews the record of the lower court's proceedings** to determine if there are adequate grounds to grant the appeal.

The party filing the appeal is called the **appellant** and the other party is called the **appellee**. The appellate court is usually headed by a **panel of judges** (typically three) and since there are no factual decisions to be made **no jury is ever present on appeal**. After reviewing the controlling issues in an action, the appellate court may **affirm** the decision of the lower court, **modify** it, **reverse** it, or **remand** the case for a new trial in the lower court pursuant to its order. When a decision is affirmed, the appellate court accepts the decision of the lower court. A reversal of a decision means that the appellate court agrees with the appellant that the decision was erroneously made. Then the party who lost the

IV. US Court Structure

case at the lower level becomes the winning party on appeal. In some cases, a decision might be reversed but the **lawsuit is still unresolved**. The appellate court then orders the **reversal** with the direction that the case be **remanded to the lower court** for the determination of the issues that remain unsettled.

The parties do not have a general right to have their case reheard by a third instance. Rather, if a party is displeased with the decision of the appeals court, (s)he may want to request ("petition") another review by the highest court. The formal petition that a party dissatisfied with the outcome of the appellate court's decision (the **petitioner**) has to file is referred to as "**petition for a writ of certiorari**". On this highest level the party opposing the petitioner is called **respondent**.

After evaluating the petition, the court of last resort will decide whether **to grant or deny certiorari**. Review on a writ of certiorari is not a matter of right, but of **judicial discretion**. A petition for a writ of certiorari will be **granted only for compelling reasons**. Certiorari is issued (designated as "cert. granted") if a case is of significant public interest or if the legal subject involved has been resolved differently by various courts or has not been dealt with before at all. Certiorari is denied when the highest court decides that the case does not present an appropriate matter for its consideration. When the highest court grants the writ it is addressed to the lower court, ordering it to send the record up for review. Every year, the Supreme Court receives thousands of such petitions but only accepts a small percentage of them. Some states have altogether abolished writs of certiorari under their rules of appellate practice.

The third instance court is also generally referred to as **court of last resort**, since there is no place to turn to after its decision. On the federal level the US Supreme Court has the final word on what the law is; its precedents bind all courts of appeals and trial courts within its jurisdiction.

When a court of appeals reaches a decision, the decision will be published in a **reporter** (see page 42). Some of these decisions can be found in case books which have to be studied and briefed by US law students (see page 46).

Overview

	court of first instance	intermediate appellate court	court of last resort
names	plaintiff v. defendant	appellant v. appellee	petitioner v. respondent
jurisdiction	general or limited jurisdiction original jurisdiction	appellate jurisdiction	appellate jurisdiction
jury / judge	jury or one judge	panel of judges	US Supreme Court sits en/in banc

IV. US Court Structure

	civil	civil & criminal	criminal
words expressing the initiation of a legal dispute	to litigate a case, to initiate a civil lawsuit to sue someone	to file/bring a (civil / criminal) action to file a (civil / criminal) complaint	to charge (someone with a crime) to arraign to indict
other words for lawsuit	civil case (civil) lawsuit	case, lawsuit, action proceedings, litigation legal dispute, legal controversy	criminal case criminal lawsuit
words for judgment	final order, decree default judgment	decision, ruling dismissal verdict	conviction, acquittal words for punishment: sentence, penalty

what trial judges do what the jury does	to render / award / impose a judgment to render / reach a verdict	what appellate judges do	to affirm (= confirm, sustain) to reverse (= set aside) to vacate (= annul) to dismiss (= to formally stop the trial) to remand (= send back)

	court of first instance	intermediate appellate court	court of last resort
issue	fact and law	law	law
further	court of first impression court of record	appeal generally as a matter of right	petition for a writ of certiorari has to be granted

State System

Each US state has its own legal system, its own state constitution, a state governor as the head of the executive branch, state legislature (usually a house of representatives and a senate) and a state judiciary (state court system). The jurisdiction of the state courts extends to basically any type of case that does not fall within the exclusive jurisdiction of the federal courts. Examples of cases within the jurisdiction of the state courts usually include cases involving the state constitution, state criminal offenses, tort/contract/probate/family law, the sale of goods, real property issues, corporations and business organization as well as traffic regulation. Unlike federal judges, most **state court judges** are not appointed for life but are either **elected or appointed** (or a combination of both) for a certain number of years.

The **structures of the individual state court systems vary drastically**, as do the names given to the courts within these systems. Most state court systems are **three-tiered**, comprising

(1) two sets of trial courts (trial courts of limited and of general jurisdiction),
(2) intermediate appellate courts and
(3) one highest state court (called by various names).

Some states only have a two-tiered court system, though, with one trial and one appellate court (then usually called "supreme court").

Because the individual states **apply different names to their courts**, it is often not evident whether a court has general or limited jurisdiction or whether it is a trial or an appellate court. The highest court of a state is not always called "supreme court" either. In New York State, for instance, the trial court of general jurisdiction is called the "Supreme Court of New York." Trial courts of limited jurisdiction are often referred to as "county courts", "municipal courts" or "justice of the peace courts".

Trial Courts of Limited Jurisdiction

Trial courts of limited jurisdiction are courts dealing with only specific types of cases that are usually presided over by a single judge sitting without a jury.

Examples of trial courts of limited jurisdiction include:

- **family courts** – dealing with divorce, alimony, custody, child support, adoption issues, paternity suits and domestic violence disputes etc;
- **juvenile courts** – that usually handle delinquency and dependency cases;
- **probate courts** – handling matters concerning the administration of a deceased person's estate and the implementation of his/her will;
- **traffic courts** – which usually hear non-felony cases alleging violations of traffic laws;
- **small claims courts** – concerned with suits between private persons of a relatively low amount in controversy;
- **municipal courts** – which usually deal with cases involving the violation of city ordinances (relating to fire safety, zoning regulations, public health or sanitation) and petty offenses, often also DUI- and DWI-cases.

Trial Courts of General Jurisdiction

Trial courts of general jurisdiction are the main trial courts in the state system. They hear any case which is not required to be first heard in a court of limited jurisdiction. Most of these cases are civil disputes involving larger sums of money or criminal litigations arising from serious state crimes like rape or murder. Cases are usually heard by one judge who regularly sits with a jury. These courts are called by a variety of names, including "Circuit Court", "Superior Court", "Court of Common Pleas" and even "Supreme Court". In certain cases, these courts can hear appeals from trial courts of limited jurisdiction in a *trial de novo* (see page 28).

Intermediate Appellate Courts

Most US states have intermediate appellate courts between the trial courts of general jurisdiction and the highest court in the state. Any party – except the prosecutor in a criminal case after the defendant has been acquitted – who is not satisfied with the judgment of a state trial court may appeal the matter to an appropriate intermediate appellate court. Such appeals are usually a matter of right (meaning the court must hear them).

However, these courts address only alleged **procedural mistakes** and **errors of law** made by the trial court. The court of appeals decision is usually be the final word in the case, unless it sends the case back to the trial court for additional proceedings, or the parties ask the highest state court to review the case.

Highest State Courts

All states have some sort of highest court. While they are usually referred to as supreme courts, some are known as "court of appeal". In states with intermediate appellate courts, the highest state courts usually have **discretionary review** as to whether to accept a case. In states without intermediate appellate courts, appeals may usually be taken to the highest state court as a matter of right. Appeals heard by the highest court usually allege a mistake of law and not fact. In addition, many state supreme courts have original jurisdiction in certain matters (such as regarding elections).

Federal System
Federal Question Jurisdiction and Diversity Jurisdiction

The law that applies to everyday situations is primarily **state law** whereas the federal legal system and the federal courts come into play only in a limited number of cases, namely when **federal questions** are raised (federal question jurisdiction):

- In a **civil case** such questions arise when the plaintiff claims that he or she has been wronged by an action that violates a **federal law**, the **Constitution**, or a **treaty** involving the US.
- In the **criminal context**, the question of jurisdiction is relatively simple. If the accused allegedly committed a federal crime, the federal court that sits in the state where the offense was committed has personal jurisdiction over the defendant. A **federal crime** is a conduct that is forbidden by federal legislation. A number of federal crimes are listed in Title 18 of the US Code. However, if the charges allege a violation of state law, the defendant will face prosecution in a state trial court (that has jurisdiction over the area in which the offense was committed). If a crime violates both federal and state law, the defendant may be tried twice: once in state court and once in federal court.
- Another way in which a federal court can have authority to hear a case is through **diversity jurisdiction**. This refers to a situation in which the federal court of the US is vested with the right to decide a case that normally would be heard in a state court.

    Example
    When opposing parties in a lawsuit are citizens of different states or a citizen of a foreign country the case is placed under federal court jurisdiction pursuant to Article 3 section 2 of the US Constitution, and the federal Judicial Code, if the amount in controversy exceeds $ 75,000.

Furthermore, federal courts also have jurisdiction over all bankruptcy matters (see bancrupcy court below)

Structure of the Federal Courts

The federal court system provides a three-tier structure. Therefore, a person involved in a federal lawsuit may proceed through **three levels** of decision:

- On the first level his/her case will be heard and decided by one of the 94 **US District Courts**.
- If (s)he is dissatisfied with the decision rendered by the district court, (s)he may have the decision reviewed by the **US Court of Appeals** for the respective district (also called "**US Circuit Court**", indicating the circuit where the district court rendering the opinion is situated).
- If dissatisfied again, the party may see seek additional review by the **US Supreme Court** which is located in Washington D.C.
  Supreme Court judges are referred to as **justices.**

Federal judges who are at least 65 years old and have served as active judges for a minimum of 15 years sometimes gain **senior status**. As senior judges they may continue to hear cases or serve on special commissions and committees. Nearly 15 percent of the US federal courts' caseload is handled by senior judges.

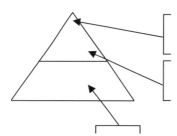

If the federal court system is regarded as a pyramid, the **US Supreme Court** – the highest court in the federal system – is located at the top. On the next lower level there are the **13 US Courts of Appeals ("US Circuit Courts")** and the US Court of Appeals for the Armed Forces.

On the lowest (first instance) level are the **94 US District Courts and various federal specialized courts** (such as the Tax Court, the Court of Federal Claims or the Court of International Trade).

US District Courts – Federal Trial Courts

The US District Courts are the general trial courts of of the federal court system. They hear both (federal) civil and (federal) criminal cases. Every state has at least one district court, and some large states, such as California, have as many as four. All federal district courts are **courts of limited jurisdiction**, because they may only decide certain types of cases (see page 33). There are **94 federal judicial districts**, almost all of them include a **US bankruptcy court** as a separate unit.

There are **two special trial courts** that have nationwide jurisdiction over certain types of cases: the **Court of International Trade** that addresses cases involving international trade and customs issues and the **US Court of Federal Claims** which has jurisdiction over most claims for money damages against the US, disputes over federal contracts, unlawful "takings" of private property by the federal government and a variety of other claims against the US.

US Circuit Courts – Federal Appellate Courts

The 94 judicial districts are organized into **12 regional circuits**, each of which has a **US Court of Appeals** (also referred to a US Circuit Court) hearing appeals from the district courts located within its circuit, as well as appeals from decisions of federal administrative agencies.

In addition, the Court of Appeals for the Federal Circuit has nationwide jurisdiction to hear appeals in specialized cases, such as those involving patent laws and cases decided by the Court of International Trade and the Court of Federal Claims.

The US Supreme Court

The US Supreme Court is the highest court in the federal judiciary. It consists of **the Chief Justice of the US** and **eight associate justices.** Like the Chief Justice, all Associate Justices are nominated by the President and confirmed by the US Senate by majority vote. The number of Associate Justices is determined by the US Congress; it is currently set at eight by the Judiciary Act of 1869.

The Supreme Court only hears a very **small number** of the petitions it receives each year. Most cases accepted on appeal involve decisions that conflict with the Supreme Court's interpretation of federal law or that the justices believe need clarification in order to establish a precedent. The Supreme Court hears cases **en banc**, meaning that all justices sit together in open court. About three-fourths of its decisions are announced in fully published opinions. When the justices decline to rule on a particular case, the decision of the lower court becomes final.

The Supreme Court also hears a limited class of cases under **original jurisdiction** (such as disputes between states), in this case being the first and only court to hear the dispute.

> **OVERVIEW – FEDERAL SYSTEM**
>
> **US District Courts** – federal trial courts
> - they have original and limited jurisdiction;
> - usually there is one judge or jury (in rare cases: three-judge panel with no jury);
> - there are also specialized trial courts such as the US Court of Federal Claims and the Court of International Trade.
>
> **US Court of Appeals / US Circuit Courts** – federal appellate courts
> - there are 13 courts of appeals (11 circuits with one court each, the D.C. circuit and the Federal Circuit, which is unique among the courts of appeals as it is the only court that has its jurisdiction based wholly upon subject matter rather than geographic location);
> - they convene in three-judge panels – simple majority is sufficient; they write a majority opinion indicating their holding;
>
> **US Supreme Court**
> it consists of one chief justice and eight associate justices and has original and exclusive jurisdiction of all controversies between two or more States;
> it has appellate jurisdiction over
> - direct appeals from the decisions of the federal district courts when the judges hear a case as a three-judge panel (in this exceptional case the parties skip over the intermediate court);
> - final decisions of a US Court of Appeals that are petitioned via the writ of certiorari and
> - appealed judgments of the highest court of a state if the appeal raises questions under the US Constitution.

IV. US Court Structure

SIMPLY
There are two court systems in the US: federal and state. In short, each system is three-tiered, including trial courts, appellate courts and courts of last resort. In some (smaller) states, there are only two tiers: the trial and the appellate level.

Concepts

cert. denied

the abbreviation used in legal citations to indicate that the highest court denied a petition for writ of certiorari (see below) in the case being cited.

certiorari [sur-shee-uh-rair-ahy / -rair-ee]

a Latin word meaning "to be informed of", or "to be made certain in regard to"; it is also the name given to certain appellate proceedings for re-examination of actions of lower courts.

(juvenile) delinquency case

a case dealing with an offense committed by a minor (juvenile criminal case).

dependency case

a case dealing with juveniles who are abandoned, abused or neglected by parents or other custodians, surrendered for the purpose of adoption or who are ungovernable.

en banc [on bonk]

also: in banc

a French term (meaning "on a bench") used to refer to the hearing of a legal case where all judges of a court will hear the case (an entire "bench"), rather than a panel of them. It is often used for unusually complex cases or cases considered of unusual significance (rehearing en banc: see page 45).

guardian

a person that has been appointed by a judge to take care of a minor, a child or an incompetent adult (both called "ward") personally and/or to manage that person's affairs. To become a guardian of a child either the party intending to be the guardian or another family member, a close friend or a local official responsible for a minor's welfare will petition the court to appoint the guardian. In the case of a minor, the guardianship remains under court supervision until the child reaches majority at 18.

jurisdiction

the authority of a court to adjudicate a case.

juvenile court

special court or department of a trial court which deals with underage defendants charged with crimes or who are neglected or out of the control of their parents.

matter of law/ question of law/ issue of law

whatever is to be ascertained or decided by the application of statutory rules or legal principles.

motion

a written or oral application requesting that the court make a specified ruling or order. Motions are made in court all the time for many purposes: Motions before (**pre-trial**) and after (**post-trial**) the trial usually require a written brief of legal reasons for granting the motion, written notice to the attorney for the opposing party and a hearing before a judge. Oral motions are common during a trial or a hearing.

paternity suit

a lawsuit, usually by a mother, to prove that a named person is the father of her child (or the fetus she is carrying). Evidence of paternity may include blood tests (which can eliminate a man as a possible father), testimony about sexual relations between the woman and the alleged father, evidence of relationship of the couple during the time the woman became pregnant, admissions of fatherhood, and, increasingly, DNA evidence. In addition to the desire to give the child a known natural father, proof of paternity triggers the obligation to pay child support.

petition

a formal written request to a court for a certain order. It is distinguished from a complaint, which asks for damages and/or performance by the opposing party. Petitions include demands for writs, orders to show cause, modifications of prior orders, continuances, dismissals of a case, reduction of bail in criminal cases and a host of other matters arising in legal actions.

petition for (a) writ of certiorari

informally called "Cert. Petition"; it is a document which a dissatisfied party files with the court of last resort asking it to review the decision of a lower court. It includes a list of the parties, a statement of the facts of the case, the legal questions presented for review and arguments as to why the court should grant the writ.

pleadings

the specific papers by which the allegations of the parties are presented in proper form; specifically the complaint of a plaintiff and the answer of a defendant plus any additional responses (replication, rejoinder – see page 114) to those papers that are authorized by law.

probate

(1) the process of proving a will is valid and thereafter administering the estate of a dead person according to the terms of the will; (2) a general term for the entire process of administration of estates of dead persons, including those without wills, with court supervision; (3) adj: reference to the appropriate court for handling estate matters, as in "probate court".

record

in the context of legal proceedings the term "record" indicates the total of the proceedings which are transcribed by a court reporter as well as all the documents filed in the case. On appeal the court can consider only the record, unless there is a claim of newly discovered evidence.

senior status

higher rank than that of others especially by reason of longer service.

small-claims courts

a special court, sometimes called "conciliation court", that provides quick, informal, and inexpensive adjudication of small claims. Depending on state law, small claims courts are limited to claims up to between $5,000 and $ 15,000. The types of cases tried in small claims courts are also limited, including disputes over security deposits and claims based on bad checks. The rules of civil procedure and of evidence are typically simplified in order to make the procedures economical. Individuals are usually allowed to conduct their own cases and to represent themselves.

trial de novo

"*de novo*" is a Latin expression meaning "anew" or "over again"; hence, the term trial de novo stands for a new trial by a different tribunal. It is usually ordered by an appellate court when the original trial failed to make a determination in a manner dictated by law. Appellate proceedings differ from a trial de novo in that an appeal must generally be based solely on points of law (legal matters) and not on points of fact (factual issues).

writ of certiorari

a writ, or order, sent from the highest court to a lower one ordering it to turn over transcripts and documents related to a specific case ("the record of the case") for review. The decision to grant such a writ is made at judicial discretion.

Explain

- *the unique characteristic of the US judiciary*
- *the hierarchy of the three-tiered court system*
- *the role of trial courts as opposed to the role of appellate courts*
- *the names of the parties on the three levels*
- *the terms "court of first impression" – "court of record" – "court of last resort"*
- *the role of the judge as opposed to the role of the jury*
- *the main task of trial courts / of appellate courts*
- *the terms original/ appellate / general / limited jurisdiction*
- *record – transcript – court reporter – pleadings – petition*
- *the phrases "en/in banc" and "panel of judges"*
- *Is there a jury in every trial?*

Vocabulary

to abolish	abschaffen
to adjudicate	(gerichtlich) entscheiden, urteilen, zuerkennen
to affirm	bestätigen, bejahen, *also:* behaupten
alimony	(Ehegatten)Unterhalt(szahlungen), Alimente
amount in controversy	Streitwert
appeal	Berufung
appellant	Berufungswerber, Rechtsmittelführer, Rechtsmittelkläger
appellate	die Berufung betreffend, Berufungs-
appellate court, court of appeals	Rechtsmittelgericht, Rechtsmittelinstanz
appellate jurisdiction	Zuständigkeit der Rechtsmittelinstanz
appellee	Berufungsgegner, Rechtsmittelgegner/-beklagter
to appoint a judge	einen Richter ernennen
to arraign	anklagen, Anklage erheben
to arraign somebody for something	jemanden wegen etw vor Gericht bringen
bancruptcy court	Insolvenzgericht(sabteilung)
a case on appeal	beim Berufungsgericht anhängige Rechtssache
cause of action	Klagsgrund
(writ of) certiorari	Anordnung zur Vorlage der Akten an ein höheres Gericht
chamber	Richterzimmer, Kammer
to charge somebody (with)	jemanden unter Anklage stellen, anklagen, anschuldigen
child custody	Obsorge, Sorgerecht (für Kinder)
city ordinance	Stadtverordnung
to close a contract	einen Vertrag abschließen
compelling	überzeugend, zwingend
to comprise, contain, include	beinhalten, umfassen, enthalten
to conduct a trial / noun: conduct	einen Prozess führen / leiten
to confirm	bestätigen, bekräftigen, zusagen
to consist of	bestehen aus
to constitute	zusammensetzen, bilden
to convene / assemble	zusammentreffen, versammeln
court file	Gerichtsakte
court of last resort	letzte Instanz
deceased person	verstorbene Person
decree	Beschluss / Urteil (des Equity-Gerichtes), *also:* Verfügung
default judgment, judgment by default	Versäumnisurteil

IV. US Court Structure

discretionary review	im Ermessen des Rechtmittelgerichts liegende Überprüfung der Entscheidung (der untergeordneten Instanz)
to be dismissed for misbehavior in office	wegen schweren Verfehlungen entlassen werden
to dispose of sth	erledigen, regeln; *also:* loswerden
dissatisfied party	unzufriedene Partei
DUI (driving under the influence)	Alkohol am Steuer
DWI (driving while intoxicated)	unter Drogeneinfluss am Steuer
to be empowered to hear a case	berechtigt sein, einen Fall zu hören / behandeln
error of law	Rechtsfehler, Rechtsirrtum
evidence	Beweis(e), Beweismittel
failure to pay child support	Verletzung der Unterhaltspflicht
file	*here:* Akte, Aktenmappe
to file (suit, an appeal)	einreichen, schriftlich einbringen
general jurisdiction	allgemeine Zuständigkeit
grant (deny) certiorari	die Revision (nicht) zulassen
to grant for compelling reasons	aus zwingenden Günden gewähren
guardianship	gesetzliche Vertretung / Sachwalterschaft
implementation	Durchführung, Umsetzung
to indict	von der Grand Jury (siehe Seite 91) in den Anklagestand versetzt werden
indispensable	unverzichtbar, unumgänglich, notwendig
judicial discretion	richterliches Ermessen
judiciary	Justiz, Richterschaft
jurisdiction	Zuständigkeit(sbereich), *also:* Jurisdiktion
juvenile court	Jugendgericht
labor court	Arbeitsgericht
landlord / tenant	Bestandgeber / Bestandnehmer
law dispute / legal dispute	Rechtsstreit
layer	Ebene, Schicht
legislative enactment	Gesetzgebung
limited jurisdiction	eingeschränkte Zuständigkeit (*also:* begrenzte Rechtsprechung)
litigation	Prozess, Verfahren
merit	Verdienst, Leistung
mistake in venue	fehlende örtliche Zuständigkeit
to modify (a judgment)	(eine gerichtliche Entscheidung) abändern, modifizieren
motion	*here:* Antrag
negotiation	Verhandlung, Besprechung
obligation to pay child support	Unterhaltspflicht
to be obliged to do sth	verpflichtet sein, etwas zu tun

original jurisdiction	originäre Zuständigkeit
paternity suit	Vaterschaftsprozess, Vaterschaftsklage
pleading	Plädoyer, general: Bitte, Fürsprache
(preliminary) pleadings	*here:* (prozessvorbereitende) Schriftsätze
post-trial	nach dem Prozess
pre-trial	vorprozessual
probate court	Verlassenschaftsgericht
procedural mistake / error	Verfahrensfehler
to proceed	fortfahren, weitermachen
to remand (a case)	eine Rechtssache an die untere Instanz zurückverweisen
to render / reach a verdict	eine Entscheidung finden, ein Urteil fällen (bezogen auf die Geschworenen)
to reside	sich niederlassen
retention vote	Abstimmung / Wahl über Beibehaltung
reversal of a decision / a verdict	Urteilsaufhebung
to reverse and remand	*here:* eine Entscheidung aufheben und an die untere Instanz zur neuerlichen E zurückverweisen
to review	überprüfen
senate, panel	Senat
to serve as a judge	als Richter tätig sein
to be subject to	unterworfen
three-tiered hierarchy	dreistufige Hierarchie
tier [tī'ər]	Rang, Reihe, Etage
tiered	gestaffelt
traffic court	Verkehrsgericht
transcript	Protokoll
trial court	Prozessgericht, erstinstanzliches Gericht
trust	Treuhand, Vermögensverwaltung
two-tier	zweigeteilt, zweigestuft
unresolved	offen, ungelöst
to vacate, to declare void	*here:* (eine Entscheidung) als nichtig aufheben, annullieren
to waive a right	auf ein Recht verzichten
will	Testament, letzter Wille
zoning regulations	Bauordnungsbestimmungen

V. Case Citation

In Common Law countries court opinions are legally binding under the rule of *stare decisis* (see page 3). That rule requires a court to apply a legal principle that was set forth earlier by a court of the same jurisdiction dealing with a similar set of facts. Thus, the regular **publication** of such opinions is important so that everyone (lawyers, judges, and laymen) can find out what the law is, as declared by judges.

Reporters or **law reports** are series of books (usually published by commercial publishing companies) that contain judicial opinions. They either include a particular court's cases (such as the *Supreme Court Reporter* which contains only US Supreme Court cases) or compile the decisions of a number of state or federal courts (eg the *Atlantic Reporter*).

Because it is the decisions of higher courts (especially the courts' of last resorts decisions) that give the Common Law lawyer information on the status of the law, most appellate court decisions are published. Some of these decisions are also printed in **casebooks** that law students have to read (and brief – see chapter VI) during law school.

The act of referring to a (precedent-setting) case in court or in a written legal court statement (brief) is a **case citation**. Although case citations are formatted differently in different jurisdictions, they generally contain the same key information (see overview below). The US Supreme Court uses its own unique citation style. Nevertheless, the most widely used **legal citation system** in the US is prescribed by the so called **"Bluebook"**. The Bluebook governs the style and formatting of various references and elements of legal publications, including the use of citations, typefaces for **Law Reviews**, short citation forms, abbreviations, numerals, symbols, cases, statutes, legislative materials as well as international materials.

Many state courts, however, have their own citation rules that take displace the Bluebook for documents filed with those courts.

Overview

Common Case Citations include the following information:
1) volume number
2) abbreviation of the reporter where it is published
3) page number
4) year
5) information to distinguish the court

Example

Smith v. Texas	384	US	436	(1966)
parties involved	volume no.	series abbrev.	page	date

V. Case Citation

In a trial court citation the first name is that of the party who has filed the complaint. On the appellate level the first name stands for the party filing the appeal (appellant), whereas the second name is that of the party against whom the appeal is directed (see overview page 30).

The first number is always the volume number of the reporter, where the published decision can be found. This number is followed by the (abbreviated) name of the reporter, which is followed by a second number designating the first page of the published decision.

Example of Federal Case Citations

State v. Ferguson, 134 F.Supp. 231 (E.D.Pa. 1955)

> The Federal Supplement (abbrev: F.Supp) reports decisions of the US District Courts; the name of the district is indicated in parenthesis together with the year; *here:* volume: 134; page: 231.
> If the state is the first party it indicates that the state filed (mostly a criminal) complaint against a defendant.

Barker v. City of Philadelphia, 159 F2d 169 (2d Cir 1947)

> The Federal Reporter (F) reports US Courts of Appeals' decisions (F., F2d., F3d. indicating the series number); *here:* US Court of Appeals for the 2d Circuit

Brown v. Board of Education, 347 U.S. 483, 74 Sup. Ct. 686, 98 L.Ed. 873 (1954)

> *here:* parallel citation of three reporters

There are three private reporter systems for Supreme Court cases:

> U.S. = United States Court Reports
> S.Ct., Sup.Ct. = Supreme Court Reporter
> L. Ed. = Lawyer's Edition

Example of a State Case Citation

Singer v. Marx, 144 Cal. App. 2d 637, 301 P.2d 440 (1956) or

Singer v. Marx, 301 P.2d. 440 (Cal. Ct.App. 1956)

> you can tell that the case was decided by a California appellate court because it is published in the California Appellate Reports (2nd series) volume 144 page 637
> Cal. – California State Court
> Ct.App. – intermediate level
> P.2d. Pacific Reporter second series volume 301 page 440

SIMPLY

> Various case citation systems are used to identify published court decisions, either in special series of books called **reporters** or **law reports**, or in a 'neutral' form which will identify a decision wherever it was reported. Although case citations are formatted differently in different jurisdictions, they generally contain the same key information (name of the case, volume and page number and the abbreviation of the reporter where the case is published).

V. Case Citation

Exercise

Analyze the following case citations:
- Regents of Univ. of Caifornia. v. Bakke, 438 U.S. 265, 274, 289 (1978)
- Gratz v. Bollinger, 539 U.S. 244 (2003)
- Grutter v. Bollinger, 539 U.S. 306 (2003)
- Hopwood v. Texas, 861 F. Supp 551 (W. D. Texas 1994)
- Hopwood v. Texas., 78 F.3d 932 (5th Cir. 1996), reh'g en banc denied, 84 F.3d 720 (1996), cert. denied, 518 U.S. 1033 (1996)

Concepts

Bluebook ("A Uniform System of Citation")

a style guide, prescribes the most widely used legal citation system in the US. The Bluebook is taught and used at a majority of US law schools, and is also used in a majority of U.S. federal courts.

citation

indication of the place where one can find a case that has been published.

concurring opinion

an opinion written by one or more justices who agree with the judgment (outcome) reached by the majority of the court's justices, but for different reasons. A case may have one or more concurring opinions.

dissenting opinion, dissent

judges who disagree with the decision reached by the majority of judges in the case sometimes write their own opinion – called a dissenting opinion or minority opinion – that explains the basis for their decision in the case. The legal arguments and conclusions in the dissenting opinion are not legally binding, but they might eventually prevail if the law changes.

(law) reports

the published decisions of (state and federal) appeals which are found in federal, state and regional series (called "reporters"). If the case is important, sometimes dissenting or concurring opinions are published following the main opinion (see chapter VI). The terms reporter and law reports are often used as synonyms.

Law Review

(or law journal): a scholarly journal focusing on legal issues, normally published by an organization of students at a law school or through a bar association. The term is also used to describe the extracurricular activity at law schools of publishing the journal. Law reviews should not be confused with legal periodicals (see below).

V. Case Citation

Legal Periodical

non-scholarly (commercial) publications for the legal profession (such as the *New York Law Journal* or *The American Lawyer*). They contain commentary on current and proposed legislation as well as on recent court decisions and administrative rulings. They may also be published by law schools (and their affiliated student organizations) or bar associations. Scholarly journals in this field are known as "Law Reviews") see page 44.

quotation

actual repetition of someone else's words, either printed or previously spoken.

rehearing en banc (short: reh'g en banc)

appellate courts in the US sometimes grant a rehearing en banc to reconsider a decision concerning a matter of exceptional public importance or a decision, appears to conflict with a prior opinion of the court. Some appellate courts (such as the US Supreme Court and the highest courts of most US states) hear all of their cases en banc (see page 36) (with the exception of cases where a judge is ill or recused). Each court of appeals has particular rules regarding en banc proceedings. Such a rehearing is usually only granted when consideration by the full court is necessary to secure uniformity of its decisions.

reporter

series of books that contain judicial (mostly appellate) opinions (law reports).

Vocabulary

abbreviation	Abkürzung(szeichen), Verkürzung
bracket	(eckige) Klammer
citation	Zitierung, Zitat, Fundstelle; *also:* Vorladung
to compile	zusammentragen, zusammenstellen
edition	Auflage, Ausgabe
formatting	Formatierung, Formatieren
numeral	Zahl(zeichen, symbol), Ziffer
parenthesis	(runde) Klammer
publication	Veröffentlichung, Publikation
publishing company	Verlag(shaus, gesellschaft)
to recuse a judge	einen Richter ablehnen
report	Bericht
reporter, law reports	*here:* Entscheidungssammlung
scholar	Wissenschaftler, Gelehrter, Schüler
series	Folge, Reihe, Serie
typeface	Schriftart, Schrift

VI. Briefing Cases

Confusion often arises over the term "brief". The term **case brief** in the context of legal education (see page 57) should not be confused with an **appellate brief** or an **amicus curiae brief**, which are written legal arguments addressed to an appellate court. If an appellate court decides to conduct an oral hearing, it will ask the parties involved to submit written briefs. These (appellate) briefs may cover many pages and are a written summary of one side's arguments. The purpose of an appellate brief is to persuade the higher court to uphold or reverse the trial court's decision. Additionally the court may receive *amicus curiae* briefs from individuals or organizations not directly involved with the case. The word "amicus" is the Latin word for "friend" and these briefs are often called "friend-of-the-court briefs", because they represent "friendly" suggestions to the Justices on how the Court should rule. The Court usually employs several clerks – young lawyers from top law schools, to review these briefs and make suggestions. Appellate briefs are rarely published. The US Supreme Court is the only court for which briefs are regularly available in published form. The *Landmark Briefs Series* includes the full texts of briefs relating to some of the many cases heard by the Supreme Court.

A **student (case) brief**, on the other hand, is a law **student's summary and analysis** of a specific case (usually contained in a casebook) which (s)he prepares for use in classroom discussion. Law school briefs are shorter than court briefs but follow a similar structure by summarizing the **facts, legal issues,** the **holding** and the **rationale** of a court opinion. They usually contain a set of notes which the student presents in class in a systematic way. Case briefing is a widely accepted pedagogical method among US law professors. Although student briefs always include the same items of information, the form in which these items are set out can vary and are sometimes given by the professor.

Typical Parts of a Case Brief
Introductory material (Citation)

Analysis of the case name and the parties:

- Who is who in the case name? Does the first name refer to the plaintiff, the appellant or the petitioner?
- Is it a trial court or an appellate court case?
- Is it a federal or a state court case?
- Who is the presiding judge?

In a criminal case, the first party is invariably the government (state or federal) and the second party is the criminal defendant. However, a case before an appellate court may result in a switch when a defendant (then the appellant or petitioner) seeks action against the state (then the appellee or respondent). So, in addition to providing the proper case citation, in this section of the case brief the role of each party has to be specified.

Facts

Substantive facts: What is the human story behind the case?

Material facts: Which part of the story constitutes a legal defense or affects the result of the action?

Procedural History / Procedural Posture

Appellate cases have already had a trial stage. Depending on at which appellate level (second or third instance) the case that is being briefed is at, it may also have been heard by an appellate court. In this part of the brief each court that has already dealt with the case has to be identified and the holdings of those lower courts should be indicated. In doing so the history of the case through the legal system is traced.

Issue on Appeal

An appeal is filed because at least one party is dissatisfied with the outcome of the lawsuit (the lower court's holding) and therefore addresses the higher court to review the lower court's opinion and proceedings. In this section of the case brief the student has to find out the specific legal question (defined as narrowly as possible) that the party filing the appeal brings before the higher court and which issues are addressed by the opposing party (the appellee or respondent).

Holding

What is the narrow factually specific legal answer that the court gives to the question that the parties ask?

Rule / Legal Precedent

What is the broad legal principle for which this case stands? Did the court articulate a new legal principle or build upon existing legal principles?

Potentially Important Dictum(a)

Is there a comment or ruling which may state a related legal principle?

Rationale (Ratio Decidendi)

What is the court's reasoning? How does it explain its decision?

Disposition

What happened as a result of the court's decision? The three most common dispositions of an appellate court are:
- *affirmed*
  - the appellate court agrees with the opinion of the lower court.

VI. Briefing Cases

- *reversed*
  - the appellate court disagrees with the opinion of the lower court and sets aside or invalidates that opinion. Reversals are often accompanied by a remand.
- *remanded*
  - the case is sent back to the court from which it came for further action consistent with the appellate court opinion. Remand often accompanies a reversal.

Dissenting Opinions

Is there an alternate published reasoning on this issue by another member of the court?

Evaluation

In this last section of the brief personal thoughts and ideas about the case can be brought in by the student and issues for further discussion should be raised.

> **SIMPLY**
>
> In the context of legal education a case brief is an organized way to express the material contained in a specific case. Case briefs are individual tools that law students use for class participation and exam preparation to better understand and remember cases.

Exercise

Explain the difference between a student (case) brief and a court (appellate) brief!

What is the difference between a concurring and a dissenting opinion?

Brief the concurring opinion of Justice Wiener (page 50) on Hopwood. v. State of Texas 78 F.3d 932 (5th Cir. 1996) using the format that was presented on pages 46–48 (read background information first)

Explain the different reasoning of Justice Wiener compared to the majority decision!

Background Information on *Hopwood v. State of Texas*

On March 6, 1961, President John F. Kennedy issued the Executive Order 10925, which included a provision that government contractors "take affirmative action to ensure that applicants are employed, and employees are treated during employment, without regard to their race, creed, color, or national origin." The intent of this executive order was to **take positive action** in order to **realize true equal opportunity** for all. The order was superseded by Executive Order 11246 in 1965, prohibiting employment discrimination based on race, color, religion, and national origin by those organizations receiving federal contracts.

In 1868 the Fourteenth Amendment to the US Constitution was enacted, which marked a great shift in American constitutionalism. The **Equal Protection Clause**, part of the Fourteenth Amendment, provides that *"no state shall ... deny to any person within its jurisdiction the equal protection of the laws."* It actually only applies to state governments, but the requirement of equal protection has been read to apply to the federal government as a component of Fifth Amendment due process.

Even after the passage of these (among other) **civil rights laws** and although the civil rights movement had some dramatic victories (such as *Brown v. Board of Education 347 U.S. 483 [1954]*) the road to equal opportunity for minorities and women remained difficult. When it became clear that antidiscrimination statutes alone were not enough to break **longstanding patterns of discrimination**, both the courts and government administrations turned to **race- and gender-conscious remedies** as a way to end entrenched discrimination. These remedies were developed because other means had failed to correct the problem of racial imbalance.

The initiatives and court decisions interpreting the civil rights guarantees within the **Equal Protection Clause** of the Fourteenth Amendment came to be known as **affirmative action**. Affirmative action consists of policies, programs and procedures that give preferences to **minorities and women** in job hiring, admission to institutions of higher education, the awarding of government contracts and other social benefits. However, in 1978 the Supreme Court placed important limitations on affirmative action programs in *Regents of the University of California v. Bakke* (see page 64). By the mid 1980s, an anti-affirmative action movement gained power and affirmative action programs were challenged in court cases, such as the cases concerning the universities of Texas (see page 50) and Michigan (see page 65).

The notable **Hopwood case** was initiated in 1992, when four white applicants to the University of Texas School of Law filed a lawsuit in federal district court alleging that the law school's admissions policies were unconstitutional (violating the Equal Protection Clause). More precisely, plaintiffs claimed that the law school's separate review processes for minority and nonminority applicants led to a preference of members of those groups over non-minority applicants with comparable **education records**.

The US District Court for the 5th circuit found there was a **compelling state interest** justifying the use of an affirmative action program at the University of Texas Law School. Nonetheless, the court found that in order to comply with existing Supreme Court jurisprudence (*Regents of Univ. of Cal. v. Bakke*, 438 U.S. 265 [1978]) the law school would have to change its admissions procedures in order to have **a more narrowly tailored program**.

The case was appealed to the Fifth Circuit, which reversed and remanded *(Hopwood v. State of Texas, 78 F.3d 932 [5th Cir. 1996] – see below)* expressly holding that any **consideration of race or ethnicity** for the purpose of achieving a diverse student body was **not a compelling interest** under the Fourteenth Amendment and that *Bakke* was not a binding precedent.

The Supreme Court **denied writ of certiorari** (*518 U.S. 1033 [1996]*) because the challenged program was no longer in effect.

HOPWOOD et al. versus STATE OF TEXAS et al.

▶ Appeals from the United States District Court
for the Western District of Texas
March 18, 1996, before SMITH, WIENER, and DeMOSS, Circuit Judges.
JERRY E. SMITH, Circuit Judge:

With the best of intentions, in order to increase the enrollment of certain favored classes of minority students, the University of Texas School of Law ("the law school") discriminates in favor of those applicants by giving substantial racial preferences in its admissions program. The beneficiaries of this system are blacks and Mexican Americans, to the detriment of whites and non-preferred minorities. The question we decide today in No. 94-50664 is whether the Fourteenth Amendment permits the school to discriminate in this way.

We hold that it does not. The law school has presented no compelling justification, under the Fourteenth Amendment or Supreme Court precedent, that allows it to continue to elevate some races over others, even for the wholesome purpose of correcting perceived racial imbalance in the student body. "Racial preferences appear to 'even the score'... only if one embraces the proposition that our society is appropriately viewed as divided into races, making it right that an injustice rendered in the past to a black man should be compensated for by discriminating against a white ." City of Richmond v. J.A. Croson Co., 488 U.S. 469, 528 (1989) (Scalia, J., concurring in the judgment).

As a result of its diligent efforts in this case, the district court concluded that the law school may continue to impose racial preferences. See Hopwood v. Texas, 861 F. Supp. 551 (W.D. Tex. 1994). In No. 94-50664, we reverse and remand, concluding that the law school may not use race as a factor in law school admissions. Further, we instruct the court to reconsider the issue of damages in accordance with the legal standards we now explain.

...

WIENER, Circuit Judge, specially concurring.

"We judge best when we judge least, particularly in controversial matters of high public interest." In this and every other appeal, we should decide only the case before us, and should do so on the narrowest possible basis. Mindful of this credo, I concur in part and, with respect, specially concur in part. The sole substantive issue in this appeal is whether the admissions process employed by the law school for 1992 meets muster under the Equal Protection Clause of the Fourteenth Amendment. The law school offers alternative justifications for its race-based admissions process, each of which, it insists, is a compelling interest: (1) remedying the present effects of past discrimination (present effects) and (2) providing the educational benefits that can be obtained only when the student body is diverse (diversity). As to present effects, I concur in the panel opinion's analysis: Irrespective of whether the law school or the University of Texas system as a whole is deemed the relevant governmental unit to be tested, neither has established the existence of present effects of past discrimination sufficient to justify the use of a racial classification. As to diversity, however, I respectfully disagree with the panel opinion's conclusion that diversity can never be a compelling governmental interest in a public graduate school. Rather than attempt to decide that issue, I would take a considerably narrower path and, I believe, a more appropriate one — to reach an equally narrow result: I would assume arguendo that diversity can be a compelling interest but conclude that the admissions process here under scrutiny was not narrowly tailored to achieve diversity.

THE LAW

A. Equal Protection

The Equal Protection Clause provides that "[n]o State shall . . . deny to any person within its jurisdiction the equal protection of the laws." Accordingly, "all racial classifications, imposed by whatever federal, state, or local governmental actor, must be analyzed by a reviewing court under strict scrutiny." Racial classifications will survive strict scrutiny "only if they are narrowly tailored measures that further compelling governmental interests." Thus, strict scrutiny comprises two inquiries of equal valence: the "compelling interest" inquiry and the "narrow tailoring" inquiry. Moreover, these inquiries are conjunctive: To avoid constitutional nullity, a racial classification must satisfy both inquiries. Failure to satisfy either is fatal.

B. Racial Classification

None dispute that the law school's admission process for 1992 employed a racial classification. Depending on an applicant's race, his request for admission was considered under one of three different (and, as explained in the panel opinion, often dispositive) TI admission ranges: one for blacks only, a second for Mexican Americans only, and a third for all other races and nationalities, including non-Mexican Hispanic Americans. In short, each applicant for admission to the law school was classified by race, and his application was treated differently according into which of those three racial classifications it fell. Thus, the law school's 1992 admissions process, like all racial classifications by the government, is subject to strict scrutiny.

C. Strict Scrutiny

The law school contends that it employs a racially stratified admissions process to obtain, inter alia, the educational benefits of a diverse student body. Translated into the constitutional idiom, the law school insists that achieving student body diversity in a public graduate school is a compelling governmental interest. The law school invokes the opinion of Justice Powell in Regents of the University of California v. Bakke to support that postulate. The panel opinion rejects that support, concluding that from its inception Bakke had little precedential value and now, post-Adarand, has none. My fellow panelists thus declare categorically that "any consideration of race or ethnicity by the law school for the purposes of achieving a diverse student body is not a compelling interest under the Fourteenth Amendment." This conclusion may well be a defensible extension of recent Supreme Court precedent, an extension which in time may prove to be the Court's position. It admittedly has a simplifying appeal as an easily applied, bright-line rule proscribing any use of race as a determinant. Be that as it may, this position remains an extension of the law – one that, in my opinion, is both overly broad and unnecessary to the disposition of this case. I am therefore unable to concur in the majority's analysis. My decision not to embrace the ratio decidendi of the majority opinion results from three premises: First, if Bakke is to be declared dead, the Supreme Court, not a three-judge panel of a circuit court, should make that pronouncement. Second, Justice O'Connor expressly states that Adarand is not

VI. Briefing Cases

the death knell of affirmative action – to which I would add, especially not in the framework of achieving diversity in public graduate schools. Third, we have no need to decide the thornier issue of compelling interest, as the narrowly tailored inquiry of strict scrutiny presents a more surgical and it seems to me a more principled way to decide the case before us. I am nevertheless reluctant to proceed with a narrowly tailored inquiry without pausing to respond briefly to the panel opinion's treatment of diversity in the context of the compelling interest inquiry

D. Is Diversity A Compelling Interest?

Along its path to a per se ban on any consideration of race in attempting to achieve student body diversity, the panel opinion holds (or strongly implies) that remedying vestigial effects of past discrimination is the only compelling interest that can ever justify racial classification. The main reason that I cannot go along with the panel opinion to that extent is that I do not read the applicable Supreme Court precedent as having held squarely and unequivocally either that remedying effects of past discrimination is the only compelling state interest that can ever justify racial classification, or conversely that achieving diversity in the student body of a public graduate or professional school can never be a compelling governmental interest. Indeed, the panel opinion itself hedges a bit on whether the Supreme Court's square holdings have gone that far, particularly in the realm of higher education. Between the difficulty inherent in applying Bakke and the minimal guidance in Adarand, the definition and application of the compelling interest inquiry seems to be suspended somewhere in the interstices of constitutional interpretation. Until further clarification issues from the Supreme Court defining "compelling interest" (or telling us how to know one when we see one), I perceive no "compelling" reason to rush in where the Supreme Court fears — or at least declines — to tread. Instead, I would pretermit any attempt at a compelling interest inquiry and accept Justice O'Connor's invitation to apply the Court's more discernible and less intrusive "narrow tailoring" precedent. Thus, for the purpose of this appeal I assume, without deciding, that diversity is a compelling interest, and proceed to the narrowly tailored inquiry .

F. Test For Narrow Tailoring

When strictly scrutinizing a racial classification for narrow tailoring, the first question is "What is the purpose of this racial classification?" The present effects rationale having proven feckless in this case, today's answer to that first question is a given: The law school's purpose is diversity. Accordingly, I perceive the next question to be, "Was the law school's 1992 admissions process, with one TI range for blacks, another for Mexican Americans, and a third for other races, narrowly tailored to achieve diversity?" I conclude that it was not. Focusing as it does on blacks and Mexican Americans only, the law school's 1992 admissions process misconceived the concept of diversity, as did California's in the view of Justice Powell: Diversity which furthers a compelling state interest "encompasses a far broader array of qualifications and characteristics of which racial or ethnic origin is but a single though important element." When the selective race-based preferences of the law school's 1992 admissions process are evaluated under Justice Powell's broad, multi-faceted concept of diversity, that process fails to satisfy the requirements of the Constitution. The law school purported to accomplish diversity by ensuring an increase in the numbers of only blacks and Mexican Americans in each incoming class to produce percentages virtually indistinguishable from quotas of approximately five and ten percent, respectively. Yet blacks and Mexican Americans are but two among any number of racial or ethnic groups that could and presumably should contribute to genuine diversity. By singling out only those two ethnic groups, the initial stage of the law school's 1992 admissions process ignored altogether non-Mexican Hispanic Americans, Asian Americans, and Native Americans, to name but a few.

In this light, the limited racial effects of the law school's preferential admissions process, targeting exclusively blacks and Mexican Americans, more closely resembles a set aside or quota system for those two disadvantaged minorities than it does an academic admissions program narrowly tailored to achieve true diversity. I concede that the law school's 1992 admissions process would increase the percentages of black faces and brown faces in that year's entering class. But facial diversity is not true diversity, and a system thus conceived and implemented simply is not narrowly tailored to achieve diversity. Accordingly, I would find that the law school's race-based 1992 admissions process was not narrowly tailored to achieve diversity and hold it constitutionally invalid on that basis. By so doing I would avoid the largely uncharted waters of a compelling interest analysis. Although I join my colleagues of the panel in their holding that the law school's 1992 admissions process fails to pass strict scrutiny, on the question of diversity I follow the solitary path of narrow tailoring rather than the primrose path of compelling interest to reach our common holding.

...

CONCLUSION

I end where I began: We should only decide the issues necessarily before this court, and then only on the narrowest bases upon which our decision can rest. This is not a class action; nothing is before us here save the claims of four individual plaintiffs. These four individual plaintiffs properly challenge only the admissions process employed by the law school in 1992 – not the admissions process that was in place and employed in 1995, not the admissions process that is being employed in 1996, and not the admissions process to be applied in any future years. In sum, I would remand, and in the process I wouldtake care not to eviscerate the discretion of the district court with excessive "commentary" or implicit directions on the precise nature of the remedy that must ensue. Rather, my remand would simply instruct the district court to apply the correct burden-shifting process articulated in Mt. Healthy, then see how the law school deals with it. That way, if the Mt. Healthy application should demonstrate the need for a remedy, the district court would be free to fashion the appropriate relief including injunctive if necessary for those among the individual plaintiffs whose individual cases warrant it. For this court to do anything beyond that impresses me as overreaching. Thus I concur in the judgment of the panel opinion but, as to its conclusion on the issue of strict scrutiny and its gloss on the order of remand, I disagree for the reasons I have stated and therefore concur specially.

SIMPLY

All racial classifications, imposed by whatever federal, state, or local governmental actors, must be analyzed by the reviewing court under strict scrutiny – a very high level of judicial inspection. This strict-scrutiny-analysis applies to any race-based law or policy, no matter whether it is intended to benefit or to disadvantage minorities. To survive strict scrutiny a(n) (*here*: law

VI. Briefing Cases

school) admission policy must be "narrowly tailored" and promote "compelling governmental interests". Hence, to avoid constitutional nullity, a racial classification must satisfy both inquiries, **the narrow tailoring and the compelling interest analysis**. An admission program fails the test if there is a less restrictive alternative, eg one that would serve the purpose just as well without using race as a criterion, as it was argued by Judge Wiener in his concurring opinion in *Hopwood. v. State of Texas.*

Concepts

affirmative action

programs and policies that grant favorable treatment on the basis of race or gender to certain "disadvantaged" individuals in order to ensure equal opportunity, as in education and employment. They are best understood as a continuation of the effort to remedy subjugation of racial and ethnic minorities and of women in US history. The typical criteria for affirmative action are race, disability, gender, ethnic origin and age.

amicus curiae brief [uh-mahy-kuhs kyoor-ee-ee / uh-mee-kuhs kyoor-ee-ahy]

an amicus curia (Latin: "friend of the court") is a person that is not a party to the litigation but who volunteers or is invited by the court to give advice upon some matter pending before it. Amicus curiae briefs are filed in many Supreme Court matters and provide valuable information about legal arguments, or how a case might affect people other than the parties to the case. Some organizations file friend-of-the-court-briefs in an attempt to "lobby" the Supreme Court, to obtain media attention or to impress members.

appellate brief

both appellant and appellee must file individual briefs to aid the appellate court in its consideration of the issues presented. Failure to do so results in a dismissal of the appeal. These (appellants') briefs must specifically discuss the alleged errors (see also page 69).

Bakke

a 1978 decision by the Supreme Court (Regents of the University of California v. Bakke) commonly referred to as "Bakke", holding that race could be used as one of many factors in (*here:* medical) school admission but that "disadvantaged minority students" were not permitted to have a certain amount of admission spots reserved for them. Bakke alleged that he was a victim of "reverse racism" that allowed less qualified minority students to be admitted to a medical school to which he had applied.

case brief

a condensed, concise outline of a court opinion. Case briefs are prepared by students as a study aid when trying to capture the essence and importance of appellate court decisions. In other words, a case brief boils down a court opinion to the key elements and discusses the essence of the court's opinion. These basic elements are the facts of the case, the particular legal issue, rule of law and its application to the facts of the case as well as the court's conclusion (holding).

VI. Briefing Cases

class action

a lawsuit brought by one or more members of a group of persons on behalf of all group members with similar legal claims usually against a company or organization. Common class actions involve cases in which a product has injured many people or occur after a plane or train accident where all the victims would sue the transportation company together in a class action suit.

Civil Rights Movement

movement led primarily by black people beginning in the 1960s in an effort to establish the civil rights of individual black citizens in the US. A high point of the civil rights movement was a rally by thousands of people in Washington D.C. in 1963 at which a leader of the movement, Martin Luther King Jr., gave his "I have a dream" speech.

dictum (plural: dicta, obiter dicta)

Latin for "remark" (plural phrase meaning "things said by the way"), indicating the judge's opinions on points of law which are not directly relevant to the case in question. Such statements are often meant to clarify the legal principle applied in the judgement. For this reason, *obiter dicta* often take the form of illustrations or conclusions based on hypothetical situations. Unlike the *ratio decidendi* (see below) *obita dicta* are not binding, but they might be adopted as *ratio (rationale)* in subsequent cases, eg when a situation that was regarded as hypothetical in the *dicta* arises in a subsequent case.

education records

records that contain information directly related to a student which are maintained by an educational agency or institution or by a party acting for the agency or institution.

holding

the central part of a court opinion which resolves the actual dispute and might become a binding precedent.

ratio decidendi, ratio

Latin phrase meaning "the reason" or "the rationale underlying the decision". It is the legal principle upon which the decision in a specific case is founded. In other words: the rationale indicates the core principal of law that the court has applied to the material facts of the case in order to arrive at its decision. It is binding on lower courts and stands in contrast to *obiter dicta* (see above). Therefore, the *ratio decideni* is a fundamental part of establishing precedents (see page 3).

Vocabulary

albeit	obgleich, obschon, wenn auch
case report / opinion	schriftliche Urteilsausfertigung
compelling interest	zwingendes Interesse
to concur	übereinstimmen, beipflichten

VI. Briefing Cases

conjunctive	verbindend
creed	(Glaubens)Bekenntnis, Credo, Überzeugung
death knell	Totenglocke
(to the) detriment (of)	(zum) Nachteil, Schaden (von)
discernible	erkennbar, wahrnehmbar
disposition	*here:* Anordnung, Verfügung
to elevate	anheben, hervorheben, erhöhen
entrenched	etabliert, fest verwurzelt
facts (of a case)	Sachverhalt, Tatsachenfeststellungen
fellow panelists	andere Mitglieder des Senats
to find the facts	*here:* den Sachverhalt feststellen
to further	fördern, voranbringen
to hedge	absichern, sich schützen
inquiry	Nachforschung, Ermittlung, Untersuchung, Befragung
to invoke	sich berufen auf, anführen, zitieren
narrowly tailored	*here:* das gelindeste Mittel
to pass / to meet muster	Anforderungen genügen
realm	Bereich, Gebiet
reluctant	widerwillig, zögernd
remedy	Abhilfe, Rechtsbehelf, Rechtsmittel
to remedy	Schaden / Mangel beheben
subjugation	Unterwerfung, Unterjochung
to supersede	ersetzen, verdrängen, an Stelle von ... treten
to target	anvisieren, abzielen auf, zum Ziel setzen
to tread	betreten, schreiten, auftreten
unequivocally	eindeutig, unmissverständliche
valence	Wertigkeit, Valenz

VII. US Legal Education

General

The American education system requires that students complete twelve years of primary and secondary education prior to attending college or university. This may be accomplished either at public (government-operated) schools or at private schools. Primary education is preceded by pre-school or nursery education (kindergarten) and most commonly consists of five years of education, referred to as first through fifth grades. Secondary school usually consists of a total of seven years, referred to as sixth through twelfth grades. In the US, the ninth through twelfth grades are referred to as high school. The diploma awarded for the completion of high school is called **high school diploma**. Students must have obtained such a diploma before they are admitted into college or university.

Students who have completed high school and would like to continue their education must attend an **undergraduate school** (= college). These are schools that offer either a two-year degree (called an associate degree) or a four-year degree (called a **bachelor's degree**) in a specific course of study. Students are required to specialize on a certain field of study (their **major**) which they have to choose by their second year.

After having obtained a bachelor's degree students can continue their education (now referred to as **graduate eduation**) by pursuing one of two types of degrees: a **master's degree** or a **professional degree** (such as the JD or MD – see below). A master's degree is usually a two-year degree that is highly specialized in a specific field. Students are sometimes admitted to a master's degree program only if they have a bachelor's degree in a related field. However, there are many exceptions to this, such as with students who want to pursue a master's degree in business administration (a so called MBA).

Those who want to advance their education even further in a specific field can pursue a **doctorate degree**, also called a **PhD**. A PhD degree can take between three and six years to complete, depending on the course of study chosen, the ability of the student, and the thesis that the student has selected. The thesis is a very intensive research paper that must be completed prior to earning the degree. Depending on the school such a paper may also be required of students pursuing a master's degree.

In the US, certain courses of study (such as medicine and law) are only available **at the graduate level**. Hence, in order to attend a US law school **a student must hold an undergraduate degree**. The professional degree granted by US law schools is the **Juris Doctor (JD)**. Like the Doctor of Medicine (MD), the JD degree is a professional doctorate. It is the degree that is required to practice as a lawyer and it requires **three years of study at a law school** after completion of an undergraduate degree.

VII. US Legal Education

Universities may offer undergraduate degrees in law-related fields. But this is not sufficient to practice as a lawyer and law schools do not require that applicants take an undergraduate degree in a particular subject. Instead, they emphasise the importance of a demanding and **well-rounded education** with experience in a variety of disciplines. Students who intend to go to law school after graduation from college should therefore seek to develop general **analytical skills** such as problem solving and critical thinking as well as oral/written communication and research skills. Given the American emphasis on liberal arts education, many of these skills are fostered in undergraduate (especially upper-level-) courses.

> **SIMPLY**
>
> In the US, law school programs are **professional programs on the graduate level**. Students are only allowed to attend a law school after having completed an undergraduate degree in some other field (typically a bachelor's degree in the humanities or social sciences). US law schools are usually **autonomous entities** within a larger university.

Law School Admission

Competition for a place at a US law school is fierce. Most law schools have at least ten applicants for every seat in the entering class; some have over twenty. This quantity of applications makes it necessary to deal with most applications based on "numbers": Of all the **selection criteria**, most law schools place the heaviest emphasis on the score from the Law School Admission Test (**LSAT**) and on the student's cumulative college grade point average (**GPA**).

The **Law School Admission Test** (LSAT) is a halfday standardized test required for admission to all ABA-approved law schools and many non-ABA-approved law schools (see law school accreditation). It provides a standard measure of reading and verbal reasoning skills that law schools can use as **one of several factors** in assessing applicants. The highest possible score is 180. Most law schools require a score of at least 150 for admission, with the more competitive schools requiring scores of over 160. No law school is likely to grant admission for scores under 145.

Another important determinant for law school admission is the applicant's college GPA. The **GPA (grade-point average)** is a number representing a student's academic performance. It is calculated by dividing the total number of grade points received by the total number of courses attended and thereby measures his/her academic achievement.

Most US high schools and colleges have a GPA-range between 0 and 4, whereby the letter grade equivalents are:

A = 4
B = 3   B+ = 3,5
C = 2   C+ = 2,5
D = 1   D+ = 1,5
F = 0

A **cumulative GPA** is the average of a student's GPA since entering an academic institution (e.g college). For the purposes of law school admission, the cumulative college GPA is sometimes "weighted", which means that additional point value is given to advanced college courses. In general, the better the law school the higher the GPA has to be to be admitted. Each law school sets its own rules on how to interpret an applicant's grade-point average, because members of law school admission committees understand that a particular grade earned at one college may not have the same meaning as the identical grade at another.

Members of the **admissions officer** usually have the power to make apriori admission decisions. If the GPA and LSAT score are above a certain level, and there is no pressing reason to reject the applicant, (s)he will be offered a seat in the incoming class. Likewise, if these numbers are below a certain level and there is no pressing reason to accept the applicant, the admissions office can reject the applicant. The two numerical ranges are referred to as the "**presumptive admit**" and "**presumptive deny**" numbers. Between these two numbers is the "**discretionary**" range including applicants whose files are worth looking at, but about whom no automatic decisions can be made. Applicants who belong to this group must show that they have **a little something extra** to offer besides their numbers.

Therefore, a student's **personal statement** or **application essay** is another important factor in law school admission. Having overcome **personal hardship** such as physical, cultural, economic or linguistic obstacles may help indicate future success in the legal field and/or explain past academic difficulties. On these grounds, racial and ethnic minorities as well as applicants with a physical disability might be admitted with numbers lower than the presumptive admit mark. The rationale in **giving these applicants special consideration** is that their lower numbers do not necessarily indicate less of an ability to succeed. Furthermore, most educators view a **diverse student body** as an important educational resource that enhances the environment for learning.

Law schools also look favorably upon **extracurricular activities** that demonstrate qualities necessary to succeed as a lawyer such as leadership or writing abilities. Therefore, law school candidates should mention their participation in student governments, debate teams, student newspapers and other organizations.

SIMPLY
Getting into law school is the first step to becoming a lawyer, but law school admission is highly competitive. There are a lot more law school applicants than there are availabe spots. Approximately 40% of the students seeking admission will not be admitted. The application process includes submitting college grades (which will be transferred into a **cumulative GPA**), a **personal essay** as well as **letters of recommendation**. Applicants also need to do well on the **LSAT**.

JD Program

Since the professional JD degree is meant for those who wish to practice law or work within the legal field in the US, the program focuses on American law. Law schools generally require three years of fulltime study for the JD degree. The **first year** is quite

VII. US Legal Education

packed with **compulsory courses** such as civil procedure, constitutional law, contracts, criminal law, legal methods, legal writing, property and torts (personal injury law). It may also include **moot court** exercises (mock trials) providing students with the opportunity to compete with one another by giving mock oral arguments before a panel of judges. The **second and third years** of law school allow a student to concentrate on particular areas of the law and to choose courses in their field of interest such as business, litigation, international or family law.

In addition, the second and third years often provide the student with the chance to get some **legal experience** through various **practical opportunities** such as **legal externships, summer clerkships, legal clinics** and **pro bono projects** (see page 63). These programs place students in law offices, courts and public interest organizations with the goal of providing **realworld legal experience** under the guidance of faculty members, licensed attorneys and sitting judges. Most of these programs are offered for **school credit** with only a few providing financial compensation.

One of the most honorable extracurricular activities that a law student can benefit from is the membership in a **law review**, a scholarly journal focusing on legal issues, which is edited and in part written by students. Membership on the law review staff is highly competitive, as it often has a significant impact on the members' subsequent careers. The paths to membership vary from school to school, but most law reviews select members after their first year of studies either through a writing competition, their first-year grades or some combination thereof.

Most law schools offer the option of academic **joint- or dual degrees** in various disciplines as a way to reach a greater number of prospective students. Joint/dual programs focus on a broader range of (interdisciplinary) studies. For students, these programs may represent a savings of both time and money when compared to the option of pursuing the same two degrees individually. Most dual (eg JD/MBA) programs can be earned in **four years** as opposed to the five years it would take to earn them separately. Consequently, these joint/dual degrees will take more time to complete due to the **added degree requirements**. The most common degrees are a JD/MBA or a JD/MA in economics or political science.

Financing Legal Education

Few students can afford to pay for college and school education without some form of financing. Most law school graduates have a combined debt from undergraduate and graduate schools. Because of the debt associated with law school graduation there is a variety of financial aid available:

- **Scholarships** do not have to be repaid and are usually awarded based on financial need, merit and/or special interests.
- **Grants** are another debt-free funding option. They are typically given to students who demonstrate financial need.

- **(Federal / State) student loans** are either sponsored by the federal- or the state government and are based on eligibility requirements. These loans must be repaid.
- **Private student loans** are an additional option when federal and/or state loans are not enough to cover all the costs.
- **Workstudy programs** involve earning money either on or off campus during the academic year. These programs provide jobs for students with financial need to pay the cost of college.

In addition, most colleges and universities offer **tuition payment plans** which allow students to spread tuition costs over several months.

Other ways of financing postsecondary education include **home equity loans** or (second) **mortgages**. The advantage of a home equity loan is that the interest may be deductible on a federal tax return.

To assist people committed to public interest work, state and federal governments have established **loan cancellation or forgiveness programs**. However, lawyers are not eligible to participate in the majority of such programs. It is widely believed that loan forgiveness should be targeted only to persons entering traditionally low paying occupations or occupations related to a national need. Therefore, law school graduates are often forced to start working in large firms if they want to pay back their loans soon.

> **SIMPLY**
> Law students finance most of their education through loans, either from the government or from private sources. Additional money for law school is available in the form of scholarships, grants or workstudy. Because most law students' financial aid come from loans, they are likely to graduate with an enormous debt.

Law School Accreditation

In most US states, a JD degree from a law school that has been approved by the **American Bar Association (ABA)** is a requirement for eligibility to take the bar examination. The ABA is a voluntary association of lawyers, judges, and other legal professionals. It seeks to improve the legal profession, ensure the availability of legal services to all citizens, and improve the administration of justice.

In order to receive the ABA's seal of approval a law school has to undergo a rigorous process known as **accreditation.** Through this process the ABA determines whether or not a law school adheres to the ABA's standards for legal education in order to insure a level of **national uniformity in legal education** and practice. As of December 2013, a total of 203 institutions were approved by the American Bar Association.

In addition to the national ABA, states have their own **state bar associations**, which administer the bar exam. In some instances, as in California, the state bar provides an additional form of accreditation. California is one of the few states that issue accreditation to some law schools not accredited by the national ABA.

Master's Degree in Law and other Postgraduate Degrees

The **LLM** (Master of Laws) is an internationally recognized **postgraduate law degree**. It is a higher academic degree that is comparable to an MBA in business and management and is usually obtained by completing a one-year full-time program. LLM programs are primarily meant for already-qualified lawyers who have several years of experience but wish to pursue further study. Common LLM programs include tax-, environmental-, family-, human rights-, commercial-, international-, information technology-, trial advocacy and insurance law. For foreign-educated lawyers some US law schools offer LLM programs in "US Law" or "US Legal Studies" which are designed to give foreign law graduates an insight into the American legal system.

Other postgraduate degrees include Master's degrees in Comparative Law (**MCL**), in Comparative Jurisprudence (**MCJ**) and in Legal Institutions (**MLI**).

Degrees awarded at the doctoral level are the **Doctor of Juridical Science** (SJD or JSD) and the Doctor of Comparative Law Studies (DCL). These are the most advanced degrees in law and generally intended for those pursuing an academic career in the legal field. Only a small number of applicants are admitted into such programs, which consist of specialized study and research as well as a substantial thesis.

Teaching Methods

Besides the vast amount of studying involved, the teaching methods used in most US law school classes can be quite intimidating to a first-year law student.

The **case method** focuses on the analysis of court opinions rather than lectures and textbooks. It was pioneered at Harvard Law School by *Christopher Columbus Langdell* and is based on the principle that the best way to study legal principles (at least in a Common Law system) is to read judicial opinions rather than studying highly abstract summaries of legal rules. Thus, student assignments entail reading cases compiled in a **casebook** (that is a collection of written judicial opinions at the appellate level). Students have to study these cases at home in order to be prepared to answer questions based on them in the next class meeting and to determine which legal rule was applied by the court and how. In doing so, students develop the ability to read and analyze cases. Furthermore, they are taught to reduce a case to its **basic components** – the **facts**, the **legal issue**, the **holding** and the court's **reasoning** (see page 46). Involving real parties with real problems cases tend to stimulate students more than textbook material does. Besides, by reading cases students learn how judges apply former precedents and **how they create law** by interpreting legal rules, which is an essential skill for a Common Law attorney.

The **Socratic method** of instruction – which is usually coupled with the case method – is founded on Socrates' belief that lecturing is not an effective method of teaching. It induces students to **orally respond** to an (often difficult) series of questions designed by the professor to help them gain further insight into the meaning of the law. Applying this teaching method, the professor usually "invites" a law student to give a thorough and detailed summary of one of the assigned cases and then questions him/her on omitted details or unresolved issues. Afterwards, the professor may slightly alter the facts of the case in order to allow the student to come to a different decision than that reached by the court. Thereby, law students learn to distinguish relevant from irrelevant facts and issues. In addition, **teaching through asking questions** does not "push ideas into students" that they may or may not be able to absorb or assimilate, but gives the professor a constant feedback and allows him/her to monitor the students' understanding when presenting the material. Needless to say, an advantage of pure lecturing is that it absorbs a lot less time.

Pro Bono Opportunities

In the law school setting "pro bono" generally refers to students providing **voluntary, law-related services** to people of limited means or to community-based nonprofit organizations. Pro bono programs help students **develop professionalism** and an **understanding of a lawyer's responsibility** to the community. Participation in such a program facilitates their involvement in the community and increases the availability of legal services to indigent citizens. Law students also benefit by gaining practical experience and by exploring alternative career opportunities. Some law schools (such as Harvard) require all of their students to contribute a minimum amount of law-related pro bono work as a condition for graduation. Law schools with voluntary rather than mandatory pro bono service policies encourage students to assist lawyers and legal aid organizations by **offering incentives**, such as awards at graduation or special notations on law school transcripts. Some law schools make **financial assistance** available to students participating in pro bono activities through fellowships, loan repayment assistance or even loan forgiveness. Other schools offer lower interest rates or **postponed payment of law school loans** to law school graduates who enter public interest employment.

Bar Exam

Upon completion of the JD degree, students must **pass a state's bar exam** in order to practice as a lawyer ("to be admitted to the bar") in that state. It is a lengthy examination conducted at regular intervals to determine whether a candidate is qualified to practice law in a particular state. Most states will not grant permission to sit the exam unless the law school has been **accredited** (approved) **by the ABA**. In some cases, though, graduates from a non-ABA-approved law school may be allowed to take the exam in the state where this particular school is located. Since it covers the law particular to that state, candidates are advised to attend a **bar review course** prior to the bar exam, in order to specifically prepare for it.

As part of their own testing of candidates to determine if they are competent to practice law, most US states also administer the **Multistate Bar Exam** (MBE), a six-hour multiple-choice question examination covering material from constitutional law, contracts, criminal law and procedure, evidence, real property and torts. The MBE score may be transferred into another jurisdiction to be used with another (but not every) state's bar examination.

VII. US Legal Education

Law School Admission and Affirmative Action

Affirmative action is a source of heated legal, political and social debate, with much of the attention focused on higher education (see page 48). Ever since Justice Powell's landmark decision on affirmative action, *Regents of the University of California v. Bakke* (1978), stating that **a university can take race into account as one among a number of factors in student admissions** for the purpose of achieving a diverse student body, affirmative action programs in student admissions (as well as in financial aid and in faculty employment) have largely been based on diversity.

Allan Bakke, a white male, applied to the University of California (UC) Davis Medical School in 1973 and in 1974. In 1973 he had a benchmark score of 468 out of 500, but no regular applicants were admitted after him with a score below 470. Bakke however, was not considered for 4 special admissions slots which had not yet been filled. In 1974 he applied again, received a score of 549 out of 600 and was denied again. In both years minority applicants were admitted under the "special admissions" program with benchmark scores significantly lower than Bakke's. He then filed suit in the Superior Court of California seeking an injunction to allow him into the medical school claiming that the school had discriminated against him on the basis of his race in violation of the **Equal Protection Clause of the Fourteenth Amendment**, the California Constitution and Title VI of the Civil Rights Act of 1964.

The California Supreme Court favored Bakke in a vote 8 to 1 and the university appealed to the US Supreme Court which, in June 1978, ruled that Bakke be admitted to the medical school. The decision was split, with 4 justices firmly against all use of race in admissions processes, 4 justices for the use of race in university admissions and Justice Powell, who was against the UC Davis Medical School quota system of admission (the program set aside 16 of the 100 places in the entering class for certain minority groups) but found that **universities were allowed to use race as a factor in admission**. Justice Powell argued that **quotas insulated minority applicants from competition** with the regular applicants and were therefore **unconstitutional** but that universities could use race as a **plus factor**. He cited the Harvard College Admissions Program as an example of a constitutionally valid affirmative action program which takes of all of an applicant's qualities – including race – into account in a "holistic review."

The nature of this split opinion created controversy over whether Powell's opinion was binding. The most noteworthy appellate court opinion rejecting the Supreme Court's 1978 *Bakke* decision is *Hopwood v. State of Texas* 78 F.3d 932 (see page 50). With the Supreme Court's July 1996 denial of certiorari, the Hopwood decision became the final law with respect to the use of race in student admissions in Louisiana, Mississippi, and Texas (the three states over which the Fifth Circuit maintains jurisdiction).

However, 25 years after *Bakke*, the Supreme Court again addressed the issue of race and access to higher education in 2003, issuing its long awaited ruling in the **University of Michigan cases**: The case *Gratz v. Bollinger* involves Michigan's undergraduate admissions program, whereas *Grutter v. Bollinger* affects its law school. In both cases the plaintiffs were white women. Jennifer Gratz was a top high school student in suburban Detroit in 1995 when her application to University of Michigan was rejected. Barbara Grutter was 49 when she applied to Michigan's prestigious law school and was rejected. In a narrow, 5–4 decision, the justices upheld the law school's admission process that considered a candidate's race, but did not assign a specific weight to this factor. In doing so, the Supreme Court reaffirmed that colleges and universities can consider race in making admissions decisions. The Court, however, struck down the undergraduate program, which automatically awarded a set number of points to minority candidates. Prior to the decisions, several organizations and individuals had filed **friend-of-the-court (amicus curiae) briefs** (see page 46) in support of equal opportunity.

Discuss

Read the syllabus of Grutter v. Bollinger and summarize the facts of the case and the legal arguments of the Supreme Court in your own words:

Grutter v. Bollinger et al.

▶ CERTIORARI TO THE UNITED STATES COURT OF APPEALS FOR THE SIXTH CIRCUIT

Argued April 1, 2003 – Decided June 23, 2003

The University of Michigan Law School (Law School), one of the Nation's top law schools, follows an official admissions policy that seeks to achieve student body diversity through compliance with *Regents of Univ. of Cal.* v. *Bakke*, 438 U.S. 265. Focusing on students' academic ability coupled with a flexible assessment of their talents, experiences, and potential, the policy requires admissions officials to evaluate each applicant based on all the information available in the file, including a personal statement, letters of recommendation, an essay describing how the applicant will contribute to Law School life and diversity, and the applicant's undergraduate grade point average (GPA) and Law School Admissions Test (LSAT) score.

Additionally, officials must look beyond grades and scores to so-called "soft variables," such as recommenders' enthusiasm, the quality of the undergraduate institution and the applicant's essay, and the areas and difficulty of undergraduate course selection. The policy does not define diversity solely in terms of racial and ethnic status and does not restrict the types of diversity contributions eligible for "substantial weight," but it does reaffirm the Law School's commitment to diversity with special reference to the inclusion of African-American, Hispanic, and Native-American students, who otherwise might not be represented in the student body in meaningful numbers. By enrolling a "critical mass" of underrepresented minority students, the policy seeks to ensure their ability to contribute to the Law School's character and to the legal profession.

When the Law School denied admission to petitioner Grutter, a white Michigan resident with a 3.8 GPA and 161 LSAT score, she filed this suit, alleging that respondents had discriminated against her on the basis of race in violation of the Fourteenth Amendment, Title VI of the Civil Rights Act of 1964, and 42 U.S.C. § 1981; that she was rejected because the Law School uses race as a "predominant" factor, giving applicants belonging to certain minority groups a significantly greater chance of admission than students with similar credentials from disfavored racial groups; and that respondents had no compelling interest to justify that use of race. The District Court found the Law School's use of race as an admis-

VII. US Legal Education

sions factor unlawful. The Sixth Circuit reversed, holding that Justice Powell's opinion in *Bakke* was binding precedent establishing diversity as a compelling state interest, and that the Law School's use of race was narrowly tailored because race was merely a "potential 'plus' factor" and because the Law School's pro gram was virtually identical to the Harvard admissions program described approvingly by Justice Powell and appended to his *Bakke* opinion.

Held: The Law School's narrowly tailored use of race in admissions decisions to further a compelling interest in obtaining the educational benefits that flow from a diverse student body is not prohibited by the Equal Protection Clause, Title VI, or § 1981. Pp. 9—32.

(a) In the landmark *Bakke* case, this Court reviewed a medical school's racial set-aside program that reserved 16 out of 100 seats for members of certain minority groups. The decision produced six separate opinions, none of which commanded a majority. Four Justices would have upheld the program on the ground that the government can use race to remedy disadvantages cast on minorities by past racial prejudice. 438 U.S., at 325.

Four other Justices would have struck the program down on statutory grounds. *Id.*, at 408. Justice Powell, announcing the Court's judgment, provided a fifth vote not only for invalidating the program, but also for reversing the state court's injunction against any use of race whatsoever. In a part of his opinion that was joined by no other Justice, Justice Powell expressed his view that attaining a diverse student body was the only interest asserted by the university that survived scrutiny. *Id.*, at 311. Grounding his analysis in the academic freedom that "long has been viewed as a special concern of the First Amendment," *id.*, at 312, 314, Justice Powell emphasized that the " 'nation's future depends upon leaders trained through wide exposure' to the ideas and mores of students as diverse as this Nation." *Id.*, at 313. However, he also emphasized that "[i]t is not an interest in simple ethnic diversity, in which a specified percentage of the student body is in effect guaranteed to be members of selected ethnic groups," that can justify using race. *Id.*, at 315. Rather, "[t]he diversity that furthers a compelling state interest encompasses a far broader array of qualifications and characteristics of which racial or ethnic origin is but a single though important element." *Ibid.* Since *Bakke*, Justice Powell's opinion has been the touchstone for constitutional analysis of race-conscious admissions policies. Public and private universities across the Nation have modeled their own admissions programs on Justice Powell's views. Courts, however, have struggled to discern whether Justice Powell's diversity rationale is binding precedent. The Court finds it unnecessary to decide this issue because the Court endorses Justice Powell's view that student body diversity is a compelling state interest in the context of university admissions. Pp. 9—13.

(b) All government racial classifications must be analyzed by a reviewing court under strict scrutiny. *Adarand Constructors, Inc.* v. *Peña*, 515 U.S. 200, 227. But not all such uses are invalidated by strict scrutiny. Race-based action necessary to further a compelling governmental interest does not violate the Equal Protection Clause so long as it is narrowly tailored to further that interest. *Eg, Shaw* v. *Hunt*, 517 U.S. 899, 908. Context matters when reviewing such action. See *Gomillion* v. *Lightfoot*, 364 U.S. 339, 343—344. Not every decision influenced by race is equally objectionable, and strict scrutiny is designed to provide a framework for carefully examining the importance and the sincerity of the government's reasons for using race in a particular context. 13—15.

(c) The Court endorses Justice Powell's view that student body diversity is a compelling state interest that can justify using race in university admissions. The Court defers to the Law School's educational judgment that diversity is essential to its educational mission. The Court's scrutiny of that interest is no less strict for taking into account complex educational judgments in an area that lies primarily within the university's expertise. See, eg, *Bakke*, 438 U.S., at 319, n. 53 (opinion of Powell, J.). Attaining a diverse student body is at the heart of the Law School's proper institutional mission, and its "good faith" is "presumed" absent "a showing to the contrary." *Id.*, at 318—319. Enrolling a "critical mass" of minority students simply to assure some specified percentage of a particular group merely because of its race or ethnic origin would be patently unconstitutional. *Eg, id.*, at 307. But the Law School defines its critical mass concept by reference to the substantial, important, and laudable educational benefits that diversity is designed to produce, including cross-racial understanding and the breaking down of racial stereotypes. The Law School's claim is further bolstered by numerous expert studies and reports showing that such diversity promotes learning outcomes and better prepares students for an increasingly diverse workforce, for society, and for the legal profession. Major American businesses have made clear that the skills needed in today's increasingly global marketplace can only be developed through exposure to widely diverse people, cultures, ideas, and viewpoints. Highranking retired officers and civilian military leaders assert that a highly qualified, racially diverse officer corps is essential to national security. Moreover, because universities, and in particular, law schools, represent the training ground for a large number of the Nation's leaders, *Sweatt* v. *Painter*, 339 U.S. 629, 634, the path to leadership must be visibly open to talented and qualified individuals of every race and ethnicity. Thus, the Law School has a compelling interest in attaining a diverse student body. 15— 21.

(d) The Law School's admissions program bears the hallmarks of a narrowly tailored plan. To be narrowly tailored, a race-conscious admissions program cannot "insulat[e] each category of applicants with certain desired qualifications from competition with all other applicants." *Bakke, supra*, at 315 (opinion of Powell, J.). Instead, it may consider race or ethnicity only as a " 'plus' in a particular applicant's file"; *i.e.*, it must be "flexible enough to consider all pertinent elements of diversity in light of the particular qualifications of each applicant, and to place them on the same footing for consideration, although not necessarily according them the same weight," *id.*, at 317. It follows that universities cannot establish quotas for members of certain racial or ethnic groups or put them on separate admissions tracks. See *id.*, at 315—316. The Law School's admissions program, like the Harvard plan approved by Justice Powell, satisfies these requirements. Moreover, the pro gram is flexible enough to ensure that each applicant is evaluated as an individual and not in a way that makes race or ethnicity the defining feature of the application. See *Bakke, supra*, at 317 (opinion of Powell, J.). The Law School engages in a highly individualized, holistic review of each applicant's file, giving serious consideration to all the ways an applicant might contribute to a diverse educational environment. There is no policy, either *de jure* or *de facto*, of automatic acceptance or rejection based on any single "soft" variable. *Gratz* v. *Bollinger, ante*, p. __, distinguished. Also, the program adequately ensures that all factors that may contribute to diversity are meaningfully considered alongside race. Moreover, the Law School frequently accepts nonminority applicants with grades and test scores lower than underrepresented minority applicants (and other nonminority applicants) who are rejected. The Court rejects the argument that the Law School should have used other race-neutral means to obtain the educational benefits of student body diversity, eg, a lottery system or decreasing the emphasis on GPA and LSAT scores. Narrow tailoring does not require exhaustion of every conceivable race-neutral alternative or mandate that a university choose between maintaining a reputation for excellence or fulfilling a commitment to provide educational opportunities to members of all racial groups. See, eg, *Wygant v. Jackson Bd. of Ed.*, 476 U.S. 267, 280, n. 6. The Court is satisfied that the Law School adequately considered the available alternatives. The Court is also satisfied that, in the context of individualized consideration of the possible diversity contributions of each applicant, the Law School's race-conscious admissions program does not unduly harm nonminority applicants. Finally, race-conscious admissions policies must be limited in time. The Court takes the Law School at its word that it would like nothing better than to find a race-neutral admissions formula and will terminate its use of racial preferences as soon as practicable. The Court expects that 25 years from now, the use of racial preferences will no longer be necessary to further the interest approved today. Pp. 21–31.

(e) Because the Law School's use of race in admissions decisions is not prohibited by Equal Protection Clause, petitioner's statutory claims based on Title VI and § 1981 also fail. See *Bakke*, supra, at 287 (opinion of Powell, J.); *General Building Contractors Assn., Inc. v. Pennsylvania*, 458 U.S. 375, 389–391. Pp. 31–32.

288 F.3d 732, affirmed.

O'Connor, J., delivered the opinion of the Court, in which Stevens, Souter, Ginsburg, and Breyer, JJ., joined, and in which Scalia and Thomas, JJ., joined in part insofar as it is consistent with the views expressed in Part VII of the opinion of Thomas, J. Ginsburg, J., filed a concurring opinion, in which Breyer, J., joined. Scalia, J., filed an opinion concurring in part and dissenting in part, in which Thomas, J., joined. Thomas, J., filed an opinion concurring in part and dissenting in part, in which Scalia, J., joined as to Parts I–VII. Rehnquist, C. J., filed a dissenting opinion, in which Scalia, Kennedy, and Thomas, JJ., joined. Kennedy, J., filed a dissenting opinion.

SIMPLY

In *Grutter v. Bollinger* the US Supreme Court reaffirmed that universities may take race into consideration as one factor among many factors when selecting incoming students. In other words, the **US Supreme Court upheld the constitutionality of race-conscious admissions policies** designed to promote diversity in higher education.

Discuss

What are the general admission requirements to get into a US law school?

Explain the different requirements in your legal education system!

Which "numbers" are used to rank law school candidates in admission procedures?

VII. US Legal Education

Which skills should a prospective law school candidate seek to develop during undergraduate education?

How do the case method and the Socratic method differ from the lecture method?

Explain the term "accreditation" in the context of legal education!

How do you qualify to practice law in the US / in your country?

Why is it advisable to attend a bar review course?

Explain the following terms and abbreviations: LAW REVIEW – EXTERNSHIP – CLINICAL COURSE – PRO BONO WORK – CASEBOOK – LAW SCHOOL TRANSCRIPT – GPA – LSAT – ABA – BA – MBA – JD

Concepts

accreditation [ə-krĕd'ĭ-tā'shən]

the granting of approval to an institution of learning by an official review board (*here:* the ABA) after the school has met specific requirements.

alumnus, alumna, almuni

an alumnus (masculine) or alumna (feminine) is a former student of a college, university, or school. Alumni/ae (plural) reunions are popular events at many institutions. They are usually organized by alumni associations and are often social occasions for fundraising.

Bachelor's degree

an academic degree conferred by a college or university upon those who complete the undergraduate curriculum; also called baccalaureate [bak-uh-lawr-ee-it]. The two most common bachelor degrees awarded by US schools are the Bachelor of Science degree (also called the B.S.) and the Bachelor of Arts degree (also called the B.A.).

bar review course

privately organized course that law students attend after graduation from law school in order to prepare for the state bar exam. Bar preparation courses supply participants with outlines of the topic areas and with sample multiple-choice questions. A substantial majority of law school graduates attend a six-week course provided by "BarBri", a US company with market dominance in the sector of bar exam preparation.

brief

a written legal argument, usually in a format prescribed by the courts, stating the legal reasons for a lawsuit in order to provide the judge with reasons to rule in favor of the party represented by the brief writer. Ironically, although the term was originally intended to mean a brief or summary argument (shorter than an oral presentation), legal briefs are quite often notoriously long.

VII. US Legal Education

case method

a method of instruction which uses case studies and focuses on the analysis of court opinions rather than lectures and textbooks with the goal that students discover insight on their own. In combination with the Socratic method, case teaching is the predominant method of instruction in US law schools.

case syllabus [sil-uh-buhs]

(1) short summary of the legal basis of a court's decision appearing at the beginning of a reported case; (2) a book containing summaries of the leading cases in a legal field, used especially by students.

casebook

a type of coursebook used in US legal education to teach students under the case method system. Rather than simply laying out the facts of a particular area of study, a casebook contains judicial decisions as well as excerpts from legal cases which illustrate the application of particular principles of a specific field of law.

college / university

the usual practice in the US is to call an institution made up of several faculties and granting a range of higher degrees a "university", while a smaller institution only granting bachelor's or associate's degrees is called a "college." The term "college" derives from Latin (collegium) and (in American English) is reserved for institutions of higher education, which are empowered to grant degrees.

externship

through an externship, a student can gain real work experience in his/her specific area of interest outside the school. Students taking part in such a program are usually supervised by attorneys and/or faculty members.

fraternity / sorority

student societies formed in US colleges primarily for social purposes. Most of these societies were originally founded on dedication to principles such as community service and sound learning. Fraternities (men's societies) and sororities (women's societies) are usually named by two or three Greek letters and are also known as "Greek-letter societies".

freshman / sophomore / junior / senior (students)

a freshman is a first-year student, a sophomore a second-year student, a junior is a student in the penultimate (usually third) year and a senior is a student in the last (usually fourth) year at a high school, college or university. A student taking more time than normal to graduate is sometimes referred to as a "super senior".

grade

in the US education system the word grade has two meanings: (1) the score achieved on an exam or in a course and (2) a year of education in primary or secondary school.

VII. US Legal Education

GPA

in the US, grades are generally assigned by a letter: A (highest grade, excellent), B (above average), C (average), D (usually the minimum passing grade), and F (failed). Most schools calculate a student's grade point average (GPA) by assigning each letter grade a number and using a mathematical formula to come up with a numerical representation of a student's work. Generally, US schools equate an A with a numerical value of 4.0 (see page 58).

ivy league law school

a league of universities and colleges in the northeastern US that have a reputation for scholastic achievement and social prestige.

J.D.

short for: Juris Doctor; the law degree granted upon graduation by US law schools.

law review

a periodical published by a law school or bar association that contains articles analyzing and evaluating subject areas and developments in the law; the term is also used to describe the (prestigious) extracurricular law school activity of publishing the journal.

legal clinics

legal clinics offer an opportunity for second and third year law students to apply classroom knowledge to real-life legal situations. Students perform "real" legal work under the supervision of a faculty member and/or practicing attorney.

LL.M.

Latin abbreviation for "Master of Laws," whereby the second L indicates the plural form which – in an abbreviated word in Latin – is always identified as a double letter. The LLM is an advanced degree that is awarded to an individual who already holds a JD after having completed a prescribed course of further legal studies. There is a wide range of LLM programs available worldwide which enable students to focus on almost any area of the law.

LSAT

short for: Law School Admissions Test; a standardized examination whose result is used by law schools as one factor in accepting applicants.

major

here: a field of study chosen as an academic specialty.

minor

a second area of specialized academic study, requiring fewer courses or credits than a major.

VII. US Legal Education

moot court

law school exercise in which students argue both sides of a fictitious lawsuit in a mock court. There are also moot court contests between teams from different law schools.

Socratic method

developed from Plato's Socratic Dialogues, the Socratic method of teaching is a student-centered approach that challenges learners to develop their critical thinking skills and engage in analytic discussion.

undergraduate/ graduate education

in some educational systems, the term undergraduate education generally stands for post-secondary education up to the level of a bachelor's degree. Students of higher degrees are known as postgraduates (or often simply "graduates"). In the US and Canada, most undergraduate education takes place at four-year colleges.

Vocabulary

to accredit	zulassen, akkreditieren, anerkennen
advance training	Fortbildung
aid	Förderung, Unterstützung
applicant	Bewerber, Antragsteller; *also:* Beschwerdeführer
assessment	Beurteilung, Einschätzung, Bewertung
associated with	verbunden mit, einhergehend mit
Bachelor's degree	Bakkalaureus, niedrigster akadem. Grad
benchmark	Bezugspunkt, Richtgröße, Vergleichspunkt
benchmark score	Richtwert (Punktezahl)
brief	Kurzdarstellung, Abriss; adj.: knapp, kurz
to brief	jm einweisen, instruieren
brief-case	Aktentasche
clinical course	praxisbezogener Kurs
completion	Beendigung, Abschluss
compulsory	verpflichtend, bindend
to convert	umwandeln, transformieren
coveted	begehrt
creditworthy debtors	kreditwürdige Schuldner
curriculum	Lehrplan, Studienplan
decline	Verfall, Untergang, Rückgang
deductible	abzugsfähig, absetzbar
to defray	(Kosten) tragen, bestreiten
demanding	anspruchsvoll
diversity	Vielfalt, Unterschiedlichkeit, Diversität
elite law school	Eliteuni

elitism	Elitismus
to enjoin sb from doing sth	jm untersagen etwas zu tun
equivalent	Äquivalent, Gegenwert, Gegenstück
to be equivalent to	gleichwertig sein mit
examination board	Prüfungskommission
to expedite sth	etwas vorantreiben, beschleunigen
fellowship / scholarship / grant	Stipendium
field of interest	Interessensgebiet
to foster (certain skills)	fördern (gewisse Begabungen)
grade	Note
(law school) graduation	Abschluss (des rechtswiss. Studiums)
to grant admission	Zulassung gewähren
home (equity) loan	Hypothek auf Wohnhaus
humanities	Humanwissenschaften, Geisteswissenschaften
impoverished	dürftig, arm, verarmt
to insulate	isolieren
interdisciplinary	fächerübergreifen, interdisziplinär
intimidating	einschüchternd
to invalidate	annullieren, entkräften, unwirksam machen
joint-degree program	Doppelstudium
landmark	Grenzstein, Meilenstein, Wahrzeichen
landmark decision	bahnbrechende Entscheidung
law class	juristische Lehrveranstaltung, Vorlesung
law school admission	Zulassung / Aufnahme zur juristischen Fakultät
lecture, course taught in the confrontational manner	Vorlesung
legal ethics	Rechtsethik
liberal arts, humanities	Geisteswissenschaften
lingering	nachklingend, zurückbleibend, verweilend
to live off campus	abseits des Campus wohnen
loan, credit	Kredit
loan repayment assistance	Kreditrückzahlungshilfe
lofty	stolz, erhaben, hochmütig
merit	Verdienst, Wert, Verdienstlichkeit
mock court / moot court	*here*: Scheingericht, hypothetisches Gericht
mock trial	Scheinprozess, Probeverfahren
moot	Streit; adj.: strittig
notation	Vermerk, Bezeichnung
to omit	unterlassen, auslassen, weglassen
to pass the bar (exam)	die Anwaltsprüfung schaffen
penultimate	vorletzte(r)

VII. US Legal Education

to place emphasis on sth	etwas betonen, hervorheben
population stratum	Bevölkerungsschicht
predominant	vorwiegend, vorherrschend, überlegen
professionalism	Professionalität, fachliche Qualifikation
to pursue an academic career	eine akademische Laufbahn verfolgen
(fixed) quota system	(festes) Quoten-, Kontingentierungssystem
to rank law school candidates	Bewerber nach Qualifikationen reihen
recommendation	Empfehlung, Vorschlag
to recruit	anwerben
to register, to enroll	inskribieren
registration, enrollment	Inskription
to reject an application	eine Bewerbung ablehnen
to be required to sit a test	eine Prüfung machen müssen
to reside on campus	am Campus wohnen
resume, curriculum vitae	Lebenslauf
to retain (= to hold within, to remain in a place)	behalten, einbehalten, zurückbehalten
sample	Beispiel
score	Punktezahl
scrutiny	genaue Überprüfung, Untersuchung
second mortgage	zweitrangige Hypothek
selection criteria	Auswahlkriterien
seminar style course	Seminar
social sciences	Sozialwissenschaften, Gesellschaftswissenschaften
sophomore	Student im zweiten Studienjahr
stipend	Gehalt, Bezüge
stratification	Schichtung, Stratifizierung
stratum, strata	Schicht(en)
to take the bar exam	zur Anwaltsprüfung antreten
tax return	Steuererklärung
to team-teach	gemeinsam / als Team unterrichten
thesis	Diplom- / Doktorarbeit
(academic) transcript	here: amtliches Zeugnis / Aufstellung aller Einzelnoten
transcript (of grades)	here: Abschrift der Noten, Zeugnis mit allen Noten
tuition	Studiengebühr
unresolved issues	ungelöste Fragen

Legal Subjects

administrative law	Verwaltungsrecht
bankruptcy law	Insolvenzrecht
canon law	Kanonisches Recht

civil law	Zivilrecht
civil procedure	Zivilprozessrecht
commercial law	Handelsrecht
competition law	Wettbewerbsrecht
conflict of laws	Kollisionsrecht
constitutional law	Verfassungsrecht
corporate law	Gesellschaftsrecht
criminal law	Strafrecht
criminal procedure	Strafprozessrecht
elder law	Altenrecht
environmental law	Umweltrecht
EU law	Europarecht
family law	Familienrecht
inheritance law	Erbrecht
labor law	Arbeitsrecht
law of contracts	Vertragsrecht
law of torts / tort law	Schadenersatzrecht
private law	Privatrecht
property law	Sachenrecht
public international law	Völkerrecht
real estate law	Immobilienrecht
securities law	Wertpapierrecht
social law	Sozialrecht
tax law	Steuerrecht

VIII. The US Legal Profession

Legal Jobs

Attorney, Attorney-at-Law

An attorney is a person who is qualified to provide legal services, including the appearance in a state or federal court. After passing the bar exam(ination), a law school graduate holding a JD degree is able to practice law in the particular state where he took the exam and to **approach the bar in that state's courts**. Some states will accept attorneys who passed the bar exam in another state, but many will not grant this "reciprocity" and require at least a basic test for out-of-state attorneys.

In order to be licensed to appear before a federal court a lawyer must apply to become a member of the Bar in the specific federal district, pay a fee and take an oath of admission. Attorneys who are not licensed in a particular state or before a certain (federal) court, but who wish to represent a client in a particular matter in that state/before that court, may petition the court to provide direct representation **pro hac vice** (Latin: "for this one case").

Corporate Attorney, Corporate Counsel

Most corporate lawyers work within the legal department of a corporation or as part of a corporate law firm. Some specialize in specific areas of business like finance, taxation, insurance, real estate transactions or mergers & acquisitions. Corporate attorneys must be licensed to practice law in at least one state; if they work for a national firm (a company that has a national presence), they might need to be a member of the bar in multiple states. They are "salaried", which means their pay does not vary according to the hours worked.

Judge, Justice

The judge is the official who presides over a court and passes judgment. The powers, functions, methods of appointment and training of judges vary widely across different jurisdictions. Judges are sometimes considered to be the "leaders" of the **judiciary**, which is one of the three branches of government. The doctrine that decisions of the judiciary should be impartial and not subject to influence from the other branches of government or from private or political interests is referred to as **judicial independence**. In most cases, judicial independence is secured by giving judges long (often **lifetime**) **tenure** or by making it difficult to remove them from office. In the US, a judge is addressed as "Your Honor" when presiding over the court. The judges of the Supreme Court of the US and the judges of many higher courts are called "justices". Judges of courts of specialized jurisdiction (such as bankruptcy courts) are sometimes officially referred to as "referees," but the use of this title is in decline. Judges sitting in Courts of Equity in Common Law systems are often called "chancellors".

In civil law jurisdictions lawyers have to undergo a special and **selective judge-training-program** after graduating from a university if they intend to work as a judge. In Common Law countries judges are usually not trained separately from attorneys but either **appointed or elected** from the pool of practicing attorneys.

Justice of the Peace (JP)

A JP is a magistrate working at the lowest level of some US state courts. They deal with minor (such as traffic) offenses, perform marriages or administer oaths and send cases to a higher court for trial. In the US, they are **usually not required to have a formal legal education** in order to qualify for the office; instead there are various forms of JP-trainings.

Law Clerk / Judicial Clerk

A law clerk / judicial clerk is a person who provides assistance to a judge (in federal or state courts) in researching issues before the court and in writing opinions. Law clerks are not court clerks (see page 24) or courtroom deputies, who belong to the administrative staff of a court. Most law clerks are recent law school graduates who performed at or near the top of their class. Working as a law clerk generally opens up career opportunities.

Magistrate

The term "magistrate" is a generic term for any judge of a court or anyone officially performing a judge's functions. In a few US states the term magistrate specifically stands for an officer of the court at the lowest level who hears small-claims-lawsuits, serves as a judge for charges of minor crimes and/or conducts preliminary hearings in criminal cases to determine if there is enough evidence presented by the prosecution to hold the accused for trial. In federal courts the term is used for an official who conducts routine hearings assigned by the federal judges, including preliminary hearings in criminal cases.

Notary Public

A notary public is a person **authorized by the state** in which the person resides to administer oaths (acts of swearing the truth of a statement), to take acknowledgments, to certify documents and sometimes to take depositions (if the notary is also a court reporter). The signature and seal or stamp of a notary public is necessary to attest that the person **making an affidavit** was under oath or to attest that a person acknowledged in the presence of the notary that (s)he accepted a deed. A notary public must see proof of identity of those swearing and must keep an **official journal of documents notarized.** In the US, the notary is commissioned by the state and may act only within the territory authorized by state statutes. Most states set maximum fees for notarial services and require that a **notarial seal or stamp** be impressed on documents authenticated by a notary public. In the US a notary public has far less power compared to the powers of a civil law notary in Western Europe. The role of a civil-law notary is more or less equivalent to that of a lawyer who specializes in real estate, sales, mortgages and the settlement of estates but who may not appear in court. In civil law countries notaries are required to undergo specific training and must also first serve as an apprentice before being commissioned or licensed to practice their profession.

Paralegal

Individuals who have not graduated from a law school and perform routine tasks for various lawyers or law firms (thus **requiring some knowledge of the law**) are called "paralegals". They are either employed by a law office or work freelance. Most of them have taken a prescribed series of courses in law and law related fields, which is much less demanding than those required for a licensed attorney. Paralegals are **increasingly popular** and handle much of the paperwork in probates of estates, divorce actions, bankruptcies, investigations, analyzing depositions, preparing and answering interrogatories and procedural motions and other specialized jobs. The hourly rate charged by a law firm for work done by paralegals is much less than that for qualified attorneys.

Summer Associate

Law firms usually have **summer associate programs** to expose (primarily second year) law students to the practice of law at their office and to determine whether they meet the firm's expectations. If that is the case the summer associate gets a job offer from that firm, returns to the firm after law school graduation and eventually brings money into the firm.

Being a summer associate is comparable with giving a **very long interview**. Since the firm's goal is to decide whether to give the student a permanent offer of employment, his or her qualifications and personality are assessed in order to find out whether (s)he fits with the firm's culture and goals and whether (s)he has the ability to be a good lawyer. The summer associate's goal is not only **to get an offer** but also to evaluate whether the firm meets his/her career goals and sometimes simply to return to the law school after the summer with attorneys to add to his/her network, a reference and a writing sample.

Stratification of the Legal Profession

Sociologists like to put societies into different classes (also referred to as strata) based on people's power and reputation within society (**social stratification**). From a sociological perspective, the US legal profession can be divided into **three strata**: The most **renowned and prestigious** category of lawyers (**stratum 1**) is sometimes called the "Cravath" strata. Lawyers of this category work for large, national law firms such as *Cravath, Swaine & Moore LLP* (short: "Cravath"). This law firm is considered one of the most prestigious and selective in the US. Some stratum 1 lawyers work for Wall Street firms (then also called **Wall Street lawyers**), whereby the phrase "Wall Street" is used shorthand for all big finance oriented businesses, whether based in New York or not. The term is also used to refer to American financial markets and financial institutions as a whole. **Cravath and Wall Street lawyers** are expected to be wholly devoted to the firm and their clients. They are chosen among the top students of the graduating classes of top US law schools and then undergo a merciless training period in their first year, which is sometimes compared with **boot camp training**, during which the firm sorts the wheat from the chaff. A first year associate's ability to remain with the firm and eventually "make it" is largely determined by his/her **hours billed** (see page 81). New associates usually do general work for a number of the firm's partners for a few years before being placed in an area of specialization.

The largest firms like to call themselves **full-service firms** because they have departments specializing in every type of legal work that pays well, which in the US usually means M&A (mergers & acquisitions) transactions, banking and real estate transactions. These firms rarely do personal injury (PI) work. Sometimes the term "BigLaw" is used to indicate the vast amount of lawyers working for such a firm. In addition to their large salaries, biglaw associates are compensated with year-end bonuses. Because the business model of a biglaw firm requires lower-level associates to significantly outnumber the partners and senior associates who supervise them, there are **high attrition rates in biglaw**. Starting around their third or fourth years with the firm, some associates are asked to start seeking work elsewhere, while others choose to leave, transferring to other large firms or taking jobs as **in-house counsels** for former clients.

Attorneys working for **middle-sized law firms** or in legal departments of business corporations as well as lawyers working for the government, such as judges and prosecutors, are considered to belong to a slightly lower stratum of the legal profession, the **stratum 2 category**. Numerically most stratum 2 attorneys are employed by corporations on a **salary basis**. Since corporations prefer to hire experienced lawyers as **corporate attorneys**, they often recruit their **in-house legal staff** from (national) law firms. Sometimes corporations train their own lawyers and compete with law firms in recruiting from elite law schools.

Legal divisions of major corporations are self-contained entities with a special **ranking system.** The size of their staffs exceeds that of many law firms. They are usually headed by a senior management official, referred to as a **general counsel**. Underneath him/her there are deputy- or associate administrators who supervise the lower staff attorneys. **Seniority considerations** play a central role in the advancement of a corporate counsel, whose client is the corporation. In-house counsels are usually involved with all kinds of legal concerns connected with modern corporate activity. They monitor business activities to ensure compliance with statutory requirements and also serve as the corporation's liaison to the law firm that is **on retainer to the corporation.**

The lowest social stratum, **stratum 3**, is composed predominantly of **solo practitioners**, but also includes attorneys working for small law firms, small corporations and state governments. The prestige and the income of stratum 3 attorneys are usually far below those of their stratum 1 and 2 colleagues, although income is not the decisive factor. In fact, due to the frequency of **contingency fee agreements** in tort cases, there are some stratum 3 trial attorneys whose income surpasses that of most strata 1 and 2 lawyers. Millionaire trial attorneys, also known as **kings of torts,** are the rare exception among the large stratum 3 category of lawyers, though. A typical stratum 3 **solo attorney** lacks a prestigious legal education and does not have the readily available research resources at his/her disposal such as large law firms do. Solos often deal with so called "**one shot cases**" such as divorce and personal injury work, which may be strenuous and distasteful. They do not close contracts with the world of big business but work for a broad range of individuals. Some solo lawyers practice in their homes or in offices built as special additions to their homes, since they cannot afford to rent a fancy office downtown.

> **SIMPLY**
> Some sociologists identify three groups (strata) of lawyers: attorneys who work for large national law firms and Wall street firms are considered most prominent (**stratum 1**), corporate attorneys who work for leading companies and attorneys working for the government belong to **stratum 2**, leaving the remaining (solo and small firm) lawyers in **category 3**.

Partnership Track

Many first year associates are hired with the explicit or at least implied promise that partnership in the firm is a realistic prospect. With hard work and diligence a new associate can expect to be offered **partnership participation** on a well defined track requiring a minimum number of years spent with the firm. In recent years the so called partnership track has moved from a 5–7 year consideration time period to as much as 7–10 years in major law firms. Over the years, other changes (in the traditional partner-associate structure) have occurred too: Permanent associates, temporary attorneys, staff- or contract lawyers and so called non-equity partners (NEPs) have all been added to the mix.

Non-equity partnership is offered to senior associates as a **temporary** step in order to take some of the economic pressure off associates for a period of time, but it can also be permanent. The role of the non-equity partner varies greatly among law firms. In some firms, non-equity partners enjoy all partnership-privileges, including the right to attend partnership meetings, receive financial reports and vote in partnership affairs. In other firms, non-equity partners are viewed as advanced-level associates with few of the advantages of partnership. Firms also use non-equity status as a **means of observation** before they offer an associate equity partnership.

Having reached **equity-status**, the new partner is assigned a percentage ownership and thus shares the firm's profits and losses. He is typically required to make a **capital contribution** to the firm which is to remain until withdrawal, termination, death or dissolution of the partnership and he is given a vote on matters relating to the firm's governance. What role a new **equity partner** plays depends largely on the culture and size of the firm. While most equity partners participate in the firm's governance and have a right to vote on firm matters and serve on management committees, in some firms, power is institutionalized in the hands of a few partners and new equity partners in fact exercise little control. **Firm culture** also determines how equity partners are evaluated and rewarded. It is usually some **combination of factors** such as his/her skills, areas of expertise, billable hours, marketing success, management ability and enhancing the image of the firm. The percentage of ownership, which is assigned to each equity partner and from which profits will be allocated, usually depends on one or more of those factors. Some firms have a lock-step system, where those who became partner in the same year will receive the same percentage. Some use a formula for assigning shares of the earnings pie. In any case, an equity partner is a "business-owner" and may therefore be asked to **guarantee the firm's loans.**

> **SIMPLY**
>
> A **non-equity partner** (also known as **non-capital partner, contract partner** or **income partner**) is a partner who does not share in profits and losses but receives a fixed compensation, makes no capital contribution and has either no voting rights or limited voting rights on firm matters. An **equity partner** is personally liable for his/her share of the debts and losses of the law firm. He does not receive a salary but a draw against future profits. He is no longer protected by the employment laws; instead, his rights are governed by partnership law.

Billable Hours

Nearly all US law firms make their money by **billing their clients by the hour**. Most law firms have a set target of billable hours (reaching 2300 hours a year) that must be achieved by each associate. The formula is quite simple: The more hours billed the more money the firm makes. If lawyers do not bill enough hours each year, they will not make enough money to cover their income, since the firm's billable hours also cover overheads, salaries and partners' profit share. When calculating how much time attorneys spend at work, one has to keep in mind that not every hour spent in the office is a billable hour. Thus, not all lawyers are enthusiasts about this **method of charging**, especially since the pressure to maintain the amount of billable hours often means losing out on other aspects of being an attorney. An associate also may have to turn down more satisfying cases for worthy causes and pro bono service in order to work for paying clients. Therefore, smaller law firms and public interest law firms often **require less billable hours**. These firms may place more emphasis on training, community-related activities and client development. Public interest and government employers do not have any billable hour requirements, as they do not bill their hours to a paying client.

Understandably, the threat of long office hours associated with the billable hour concept often deters law school graduates from working for biglaw firms. One could say that **the larger a firm is, the more likely it is that it relies on billable hours** as the measure for charging clients and assessing its lawyers' productivity. Some firms even set penalty clauses to make sure that each lawyer achieves their billable hour quota. This can exert pressure on both home and work life.

> **SIMPLY**
>
> The billable hour is a practice that has been used by US law firms since the early 1960s. It is a charging scheme which divides the time that a lawyer spends on his/her client's case. Both partners and associates are routinely required to bill clients a high number of hours a year.

Legal Ethics

The term "legal ethics" refers to **ethical codes governing those in the practice of law**.

Almost everywhere lawyers are bound by ethical codes, whose contents differ from place to place. Such codes of conduct tend to have some common ideas, though, including provisions dealing with conflict of interests, incompetence, bribery, coercion, communications with jurors, coaching witnesses etc. Ethical codes for attorneys are often designed and enforced **by self-governing bar associations**, which have the authority **to punish members who engage in unethical professional behavior**. Also judges abide by ethical principles and guidelines adopted and executed by independent judicial institutions. US law schools are required to offer a **legal ethics course**, encompassing both legal ethics and various other matters of professionalism that are not essentially of ethical concern. In addition to the bar exam, most states also require applicants to pass a separate written ethics examination before letting them practice law in their courts.

US federal judges abide by the **Code of Conduct for US Judges**, a set of ethical principles and guidelines adopted by the Judicial Conference of the US. This code provides guidance for judges on issues of judicial integrity and independence, judicial diligence and impartiality, permissible extra-judicial activities, and the **avoidance of impropriety or even its appearance**. Judges may not hear cases in which they have either personal knowledge of the disputed facts, a personal bias concerning a party to the case, earlier involvement in the case as a lawyer, or a financial interest in any party or subject matter of the case.

▶ **Code of Conduct for United States Judges**

(from http://www.uscourts.gov/)

The code of conduct of the Judicial Conference of the United States applies to all federal judges but is only advisory and nonbinding on Supreme Court justices. The rules explicitly permit judges to accept and participate in awards programs and to receive certain benefit from legal publishers. Below are the official canons, followed by excerpts of commentary provided by the Judicial Conference.

Canon 1: A judge should uphold the integrity and independence of the judiciary. ("Public confidence in the impartiality of the judiciary is maintained by the adherence of each judge to this responsibility.")

Canon 2: A judge should avoid impropriety and the appearance of impropriety in all activities. ("A judge must expect to be the subject of constant public scrutiny. A judge must therefore accept restrictions that might be viewed as burdensome by the ordinary citizen and should do so freely and willingly.")

Canon 3: A judge should perform the duties of the office impartially and diligently. ("A judge shall disqualify himself or herself in a proceeding in which the judge's impartiality might reasonably be questioned, including but not limited to instances in which the judge has a personal bias or prejudice concerning a party … ")

Canon 4: A judge may engage in extrajudicial activities to improve the law, the legal system and the administration of justice. ("A judge, subject to the proper performance of judicial duties, may engage in … law-related activities, if in doing so the judge does not cast reasonable doubt on the capacity to decide impartially any issue that may come before the judge.")

Canon 5: A judge should regulate extrajudicial activities to minimize the risk of conflict with judicial duties. ("Complete separation of a judge from extrajudicial activities is neither possible nor wise; a judge should not be isolated from the society in which the judge lives. The changing nature of some organizations and of their relationship to the law makes it necessary for a judge regularly to reexamine the activities of each organization with which the judge is affiliated to determine if it is proper for the judge to continue the judge's relationship with it. For example, in many jurisdictions charitable hospitals are now more frequently in court than in the past.")

Canon 6: A judge should regularly file reports of compensation received for law-related and extrajudicial activities. ("A judge may receive compensation and reimbursement of expenses for the law-related and extrajudicial activities permitted by this Code, if the source of such payments does not give the appearance of influencing the judge in the judge's judicial duties or otherwise give the appearance of impropriety...").

SIMPLY

Legal ethics consists of the standards and norms that bear on law practitioners covering such matters as conflict of interests, bribery, embezzlement, coercion, communications with jurors, coaching witnesses etc. Judicial ethics is part of the larger legal category of legal ethics.

Discuss

Which three strata are distinguished in the legal profession?

Explain the term "Wall Street firm"!

Guess from what kind of families Cravath- and Wall Street lawyers come from and what kind of law schools they went to?

Which areas of work do Cravath- and Wall Street lawyers deal with? What kind of cases do solo practitioners handle?

What is the original meaning of "boot camp"?

What is a full-service firm?

Which areas of legal work are considered to pay well and why?

What does the nickname 'BigLaw' indicate?

Explain the ranking system of a large corporation's legal department!

What is meant by "seniority considerations"?

Is there a difference between working for a law firm and working as a corporate attorney?

Who is the corporate counsel's client?

Why aren't all lawyers enthusiastic about the concept of billing hours?

Would you apply for a job with a law firm that uses this charging scheme?

Think of the reasons why public interest and government employers do not bill their hours to a paying client!

Which forms of punishment for unethical behavior can you think of?

Excercise

Study the following job ad and find out the profile of a prospective candidate:

LITIGATION ASSOCIATE
Adler Brown Hahn & Whitelaw LLP, a 30-attorney litigation boutique located in ..., is seeking an associate with 5+ years products liability, toxic tort, and/or environmental litigation experience. The associate will become part of a litigation team involved in the defense of Fortune 500 companies. Ideal candidates will have applicable experience, including motion practice, taking and defending depositions and working with experts. Strong analytical and writing skills are a must. The practice group emphasizes a team approach and is working closely with sophisticated clients. Please e-mail your cover letter, resume and a writing sample to ... For additional information about the firm, visit our web site at ... We are proud to be an equal opportunity employer.

Concepts

affidavit

a written document in which the signer swears under oath before a notary public (or someone else authorized to take oaths) that the statements contained in the document are true. In some US states the term affidavit also stands for a declaration under penalty of perjury, which is the equivalent of an affidavit and does not require the oath-taking before a notary.

ambulance chaser

a colloquial phrase that is used derisively for a person (not necessarily but often a lawyer) who is hired by an attorney to seek out negligence cases (eg using a personal police/fire radio scanner) at the scenes of accidents or in hospitals where prospective clients are treated. The term is derived from lawyers "following ambulances to hospitals" after a person is injured, in order to try and convince the victim that (s)he needs to sue when (s)he is still injured and may be easily talked into suing. In most jurisdictions, lawyers can be disbarred if caught engaging in such unethical behavior.

BigLaw

nickname for the largest law firms in the US. BigLaw firms are full-service law firms that traditionally employ a large number of attorneys (exceeding one hundred), rank among the highest-grossing firms, pay top-market salaries, recruit from top US law schools and maintain a national or even global presence.

censure

here: a procedure for publicly reprimanding a judge for inappropriate behavior.

(in house) counsel / corporate attorney

an attorney who works only for a particular business or corporation and is part of the staff of the company (also referred to as staff attorney); they usually work on a salary basis.

disbarment

the ultimate punishment of an attorney, which takes away his/her license to practice law either for a certain amount of time or for life. Disbarment only comes after investigation and opportunities for the attorney to explain his/her improper conduct. Sometimes an attorney may be reinstated upon a showing of rehabilitation.

impeachment

a process that is used to charge, try, and remove public officials for misconduct while in office.

king of torts

successful tort litigators are sometimes referred to as "kings of torts". They practice personal injury law on a contingency fee basis and have an income even surpassing that of an associate working for a big law firm.

lifetime tenure

here (in the context of public employees like judges or professors): a guaranteed right to a job once a probationary period has passed with the exception of substantial inability to perform or some wrongful act.

litigation team/ trial unit

big law firms as well as prosecutors' offices are often internally structured, comprising various departments and units (such as the felony or homicide unit in a state attorney's office) with individual lawyers specializing in certain fields of law. A law firm's (often prestigious) litigation team focuses on the representation of its clients in court. The trial lawyer (= litigator) or unit (if more lawyers act in court) is the person / unit of the litigation team that actually deals with the jury during the trial. A good litigator has excellent rhetorical skills as well as experience with filing & arguing motions, preparing briefs and taking depositions.

M&A – mergers and acquisitions

a general term used to refer to the consolidation of companies. In corporate law, a merger is the joining together of two corporations in which one corporation transfers all of its assets to the other, which continues to exist. In effect one corporation "swallows" the other, but the shareholders of the swallowed company receive shares of the surviving corporation. The term acquisition is used when one company purchases a majority interest in another. They can either be friendly or unfriendly: Friendly acquisitions occur when the target firm agrees to be acquired, unfriendly acquisitions when they don't.

on retainer

when a client keeps an attorney or a law firm on retainer, (s)he thereby prevents the attorney from acting for an adversary, by employing the attorney to act only on his/her behalf. The term retainer is generally used to refer to a payment in advance to cover services expected to be performed and is frequently used by attorneys and consultants. The

VIII. The US Legal Profession

term also stands for the contract between attorney and client specifying the nature of the services to be rendered and the cost of the services.

one shot client

one shot clients usually hire an attorney to deal with a case ("**one shot case**") that, due to its nature, typically occurs only one time, such as a personal injury or divorce case. Contrary to law firms that are kept on retainer by big corporations, a lawyer dealing with one shot clients who has no retainer contract with the world of big business constantly has to look for new clients.

recusal

the disqualification of a judge or jury by reason of prejudice or conflict of interest. A judge can be recused by objections of either party or disqualify him(her)self.

salaried attorney

most beginning lawyers start in salaried positions. Most salaried lawyers hold positions in government or with corporations or nonprofit organizations. Salaried lawyers usually have structured work schedules. Law firms also hire new associates, who initially work with more experienced associates or partners (on a salary basis).

solo attorney, solo practitioner

an attorney who works in a solo practice. Solo attorneys manage their office by themselves and also enjoy greater freedom than associates and partners in big law firms. Some solo practitioners find it difficult to survive financially. Most of them cannot afford to rent an office by him(her)self and have to share it with other solo practitioners. They generally work for individuals and often deal with their clients only once ("one shot clients") due to the nature of the case (such as divorces or traffic accidents).

summer/ first year/ senior associate

in large law firms, law students hired by a law firm for the summer are called summer associates. Law firms also have junior, midlevel, senior and lateral associates, depending on how long they have been with the firm.

Wall Street lawyer

a lawyer working for a large financial institution, often dealing with legal issues affiliated with the stock exchange.

Vocabulary

acknowledgment	Bestätigung, Anerkennung, Quittierung
to be admitted to the bar	zur Anwaltsprüfung zugelassen werden
advancement	Vorwärtskommen, Beförderung, (beruflicher) Aufstieg
affidavit	eidesstattliche Erklärung
affiliated	angegliedert, angeschlossen

VIII. The US Legal Profession

affiliated group (of companies)	Konzern
allocation of earnings	Erfolgszurechnung
applicable experience	*here:* einschlägige Berufserfahrung
appointment of counsel	Bestellung eines Vertreters / Anwaltes
apprentice	Lehrling, Auszubildende ('Azubi')
attachable earnings	pfändbare Bezüge
attachment of earnings	Lohnpfändung
to attest	attestieren, beglaubigen, bescheinigen
attrition rate	Schwundquote
to authenticate	beurkunden, legalisieren, bescheinigen
avoidance	Vermeidung, Meiden
boot camp	*military:* Ausbildungslager
boot camp training	*here:* Grundausbildung
bribery	Bestechung
capital contribution	finanzieller Beitrag
chancellor	Richter des Equity Gerichts, *also:* Kanzler
to charge	*here:* in Rechnung stellen
chief justice	vorsitzender Richter
to coach a witness	einen Zeugen vorbereiten (auf die Verhandlung)
coercion	Zwang, Nötigung
compliance (with)	Befolgung, Einhaltung (von); *also:* Zustimmung
conflict of interests	Interessenkollision
conjecture	Vermutung, Mutmaßung
corporate tax	Körperschaftsteuer
decisive	ausschlaggebend, maßgebend, entscheidend
deed	Vertrag, Urkunde (*also:* notariell beglaubigt), Akt
deputy	(Stell)Vertreter, Bevollmächtigter
derisively	spöttisch, höhnisch
determined by	ermittelt durch
diligence	Sorgfalt, Fleiß, Eifer, Gewissenhaftigkeit
diligent	genau, sorgfältig, fleißig
dissolution	Auflösung
due diligence, due care	Sorgfaltspflicht
embezzlement	Veruntreuung, Unterschlagung
entity	Gebilde, Organisation, Einheit
to evaluate	einschätzen, beurteilen, evaluieren
to exercise control	Kontrolle ausüben
to exert pressure	Druck ausüben
expertise	Fachkenntnis, Kompetenz, Sachverstand
fancy	schick, raffiniert, hochtrabend
free-lance	freiberuflich

VIII. The US Legal Profession

governance	Kontrolle, Herrschaft, Gewalt
guarantee	Bürgschaft, Garantie
high-grossing	umsatzstark
impartiality	Objektivität, Unbefangenheit, Unparteilichkeit
to impeach	anklagen (wegen eines Amtsvergehens), *also:* anzweifeln
impropriety	Fehlverhalten, Ungehörigkeit
incompetence, incompetency	Unfähigkeit, Unzuständigkeit
justice of the peace	Friedensrichter
to lay / put emphasis on sth	etwas betonen
legal division, legal department	Rechtsabteilung
liaison	Angelegenheit, Verbindung
licensed	lizensiert, zugelassen, zugesagt
major	*here:* Studiengang, Hauptfach
merciless	unbarmherzig
mortgage	Hypothek, Pfand, Belastung
notary public / civil law notary	Notar(in) (im Common- / civil-law-System)
notary seal	Siegel des Notars
notary trust account	Treuhandkonto
overhead	*here:* Fixkosten
to perform	leisten, etw tun, vollbringen
to perform near the top of a class	bei den besten eines Jahrgangs sein, als eine(r) der besten eines Jahrgangs abschneiden
to predominate	vorwiegen, vorherrschen
prestigious	angesehen, prestigeträchtig, renommiert
probationary	zur/auf Probe
profitable	ertragreich, gewinnbringend, profitabel
proof of identity	Identitätsnachweis, Legitimation
radio scanner	*here:* Funkscanner
ranking	reihend, Rangordnung
real estate transactions	Immobilientransaktionen
to recruit	anwerben
to recuse a judge	einen Richter ablehnen
renowned	altbekannt
resource	(Einsatz-, Betriebs-, Produktions-)Mittel
retainer	*here:* Anwaltsvorschuss
revenue	Einkünfte, Einnahmen, Ertrag
to reward	belohnen, vergelten
rumor	Gerücht
salary	Gehalt, Vergütung
selective	pingelig, selektiv

settlement of estates	Nachlassabwicklung
shorthand	kurzerhand, stichwortartig; Stenografie
solo	einzeln, allein
to sort the wheat from the chaff	Spreu von Weizen trennen
to surpass	übertreffen, übersteigen, überbieten
taxation	Steuerwesen
tenure	*here:* Amtszeit, Anstellung
to undergo	erdulden, durchleben, erfahren
withdrawal	*here:* Rückzug, Ausstieg, Rücktritt

IX. The US Jury System

General

In the US legal system the **jury** finds expression in three places:

- the grand jury,
- the criminal petit jury and
- the civil petit jury.

The **terms** "grand jury" and "petit jury" are French in origin, whereby "grand" means large and "petit" means **small**. The terms refer to the **number of jurors** serving on each jury (between 16 and 23 in a federal grand jury, a maximum of 12 in trial juries).

A **grand jury** is solely part of the **criminal justice system** (see page 107). In other words, there is no grand jury in a civil case. The jury that acts as a fact-finder in a civil or criminal trial ('**trial jury**') is, on the other hand, **always "petit"** and has no more than 12 members.

Trial by (petit) jury in serious criminal cases is guaranteed in the 6th Amendment as well as in most state constitutions. Besides, Supreme Court decisions interpreting the due process clause of the 14th Amendment have applied the 6th Amendment guarantee to state criminal cases (see pages 10–11). Parties to a civil lawsuit are provided with a similar right in the 7th Amendment. Although the 6th and the 7th Amendments **guarantee the right to trial by jury**, they **do not require** that a jury actually be used for every single trial. When a criminal defendant or both parties to a civil lawsuit **waive** their right to a trial by jury, there will be a **bench trial**. Furthermore, the Supreme Court has consistently excluded **petty offenses**, as distinguished by their punishment or the nature of the offense itself, from falling under the 6th Amendment provision.

Traditionally, all trial juries consisted of 12 members. However, Supreme Court cases have held that **the number 12 is not essential**. In *Williams v. Florida*, 399 U.S. 78 (1970) the Court upheld the use of **six-person juries in state criminal cases**, reasoning that a six-person jury is "large enough to promote group deliberation, free from outside attempts at intimidation, to provide a fair possibility of obtaining a representative cross-section of the community." Since then, many states have set numbers under 12 for particular types of cases. Nowadays in most criminal (state) jurisdictions the jury consists of **six jurors for a misdemeanor trial**. On similar reasoning the US Supreme Court has held that **the traditional requirement of unanimity** is not a part of the constitutional right. In *Johnson v. Louisiana*, 406 U.S. 356 (1972) the Court held that conviction by a "nine to three" verdict in certain **non-capital cases** does not violate the due process clause.

In *Taylor v. Louisiana*, 419 U.S. 522 (1975) the Court held that the 6th and 14th Amendment require petit juries to be selected from a source **fairly representative of the community** and that this requirement (which is known as **cross-section requirement**) is violated by the systematic exclusion of women from jury panels. Thus, it is a constitutional violation if the array from which the trial jury is selected (the jury pool) is made up of only segments of the population, or if large, distinctive groups are excluded from the pool. In *Lockhart v. McCree*, 476 U.S. 162 (1986) the Supreme Court proceeded that – while the 6th Amendment requires that jury members must be chosen from a group composed of a diverse "cross-section" of the local community, including people of different races and backgrounds found in that community – it does not require that **the selected jury itself** must include all these people.

With regard to the jury system, a typical civil trial procedure is very similar to a criminal **trial process** since the duties of a civil juror are not significantly different from those of a criminal juror. In both cases, jurors are required to pay attention in court, listen to the evidence presented and **render a verdict** at the end of the trial **based upon the evidence presented** and the law as instructed by the judge. In both (civil and criminal) procedures potential jurors **(venirepersons)** initially form the **jury pool (array, venire)**, from which the trial jury is selected (see page 94).

Grand Jury

The American grand jury has its origin in England, where the first grand jury assembled in 1166. It was officially recognized by King John in the *Magna Carta* in 1215 on demand of the nobility. Today, grand juries are virtually unknown outside the US. The United Kingdom abandoned grand juries in 1933. The 5th Amendment to the U.S. Constitution still provides that *"no person shall be held to answer for a capital, or otherwise infamous crime, unless on a presentment or indictment of a Grand Jury, except in cases arising in the land or naval forces, or in the Militia, when in actual service in time of War or public danger"*. The provision has been interpreted to permit **bypassing the grand jury for misdemeanor offenses**, which can be charged without grand jury proceedings but merely by a prosecutor's criminal complaint. Besides, unlike many other provisions of the Bill of Rights, the Supreme Court has ruled that the 5th Amendment requirement **does not pertain to the state courts** via the 14th Amendment, and states therefore may elect to not use grand juries. As a result, **in many state jurisdictions** lower criminal charges are currently filed by the district attorney in a municipal or other lower court, which holds a **preliminary hearing instead of conducting a grand jury hearing** to determine if there is just cause for trial (see page 107).

A grand jury is a group of up to 23 people that is selected randomly from the general population of a court's district and usually serves for a term of a year. Once selected, they convene in private **to hear evidence presented by the prosecutor** against a person accused of a **major crime**. If a **simple majority** of the jurors agree that there is **enough evidence** against the accused to conduct a trial, an **indictment** (formal charge) is issued and the prosecution is empowered to proceed with its legal action against the accused.

One could say that the grand jury serves a **dual function**: It determines that a person should be prosecuted for a criminal act (if there is **probable cause** to believe the person has committed an offense). In doing so the grand jury **protects innocent people from unfounded accusations** and from the trouble, expense and anxiety of a criminal trial when there is, in fact, insufficient evidence. Although the grand jury acts under the authority of the courts and is considered a part of the court system, it is an **independent body** with broad powers of its own to inquire into crime and corruption. Included in this investigative power is the grand jury's right to subpoena witnesses and documents.

The **rules** governing grand jury proceedings are **very different** from those governing trials by (petit) jury. The **public is not admitted** to hearings and the procedure is **inquisitorial** rather than adversarial. The defense is not allowed to call witnesses, and the prosecutor is not obliged to present both sides of the case. Hearsay and other evidence that might be excluded at a jury trial may be introduced.

> **SIMPLY**
>
> In the US legal system, a grand jury is a group of up to 23 persons who determine whether a person should be prosecuted for an alleged crime and face trial. It is a grand jury's task and duty to protect suspects from inappropriate prosecution by the government. Grand jurors carry out this duty by hearing and examining evidence presented to them by a prosecutor and issuing **indictments,** or by investigating alleged crimes and issuing **presentments** (see page 108). A grand jury does not act in a trial but convenes in private session to fulfill this task.

Excuse / Exemption from Jury Duty

Generally, it is a civilian's **duty** to serve as a juror once summoned by the court. A common method for drafting jurors is to draw them at random from electoral rolls (also known as allotment). Prospective jurors are notified personally in the form of a written order (**jury summons**) by the jury administrator (**jury commissioner**) to attend the court on a specific day for jury selection.

There are **legal ways to escape jury duty**, though. Under Title 28 of the US Code the statutory **qualifications** for federal jury service are stated as follows:

▶ **Section 1865. Qualifications for Jury Service**

(a) The chief judge of the district court, or such other district court judge as the plan may provide, on his initiative or upon recommendation of the clerk or jury commissioner, or the clerk under supervision of the court if the court's jury selection plan so authorizes, shall determine solely on the basis of information provided on the juror qualification form and other competent evidence, whether a person is unqualified for, or exempt, or to be excused from jury service. The clerk shall enter such determination in the space provided on the juror qualification form and in any alphabetical list of names drawn from the master jury wheel. If a person did not appear in response to a summons, such fact shall be noted on said list.

(b) In making such determination the chief judge of the district court, or such other district court judge as the plan may provide, or the clerk if the court's jury selection plan so provides, shall deem any person qualified to serve on grand and petit juries in the district court unless he

(1) is not a citizen of the United States, eighteen years old, who has resided for a period of one year within the judicial district;

(2) is unable to read, write, and understand the English language with a degree of proficiency sufficient to fill out satisfactorily the juror qualification form;

(3) is unable to speak the English language;

(4) is incapable, by reason of mental or physical infirmity, to render satisfactory jury service; or

(5) has a charge pending against him for the commission of, or has been convicted in a State or Federal court of record of, a crime punishable by imprisonment for more than one year and his civil rights have not been restored.

In addition, title 28 US Code, Section 1863, specifies that the following persons are barred from jury service on the grounds that they are **exempt**:

(1) members in active service of the **armed forces** of the US;

(2) members of any governmental **fire or police departments**;

(3) **public officers** of the US, state, or local government (elected to public office or directly appointed) who are actively engaged in the performance of official duties.

While an exemption results in automatic dismissal at the summoned person's option, an **excuse is considered individually** by the judge and is not automatically granted. In the federal court system these persons may request a **permanent excuse:**

- persons over 70 years of age or older;
- persons having active care and custody of a child or children under ten years of age whose health and/or safety would be jeopardized by their absence for jury service;
- persons who are essential to the care of aged or infirm persons;
- persons who have, within the past two years, served on a federal grand or petit jury panel;
- voluntary safety personnel serving a public agency as a non-compensated firefighter or a member of an ambulance or rescue squad;
- persons with arrest powers.

In the state court system, virtually all state legislators have enacted statutes delineating **similar qualifications and disqualifications** for jury service. The qualifications vary somewhat from jurisdiction to jurisdiction, but most include US citizenship, a minimum age of 18, residence in the specific judicial district, as well as the ability to sufficiently understand English. Disqualifying conditions typically involve being incompetent to understand the court proceedings or having a record of a felony conviction. In addition, some state jurisdictions have **exemption provisions**, whose rationales tend to cluster around three ideas: the first is that there are some groups whose members are very unlikely to survive the selection process, and it is therefore inefficient to summon them (eg lawyers and police officers); the second relates to persons whose absence from their jobs could cause public inconvenience or even hardship (eg physicians); the third involves persons whose service could cause them great personal hardship, such as nursing mothers or sole proprietors of a business.

IX. The US Jury System

In the recent past the trend has been towards a **repeal of exemptions** in order to attain a broader representation for purposes of the fair cross section requirement. If an exemption is repealed, persons formerly within the exempted category can no longer simply opt out, but instead must report for jury duty. If they claim a hardship, the judge has to consider on a **case-by-case basis** whether their excuse should be granted or not.

If a qualified person who is summoned by the court and is not exempt from jury duty **wishes to be excused** according to federal or state law, (s)he has to submit a **written request** to the jury administrator prior to the summons date. The most common exclusions are for people whose job in some way precludes them, people who have health problems or people who are caring for young children. After this **initial selection** the remaining jurors undergo another procedure of examination at the beginning of the trial, known as voir dire (see below), whereby both parties can object to certain persons being a juror.

> **SIMPLY**
>
> In each jurisdiction, there are positive **qualifications** set by the legislature for eligibility to serve on a jury (such as minimum age) as well as negative disqualifying factors (**disqualifiers**), such as a felony conviction. Some jurisdictions also have **exemptions** from service for certain categories of people. These exemptions entitle a summoned person within the exempted group to opt-out of jury service simply by claiming status within the group. Virtually all jurisdictions further allow for **excuses** from jury service (often merely postponements) for certain reasons. Whether such an excuse is granted will be considered on a **case-by-case basis**.

Voir Dire

On the day of trial the clerk of the court convenes **the panel of potential jurors.** The entire group (panel) of people summoned for service form the so called "**array**" or "**venire**", whose members (the prospective jurors) are also referred to as **venirepersons.** Each court has a jury management office, whose staff communicates with the judges throughout the day so that jurors are available when needed. Jury selection from the array is the first step in a trial. In a civil case usually (depending on the state) six jurors are selected – plus two **alternates.** In felony criminal cases there are usually 12 jurors selected (again plus a minimum of two alternates).

Since the jury is a body of laypersons that decide the facts of a case and reach a verdict, **jury selection** is one of the most cruicial elements of the entire trial. The basic idea is that a **fair and impartial jury** is chosen of the array. But the truth of the matter is, both sides want to strike those jurors who are biased against their case and keep the jurors who favor their case. Courts are increasingly using **written questionnaires** in addition to **oral questioning** to enable the lawyers to learn as much as they feasibly can about the venirepersons, their thoughts and biases. Such questionnaires are a lot more efficient than oral questioning and also more respectful of the venirepersons' privacy. The panel members have to **swear an oath** to **truthfully** answer all (written and oral) questions about their qualifications to sit as jurors in the case. Deliberately untruthful answers by a juror will result in punishment.

IX. The US Jury System

The oral questioning procedure is called "**voir dire**" [vwaɹ diəɹ], an Anglo-French term meaning "to speak the truth". The methods of voir dire vary from court to court and from case to case. Voir dire examinations usually open with a short statement by the judge to inform the jurors of what the case is about and to identify the parties and their lawyers. After that the judge and/or the lawyers will question the potential jurors to varying degrees depending on the jurisdiction. Traditionally, attorneys have much latitude in conducting voir dire.

The attorneys' power to **challenge** (= make a formal objection to) prospective jurors is of central importance in the adversary system. Since it has been subject to misuse and even abuse it has been the target of considerable criticism.

The primary **purpose of voir dire** is certainly to sort out those people who **cannot render an impartial verdict**, eg if they have a personal interest in the case. The court also wants to know if any member of the panel is related to or personally acquainted with one of the parties, their lawyers, or a witness who will appear during trial. Other questions determine whether any panel members have a **prejudice** or a certain feeling about the case or a person involved that might influence them when rendering a verdict. If a juror has knowledge of the case (s)he has to explain it to the judge.

After this thorough examination and questioning, the parties (represented by their attorneys) may request that a specific venireperson be excused from service on the particular jury. These requests or demands are called **challenges**. A venireperson may be **challenged for cause** by either party if the examination shows that (s)he has characteristics that will likely make it difficult for him/her might not judge the particular case fairly and without bias. The judge has to rule on each challenge. If he grants a challenge the venireperson concerned is **dismissed from the panel**. If the judge denies the challenge, the venireperson may remain on the panel. The judge may also excuse a venireperson on his own initiative.

There is **no limit** to the number of **challenges for cause** which either party may use, and there are many bases that will support a for cause challenge. Most challenges for cause involve one of **three general principles**, that is: (1) that the venireperson knows someone involved with the case, (2) that (s)he expresses an opinion in the jury questionnaire or during voir dire indicating that (s)he cannot set aside some **preconceived notion** that will interfere with his/her ability to fairly judge the case, or (3) that (s)he has life experience from which **bias** can be inferred. For example, in a death penalty jurisdiction a venireperson who is so opposed to the death penalty that (s)he would never vote to impose it would be challengeable for cause.

An opposing party does not usually contest a for cause challenge based on the venireperson's actual knowledge of someone connected with the case. But when a juror is challenged because of his alleged inability to remain impartial, the opposing counsel will try to **rehabilitate** the venireperson through questions designed to demonstrate that (s)he can fairly judge the case, despite his/her opinion or life experience. The judge will only excuse an individual from the panel if the cause raised in the challenge is sufficient.

If the judge denies a for cause challenge, the party who lodged it might be forced to use one of their (**limited number of**) **peremptory challenges** on that venireperson. For this (second) kind of challenge **no cause** is necessary. The number of peremptory challenges that each side has is predetermined and depends on the jurisdiction. For example, in federal court, 28 U.S.C. 1870 gives each party 3 peremptory challenges in civil cases. According to Title VI, Rule 24 of the Federal Rules of Criminal Procedure each side has 3 peremptory challenges in misdemeanor cases (when the defendant is charged with a crime punishable by fine or imprisonment of a maximum one year); 6 to the prosecution and 10 to the defense in criminal cases in felony cases and 20 for each side in cases where the potential punishment is a death sentence (so called "capital cases").

They may be exercised for any reason or for no reason whatsoever, with the exception that they may not be used to exclude women or minorities from the jury merely because of their gender or race. Peremptory challenges give both sides some choice in the make-up of a jury by excluding those potential jurors that they believe would be bad for their side **without giving a reason** for it. In some courts the peremptory challenges are made openly, in others they are made from the jury list and out of the jury's sight.

After all the challenges are used the court **impanels** the jury by administering an **oath**. Each selected juror has to swear or to affirm, that (s)he will "... *try the matter in dispute and give a true verdict according to the evidence.*" **When the jurors take this oath, they turn into neutral factfinders** and are obliged to act fairly and impartially when considering the evidence presented.

> **SIMPLY**
>
> The preliminary examination of prospective jurors to determine their suitability to serve on a jury is called **voir dire**. Its purpose is to find out if members of the array are biased or cannot deal with the issues fairly. After a process of thorough questioning each attorney has the right to request that a juror be excused from the panel. There may be a **challenge for cause** on the basis that a juror has admitted prejudice or shows some obvious conflict of interest. In addition, both attorneys may use a limited number of **peremptory challenges** which are requests to excuse a juror from the panel without giving a reason for it.

Jury and Trial Consultants

Those parties to a lawsuit that can afford it sometimes retain **one or more consultant(s)** to guide their lawyers during jury selection. The idea is that jury consultants **develop profiles** of potential jurors that will help the lawyers select those more apt to favor their side or, more accurately, strike those who they consider "the worst". In really important cases or when companies are involved they might hire a **jury consulting team** or a **jury consulting firm** (consisting of social scientists, psychologists, criminologists, communication experts and/or legal experts etc.) to scrutinize how jurors relate to case facts and how they make their decisions.

The term trial consulting is a little broader (than jury consulting) and indicates that **trial consultants** assist the parties and their lawyers not only during jury selection but through the whole trial. Many jury consulting firms nowadays refer to themselves as **litigation consultants** to stress that they cover all of their clients' pre-trial, trial and post-trial needs and thus help them **through all stages of a case**. Typically, they offer trial technology services so that the lawyers can communicate their messages with maximum effectiveness. The use of visual design and technology helps to explain difficult concepts to judges and jurors but also to organize testimony and prepare witnesses. Trial or litigation consulting also involves conducting organized mock trials to 'test' a case before taking it to court. Some trial consulting firms include mock mediation and arbitration sessions and draft possible strategies to reach a settlement.

Jury and trial consulting became publicly known during the O. J. Simpson trial. Since then, critics have labelled it as "hightech jury tampering" and there has been a debate on whether the work of such a consultant is protected under the attorney-client privilege, especially when (s)he is hired by a party and not by an attorney. The *American Society of Trial Consultants* does have a **code of ethics** for members, but they are not legally binding.

The practice of law firms hiring **in-house trial consultants** is also becoming more popular. These (in-house) consultants have usually undergone a formal legal as well as a psychological training. A growing number of universities offer specialized training in legal psychology, some of them even as a **joint** (J.D. and Ph.D.) **program**.

> **SIMPLY**
> Trial and jury consulting is a growing field in major litigation. **Jury consultants** help lawyers pick jurors during *voir dire* by analyzing how jurors might react to what they see and hear during the trial. **Trial and litigation consultants** assist their clients not just with jury selection but help them through all stages of the lawsuit (prepare witnesses; improve arguments & rhetorics; develop strategies to reach a 'good' settlement).

Jury Deliberation

In both civil and criminal cases it is the **jury's duty to decide the facts of a case** in accordance with the principles of the law, as laid down by the judge. The jury's decision on the facts must solely be based on the evidence presented to them and is usually final.

While jury selection and jury trials are usually held in open court, **jury deliberations** are absolutely **secret.** There are **no prescribed procedures** for juries to follow and they are left to themselves in a locked room, guarded by the court, to reach a verdict based only on their judgment of the evidence presented during the trial. The jury is neither required nor allowed to offer their reasoning in court. They are asked only for their verdict. Thus, the final phase of a jury's work is also its most mysterious.

The jury's first task in the jury room is to select one of the jurors as a **foreman**, who leads the discussion and who should encourage everyone to join it. The idea of having **secret jury deliberations** is to have an uninhibited and open debate by the jurors based on unbiased reasoning. In most criminal jurisdictions all jurors must agree, that is, the verdict must be **unanimous.** In many civil jurisdictions **majority verdicts** are permitted, whereby the kind of majority that is required (simple or qualified) varies.

In jurisdictions with a unanimous-verdict requirement and where litigants have a choice of jury size (as between a six-person and twelve-person jury) defense lawyers in both civil and criminal cases frequently opt for the larger number of jurors, arguing "it takes only one to hang the jury", since a **hung jury** is regarded as the next best thing to a defense verdict.

Finding a decision may take a few hours or even days. Once the jury has reached its verdict, the foreperson will take it down on an official form and the bailiff will inform the judge that the jury is ready so that the jurors can **return to the courtroom** where the bailiff or the clerk reads the verdict aloud. Sometimes one of the parties will ask that the jury be **polled,** which means that the clerk asks each juror individually if this is his or her own verdict. After that the jury's service is complete and the members are discharged. If the poll reveals a lack of unanimity or lack of assent by the required number of jurors, the court may direct the jury to deliberate further or may order a new trial.

The **verdict in a criminal case** is the decision of the jury as to whether the defendant is **guilty or not guilty.** If the jury finds the criminal defendant guilty, (s)he is **convicted.** The opposite of a conviction is an acquittal. In most criminal cases, jurors will not be asked to pass a sentence on the defendant. It is the judge who imposes sentence if a jury determines that a defendant is guilty. However, in a **capital case** in which the prosecutor requests the death penalty, the jury will be asked to **recommend** whether the court should impose a death sentence or not.

In a **civil case** the jurors decide either **in favor of the plaintiff or the defendant.** In tort cases a **monetary sum** is awarded for damages caused by the opposing party. Jurors often struggle with the amount, particularly in cases in which offering money will not bring someone back to life or for incurable injuries or diseases. Much discussion centers on how irrational juries sometimes are in their assignment of damages – then occasionally referred to as "runaway juries".

> SIMPLY
> The jury members' considering, discussing and (hopefully) reaching a verdict is referred to as jury deliberation.

Jury Nullification

Juries are charged with the responsibility of reaching a verdict based on the facts of a case within the law as it is explained by the trial judge. Jury nullification occurs when the members of a jury disregard either the evidence presented to them or the instructions of the judge in order to reach a verdict based upon their own conscience. In other words, jury nullification takes place when a jury **renders a verdict in contradiction to the law,** by eg refusing to find the criminal defendant guilty, although they believe that he committed the crime, because they strongly believe that a guilty verdict would be unjust.

Jury nullification is possible because the jurors' motivations during or after deliberation remain confidential. Furthermore, two Common Law precedents support a jury's ability to nullify the law: the **prohibition on punishing jury members for their verdict** and the **prohibition on retrying criminal defendants after an acquittal**. Thus, if jury nullification is used to acquit a criminal defendant, there is no way to try the person again for the same act(s). If, on the other hand, a jury that dislikes a criminal defendant convicts him through nullification although he is innocent, the judge is obliged **to set aside** such a conviction, if it is clearly at odds with the law and the facts of the case. Jury nullification may also occur in civil suits.

Since jury deliberation is secret, nullification is both covert and controversial. Proponents argue that it is an important safeguard of last resort against wrongful imprisonment and government tyranny. Opponents view it as an abuse of the right to a jury trial that undermines the law and violates the oath sworn by jurors.

> **SIMPLY**
> Jury nullification is a jury's refusal to render a verdict according to the law, as instructed by the court, regardless of the weight of evidence presented. Instead, the jury bases its verdict on other grounds.

Exercise

Explain the concepts of VOIR DIRE – CHALLENGE FOR CAUSE – PEREMPTORY CHALLENGE – JURY & TRIAL CONSULTING – JURY DELIBERATION – JURY NULLIFICATION in your own words!

Study the following information for trial jurors serving in the federal courts (from: http://www.uscourts.gov) *and summarize a juror's do's and don'ts in your own words:*

▶ Conduct of the Jury during the Trial

Jurors should give close attention to the testimony. They are sworn to disregard their prejudices and follow the court's instructions. They must render a verdict according to their best judgment.

Each juror should keep an open mind. Human experience shows that, once persons come to a preliminary conclusion as to a set of facts, they hesitate to change their views. Therefore, it is wise for jurors not to even attempt to make up their mind on the facts of a case until all the evidence has been presented to them, and they have been instructed on the law applicable to the case. Similarly, jurors must not discuss the case even among themselves until it is finally concluded.

Jurors are expected to use all the experience, common sense and common knowledge they possess. But they are not to rely on any private source of information. Thus they should be careful, during the trial, not to discuss the case at home or elsewhere. Information that a juror gets from a private source may be only half true, or biased or inaccurate. It may be irrelevant to the case at hand. At any rate, it is only fair that the parties have a chance to know and comment upon all the facts that matter in the case.

If it develops during the trial that a juror learns elsewhere of some fact about the case, he or she should inform the court. The juror should not mention any such matter in the jury room.

Individual jurors should never inspect the scene of an accident or of any event in the case. If an inspection is necessary, the judge will have the jurors go as a group to the scene.

Jurors must not talk about the case with others not on the jury, even their spouses or families, and must not read about the case in the newspapers. They should avoid radio and television broadcasts that might mention the case. The jury's verdict must be based on nothing else but the evidence and law presented to them in court.

Jurors should not loiter in the corridors or vestibules of the courthouse. Embarrassing contacts may occur there with persons interested in the case. Juror identification badges will be provided, and they should be worn in the courthouse at all times.

If any outsider attempts to talk with a juror about a case in which he or she is sitting, the juror should do the following:
1. Tell the person it is improper for a juror to discuss the case or receive any information except in the courtroom.
2. Refuse to listen if the outsider persists.
3. Report the incident at once to the judge.

Jurors have the duty to report to the judge any improper behavior by any juror. They also have the duty to inform the judge of any outside communication or improper conduct directed at the jury by any person.

Jurors on a case should refrain from talking on any subject — even if it is not related to the matter being tried — with any lawyer, witness, or party in the case. Such contact may make a new trial necessary.

In the Jury Room

Jurors have to elect a foreperson. The foreperson presides over the jury's deliberations and must give every juror a fair opportunity to express his or her views.

Jurors must enter deliberation with open minds. They should freely exchange views. They should not hesitate to change their opinions if the deliberations have convinced them they were wrong initially. However, a juror should never change his or her mind merely because others disagree or just to finish the trial.

In a criminal case all jurors must agree on the verdict. This is also required in a civil case, unless the jury is otherwise instructed by the court.

The jurors have a duty to give MI consideration to the opinion of their fellow jurors. They have an obligation to reach a verdict whenever possible. However, no juror is required to give up any opinion which he or she is convinced is correct.

The members of the jury are sworn to pass judgment on the facts in a particular case. They have no concern beyond that case. They violate their oath if they render their decision on the basis of the effect their verdict may have on other situations.

Discuss

Explain the difference between a trial jury and the grand jury!

Explain the "cross-section requirement" in your own words!

Explain the difference between being disqualified, exempt and excused from jury duty!

What is your opinion on exemptions that permit certain categories of workers (doctors, lawyers, etc.) to be excused from jury service?

How could jury duty be made less onerous?

What does it mean "it takes only one" to hang a jury?

Does trial consulting impair the fairness of the jury? Is it fair if only one side is supported by a trial consultant?

Some commentators have suggested that very complex civil cases are beyond the power of a jury to deal with. Do you agree? Should discretion be taken from the jury?

If so, which issues could be decided by the judge?

What is your opinion on abolishing peremptory challenges?

Should non-citizens also be called to jury duty?

What is your opinion on jury nullification? Should a judge be able to punish a juror for exercising his/her power to nullify?

What arguments could be made for why juries fill an important role in a democracy?

What arguments support severely limiting their role?

Concepts

alternate juror

in order to avoid having to retry a case when a juror is excused (eg because (s)he falls sick) before the end of the trial the court may seat a few extra or 'alternate' jurors as 'replacements'. They are selected in the same manner as regular jurors and hear all the evidence, but do not take part in the decisionmaking process unless called upon to replace a regular juror.

array

here: the panel of prospective jurors (also referred to as jury panel or jury pool) from which the jurors are chosen.

capital case

criminal case in which the defendant is accused of committing a capital offense and is potentially eligible for the death penalty (also referred to as 'capital punishment'). Capital punishment continues to be used in the US despite controversy over its merits and over its effectiveness as a deterrent.

compromise verdict

a verdict resulting from improper compromises between jurors on certain issues; in other words: some jurors compromise their opinions in order to avoid a deadlock situation.

IX. The US Jury System

contempt of court

there are essentially two types of contempt: (1) being rude, disrespectful to the judge or other attorneys or causing a disturbance in the courtroom, and (2) willfully disobeying an order of the court. The court's power to punish for contempt (called "citing") includes fines and/or jail time (referred to as "imposing sanctions"). Since the judge has discretion to control the courtroom, contempt citations are generally not appealable unless the amount of fine or jail time is excessive.

deadlock

dead end; a stalemate situation in which no progress can be made or no advancement is possible: if a jury is deadlocked (see: hung jury) it is unable to reach a verdict by the required voting margin (unanimity or majority), which results in a mistrial.

directed verdict

decision following an instruction by the judge that the jury can only bring in a specific verdict (eg: "based on the evidence you must bring in a verdict of 'not guilty'"). If the party with the burden of proof has failed to present a prima facie case, the trial judge orders the entry of such a verdict

hung jury

a hung jury is a jury whose required majority can not reach or agree upon a verdict after an extended period of deliberation and is thus deadlocked. In the US, the result is a mistrial and the case has to be retried. One method of dealing with the difficulties associated with hung juries has been the introduction of majority verdicts.

impanel(l)ing

general term for all the steps of jury selection (drawing names at random, determining who is exempt/excused, voir dire and swearing in those jurors who remain seated after this process).

jury commission(er)

court official (or group of officials) with administrative duties; (s)he/they is/are responsible for organizing, coordinating and supervising the jury.

jury consultant, jury consulting team

individual or group of people that can be hired by an attorney representing a party in court in order to help him/her pick the 'right' jury for their side.

jury tampering

crime of unduly attempting to influence the composition and/or decision of a jury, eg by attempting to discredit venirepersons to ensure they will not be selected, by bribing or intimiding jurors, by making unauthorized contact with them etc.

mistrial

the termination of a trial before its normal conclusion because of a serious procedural error or because the jury is unable to reach a verdic after deliberation (see: hung jury). If a mistrial is declared, the case is tried again unless the parties to a civil lawsuit settle the case or the prosecution dismisses the criminal charges or offers a plea bargain.

polling the jury

a practice whereby the jurors are asked individually whether they assented and still assent to their verdict.

special verdict

decision by the jury on the factual issues of a case, leaving the application of the law to those facts to the judge. Typically the judge formulates questions for the jury to answer and then draws legal implications from these answers, which can be beneficial in complex civil cases.

supermajority

a supermajority or a qualified majority is a requirement for a proposal to gain a specified level of support which exceeds a simple majority in order to have effect.

venire [ven-eer-ay]

synonym for "array" or "jury panel". The term venire derives from the French infinitive "to come", that is to come to court.

venireperson

member of the venire.

verdict

the term verdict literally means "to speak the truth"; it is the decision of a jury after a trial, which must be accepted by the trial judge to be final (the judge "enters judgment on the verdict"). A judgment by a judge sitting without a jury (bench trial) is not a verdict.

Vocabulary

alternate	Ersatz-, alternativ
to be apt to do sth	dazu neigen; geneigt sein etwas zu tun
(to) award	zuerkennen, zusprechen; Zuspruch
barred from	ausgeschlossen von
bias	Neigung, Vorliebe
to bypass	umgehen
to cluster	anhäufen, gruppieren
conduct	Führung, Leitung, Verwaltung
to confound	vereiteln, verwischen, verwirren
conscientious	gewissenhaft

IX. The US Jury System

contempt of court	Missachtung gerichtlicher Anweisungen, Nichterscheinen vor Gericht
to contest	anfechten, bestreiten, bekämpfen
to deem	erachten, halten für
to delineate	beschreiben, darstellen, skizzieren
to dilute	verdünnen
discretion(ary)	Ermessen(s-)
dismissed	*here:* entlassen
to disregard	missachten, nicht beachten
to draft jurors	*here:* Geschworene einberufen
to embarrass	beschämen, in Verlegenheit bringen, verlegen machen
to evolve	herausbilden, entwickeln
excuse	*here:* Hinderungsgrund, Befreiung
exempt	ausgenommen, befreit
to exempt	befreien, freistellen
foreperson	gewählter Sprecher der Jury
to gather	(an)sammeln, erfassen
hardship	harte Umstände, Not, Mühsal
to impanel (a jury)	zusammenstellen
improper	ungebührlich, unpassend, ungeeignet
inconvenience	Unannehmlichkeit, Unbequemlichkeit
infamous crime	niederträchtige Straftat, Schandtat
to infer from	ableiten
juror identification badge	Namensschild der Geschworenen
jury summons	Geschworenenladung
latitude	Freiraum, Spielraum
to lodge	*here:* deponieren ("to lodge a claim"), *also:* wohnen
mental disability	geistige Behinderung
misuse	Missbrauch, Zweckentfremdung
monetary award	Geldersatz
non-compliance	Nichterfüllung, Nichtübereinstimmung, Diskrepanz
oath	Eid, Schwur
to object to somebody	gegen jemanden Einspruch erheben
on a case-by-case basis	im Einzelfall
onerous	beschwerlich, mühsam
to persist	beharren, fortdauern
to pertain	betreffen, gehören, gelten, zutreffen
to poll	abfragen, befragen
pool of potential jurors	Ansammlung der potenziellen Geschworenen
preconceived	vorgefasst
predetermined	vorherbestimmt, vorher festgelegt
prejudice	Vorurteil, Befangenheit

preliminary	Vorarbeit, vorbereitende Maßnahme; vorbereitende Tätigkeit
putative defendant	vemutlicher, mutmaßlicher Beschuldigter
to refrain from	etwas unterlassen, von etw Abstand nehmen
to rehabilitate	Ansehen wiederherstellen, sanieren, wieder einstellen
to repeal	aufheben, widerrufen
scruples	Skrupel, Bedenken
to show cause	seine Gründe zeigen, begründen
stalemate (situation)	Pattsituation
to strike (remove) a prospective juror from the panel	einen angehenden Geschworenen erfolgreich ablehnen
to subpoena	unter Strafandrohung vorladen
to summon	auffordern, bestellen, rufen
sympathetic	wohlgesonnen, wohlwollend, mitfühlend
unanimous	einstimmig
undue influence	unzulässige Beeinflussung
uninhibited	ungehemmt, hemmungslos
to weigh the evidence fairly and objectively	die Beweise objektiv und unvoreingenommen abwägen

X. Case Flow

General

There are three general stages of a (criminal and civil) lawsuit: **pre-trial** activities, **post-trial** procedures and – naturally – the **trial** itself. While the courtroom procedures in a criminal trial are similar to those of a civil litigation (at least as far as the sequence of events is concerned) criminal **pre-trial activities differ considerably** from pre-trial discovery in civil cases. A typical **civil** lawsuit is initiated by a private party (the plaintiff) who files a civil complaint (civil action) with the proper court. **Criminal** pre-trial proceedings, on the other hand, are dominated by the **police**. Once the case finds its way into the courtroom, criminal and civil procedures are again comparable: in both trials (civil and criminal) there is jury selection, a case presentation with witnesses that are examined by both sides as well as closing arguments, jury instructions and jury deliberation (as to the differences between criminal and civil law, see page 7).

Criminal Pre-Trial Activities

The typical pre-trial stages of a criminal case can be chronologically outlined as follows:

(1) Arrest
(2) Booking & Bail
(3) Initial Appearance
(4) *sometimes*: Plea Bargaining
(5) Preliminary Hearing
(6) Filing an Indictment or an Information
(7) Pre-Trial Motions

Criminal proceedings usually begin when police officers investigate on the basis of their observations or when they are informed about criminal activities. During the **police investigation** of an alleged crime the police interrogate suspects and witnesses, conduct lineups and use various other identification tools. When the police have reasonable belief, based on facts and circumstances, that a person has committed or is about to commit a crime, the officer may arrest that person. This belief, known as **probable cause**, may arise from various circumstances.

An **arrest** occurs when a person is taken into **police custody** and is no longer free to leave. The use of **physical restraint** or handcuffs is not always necessary. An arrest can also be complete when a police officer tells the suspect that (s)he is **under arrest** and the suspect submits without the officer's use of any physical force. Thus, the basic elements of an arrest are the **exercise of police authority** over a person and that person's voluntary or involuntary **submission**.

The next two steps of the criminal (pre-trial) proceedings are taking the person into police custody, which is known as **booking** (sometimes "processing") and a determination of his or her **eligibility for release** from custody (typically in exchange for the posting of a set amount of money). During booking a police officer typically fingerprints, photographs and searches the suspect, takes his personal data, confiscates any personal property, performs a record search of his criminal background and then places the suspect in a police station **holding cell** or local jail.

Persons arrested for minor offenses may be given a **written citation** and released immediately after signing it and promising to appear in court at a later date. The process through which an arrested suspect pays a set amount of money to obtain release from police custody is known as **bail**. For common crimes many jails have **standard bail** schedules specifying the individual bail amount. An arrested person can often get out of jail quickly by paying the amount set forth in this schedule, but there is **no absolute right to bail**. If the suspect does not obtain release by paying bail immediately after booking or if (s)he cannot afford the amount of bail on the schedule, (s)he has the right to be heard by a **judicial officer** (usually the magistrate) to formally set or lower it. Depending on the state, this request must be made either in a special **bail setting hearing** or when the criminal suspect appears in court for the first time.

The **purpose of setting bail** is to ensure a defendant's appearance at trial. When determining the necessary amount the judge or magistrate examines the **nature and circumstances of the charges**. The court also considers whether the person was on **parole or probation** at the time of the present arrest and examines the defendant's character, the nature and seriousness of threat he poses to others as well as the weight of the evidence against him. When examining the background of an arrested person, the court usually looks at his/her criminal history, family ties and the length of his/her residence in the community. If the judge comes to the conclusion that the suspect **endangers the safety of the community**, (s)he may be **held without bail**. If (s)he poses no threat to others and there is no grave danger that (s)he might flee from the court's jurisdiction (s)he is either released on personal recognizance or released on bail.

When the arrested person is granted **own recognizance release**, no bail money needs to be paid to the court, and no bond is posted. The suspect is merely released after signing a written promise to appear in court for all upcoming proceedings. Most state criminal courts impose certain conditions on this form of release in order to prohibit the suspect from leaving the area while the criminal proceedings are ongoing. Sometimes suspects are required to contact the court periodically while the case is pending. Payment of bail to the court may be made in cash or in an approved **cash substitute**. Once bail has been posted, the court will order that the defendant may be released. Released defendants must not commit any crimes during the period of their **release**.

After the arrest, booking and initial bail phases the first contact with the court is usually known as the **initial appearance** or initial arraignment. If the suspect is still under arrest, he has the right to be taken before the magistrate for a hearing **within a specific time period**, usually within 24 hours. During this hearing he magistrate typically reads the criminal charge(s) against the suspect (now called the **defendant**) and asks him/her if he or

X. Case Flow

(s)he has an attorney or needs the assistance of a court-appointed attorney (a public defender) to ensure the protection of his/her rights. If the defendant faces the possibility of jail time (s)he has a constitutional right to such assistance. Since the police may not constitutionally arrest a person unless they have probable cause to believe that a crime has occurred and that the suspect committed it, a **probable cause determination** (a so-called "Gerstein hearing") has to be made by the magistrate if the suspect was arrested without a warrant. Finally, the magistrate determines whether the arrested person should be set free or remain detained and announces the dates of future proceedings in the case, such as the preliminary hearing, pre-trial motions, and the beginning of the trial.

The **preliminary hearing** (which is conducted if there is no grand jury hearing – see page 91) is something like a "small trial" before the real trial and is usually held soon after the suspect's first appearance in court. If the defendant is detained most state laws require the courts to set the hearing at the latest two weeks after the initial court appearance. The purpose of the hearing is to decide whether there is enough evidence to force the defendant to stand trial. In making this determination, the judge uses the **probable cause legal standard**; in other words: the judge has to ascertain whether the government has produced enough evidence to convince a reasonable jury that the defendant committed the crime(s) (s)he is charged with. In reaching this probable cause decision, the judge listens to arguments from the prosecution and the defense. During the hearing both sides may call witnesses to testify and introduce physical evidence in an effort to convince the judge that the case should/should not go to trial. The defense usually seeks to convince the judge that the prosecutor's case is not strong enough and in doing so tries to call the evidence presented by the prosecution into question. If the defense succeeds, the case against the defendant will be dismissed by the judge and consequently there will be no trial. If the prosecution succeeds and the judge believes that there is sufficient evidence **to bind over the defendant for trial**, the defendant is formally charged with a (or more) crime(s). In some jurisdictions, the **formal charging document**, which is filed by the state attorney stating the individual charges and the essential underlying facts, is called **information**.

A preliminary hearing may not be held in every criminal case and in every jurisdiction, though. Some states conduct preliminary hearings only in felony cases and other states (as well as the federal government) utilize a **grand jury indictment** (see page 91) for serious matters in which a designated group of citizens decides whether the case should proceed to trial. If a majority of the grand jurors do not vote to indict the defendant, the case is **dismissed** and (s)he is discharged. Otherwise, they issue an **indictment**, which in this case is the **formal charging document** replacing the information.

A useful general term for the official charging document (encompassing indictment, information and presentment) is **criminal complaint**.

There is actually a third form of charging document, known as **presentment.** While the information is an accusation presented directly by the prosecutor without consideration by a grand jury and an indictment is issued by a grand jury after their investigation was initiated by the prosecution, a **presentment** is a formal accusation **issued by the grand jury on its own knowledge** without the prosecutor having charged the person beforehand.

Above and beyond, the possibility always exists that any time prior to the preliminary hearing a criminal case will be resolved through a **plea bargain** between the government and the defendant. In fact, a **vast majority** of criminal cases are resolved through such deals well before the case reaches trial. In a plea bargain, the defendant agrees to plead guilty – usually to a lesser charge than the one for which he faces trial – in exchange for a more lenient sentence and/or a dismissal of some charges. For both the state and the defendant the decision to enter into a plea bargain may be based on the seriousness of the alleged crime, the strength of the evidence in the case and the prospects of a guilty verdict reached in trial. In the US, plea bargains have become something of a necessity due to overburdened criminal court calendars and overcrowded jails.

Absent a plea bargain or a dismissal of the charges, a criminal complaint (see previous page) is filed with the trial court, after which the defendant is arraigned in open court. In this context the term **arraignment** is used for the formal reading of the criminal complaint in the presence of the defendant, in order to inform him of the charges against him. In response to the arraignment, the accused is expected to **enter a plea**. Acceptable pleas vary from jurisdiction to jurisdiction, but they generally include "guilty", "not guilty", and pleas of "nolo contendere" (no contest). No contest pleas occur when defendants do not want a trial to contest the charge but also do not want to openly admit that they committed the crime they are charged with. It is a common plea when there may be other charges pending against a defendant and/or there is also a likelihood of a civil lawsuit. By entering this plea the defendant does not admit to the crime, but the judge will still enter a guilty verdict and determine the punishment without conducting a trial.

If the defendant states that (s)he is not guilty or **stands mute** the case goes to trial. Before that the prosecutor and the defense usually file written **pre-trial motions** or appear before a criminal court judge arguing that certain pieces of evidence should be kept away from the jury in an effort to set the boundaries for trial. The most common motion to exclude evidence is the **motion to suppress** (evidence) which is sometimes also denoted **motion in limine**.

Civil Pre-Trial Activities

A civil case typically begins with the plaintiff filing a **complaint** (civil action) with the clerk of the proper court and paying a certain fee. The complaint is the first pleading and initiates the lawsuit. The plaintiff has to include all the relevant **allegations of fact** on which the action is based and formulate a **prayer.** Once the complaint is filed it must be served upon the defendant, in order to inform him that a lawsuit has been filed and give him the opportunity to respond. The complaint is usually **served** upon the defendant **together with a summons**. There are some alternative serving methods such as registered mail accompanied by a copy affixed to the defendant's residence (a form of service that is known as "**nail and mail**"). In any case, rendering a default judgment requires that the defendant is either served personally or by proxy. The summons directs the defendant to either appear in court or to file a response pleading within a certain time. **Several types of responses** by the defendant are available, the most common of which is the **answer**.

X. Case Flow

The defendant may also file a **motion to dismiss** or a **demurrer**, both with the intention to formally stop the lawsuit. The judge must then rule on these motions by either dismissing (overruling) or sustaining them. When the defendant files an answer, which might also include a **counterclaim**, the plaintiff gets a chance to reply with a formal **replication**.

After the exchange of these pleadings a process called **pre-trial discovery** begins. This phase of a US civil litigation differs considerably from its criminal counterpart and from continental European court proceedings. The primary purpose of pre-trial discovery (for both sides) is to find out whether it is worth taking the risk that conducting a trial involves. During pre-trial discovery both parties **gather the evidence** they need to convince the jury of their factual positions, prepare themselves and their witnesses for the trial and try to prevent surprise situations in front of the jury. The US civil process typically utilizes **extensive discovery procedures**, which can be lengthy and very expensive, which provides an advantage to financially well situated litigants and discriminates those who cannot pay these costs. Non-criminal defendants have no Fifth Amendment protection against extensive requests for information and a party may turn to the court for an **order to compel compliance**, if the opposing party refuses to cooperate during discovery. To facilitate the production of evidence, both parties have specific discovery devices at their disposal, such as **depositions, interrogatories, requests for admissions, requests for the production of documents and physical or mental examinations**. Because the jury only deals with allegations in dispute, so called **requests for admissions** ("*do you admit that…?*") help to narrow the scope of the controversy and to make the actual trial shorter. **Non-controversial** and **admitted facts**, however, need <u>not</u> be presented to the jury.

In federal courts, a **pre-trial conference** is held after discovery and both counsels usually appear without their clients to talk about the nature of the case, the standpoints of both parties, the **uncontested** or explicitly **admitted facts** (stipulations) and the ultimate **facts in dispute**. The judge may enter a **pre-trial order** to specify the witnesses to be called and the documents to be disclosed at trial. While such a conference is a regular procedure in federal courts, most state courts only hold pre-trial conferences in more complex cases and in medical malpractice cases or when a party specially asks the court for it in order to try and settle the dispute out of court.

In the US, **settlements** occur both in civil and criminal cases. In civil cases, lawyers try to reach an agreement which appeases both sides. This may take the form of a monetary amount which both sides believe satisfies their claims. In criminal cases, the prosecutor or state (district) attorney may agree on not to prosecute by means of a trial in exchange for the defendant's admittance that he or she committed a crime (so called **plea bargain** – see previous subchapter). **Settlement negotiations** usually take place between the lawyers right up to the moment the trial begins. The trial may even be delayed while the lawyers try to work out a settlement with the judge in his chambers.

Trial

The actual court litigation begins after the trial jury has been selected and impaneled (see page 96). In short, one could say that the typical (civil and criminal) trial process contains the following stages:

(1) Opening statements
(2) Presentation of evidence by both parties
(3) Rebuttal / surrebuttal
(4) Closing arguments / summation
(5) Instruction of the jury
(6) Jury deliberation
(7) Announcement of the verdict

During **opening statements** both attorneys inform the jury about their factual versions (the allegations) of the case and what they intend to prove and how. The attorney for the defense may make his/her opening statement immediately or postpone it until the plaintiff has rested his/her case. After the opening statement(s) the plaintiff presents her case; in doing so his/her lawyer (or in a criminal case the prosecution) will **call witnesses** who have to take an **oath** before giving testimony. There are two types of witnesses: lay and expert witnesses. While the **lay witness** is a person who has seen or heard something that is relevant in the case, the **expert witness** is a person who is a specialist in a specific profession and whose expert opinion is important for the understanding of a relevant factual issue by the jury. Before the expert witness is asked to express his opinion on the matter at stake, he has to be **qualified as an expert** by the party who introduced him, usually by asking him about his studies and professional activities. If the opposing party's attorney objects to the motion to have the witnessed recognized as an expert, the judge has to rule on this motion immediately.

During **direct and cross-examination**, exhibits such as documents or photographs may be introduced into evidence. If the judge rules that these exhibits are to be **admitted into evidence**, the jury is allowed to examine them and take them into the jury room during deliberation. Under certain circumstances jurors may also leave the courtroom to look at a particular site or object, but only under court supervision. The process of examining and cross-examining witnesses and introducing exhibits continues until the **plaintiff rests her case**. Before the defendant starts with the presentation of his/her evidence, (s)he may make a **motion for a non-suit**, claiming that the plaintiff has failed to make a **prima facie case** by arguing that the plaintiff has failed to provide reasonable proof of every element of her **cause of action**. When ruling on this motion, the judge simply has to assume that all the factual issues raised by the plaintiff are true and decide as a matter of law whether the plaintiff has failed to make a case.

If the motion is overruled, the trial continues with the **defendant's case in chief**. During this phase of the trial the defendant tries to weaken the jury's belief in what they saw and heard during the plaintiff's presentation of evidence and, if possible, to make a defense against the plaintiff's claims. This time the defendant's lawyer examines his witnesses first (on direct examination) and then the plaintiff's lawyer continues with cross-examination. The defendant's case continues in essentially the same manner as the plaintiff's until the defendant's lawyer states to the court that the **defense rests**. Before the plaintiff is given a chance to refute or oppose the factual allegations made by the defense (s)he may make a **motion for a directed verdict**, which is similar to the motion for a non-suit, just made at a later point in the trial with the plaintiff being the moving party. If there is no such motion or the motion is denied the plaintiff gets a chance to attack claims that were made by the defense in a **rebuttal**, after which the defendant can present his **surrebuttal**. In both rebuttal and surrebuttal the parties cannot raise any new issues but may only refer to the evidence that was already presented.

Finally, before the case is turned over to the jury, both attorneys sum up the case from their perspectives and remind the jury of what they should take into consideration during deliberation in their **closing arguments** (also called **summation**). Unlike the opening statements, which are limited to what is going to be proven during trial, the closing arguments may include opinions on the law and comments on the opposing party's evidence. Usually, the attorneys request a verdict favorable to their clients.

Post-Trial Procedures

The jury's verdict only takes legal effect once the judge enters **judgment on the verdict**. In almost all cases the judge enters judgment in accordance with the jury's decision. **Motions for a judgment notwithstanding the verdict** by the losing party are hardly ever granted. Such a motion will actually **never** be successful when the jury reaches a **not guilty verdict in a criminal case**. Even if the jury acquitted a criminal defendant by obviously ignoring (nullifying) the law the judge is not in a position to alter such a verdict. A motion for a judgment notwithstanding the verdict might be successful with regard to the **damage awarded in tort cases**, though, when a jury has obviously overreacted to the harm caused by a defendant (such a jury is referred to as a "**runaway jury**"). Another possible post-trial motion is the motion for a new trial, claiming that a prejudicial error that affected the outcome of the case occured during trial. If this motion is sustained the whole procedure is void and the case must be tried again.

The party dissatisfied with the court's ruling (losing litigant, losing party) has the right to file an **appeal** within a specified length of time (usually 30 days). The appellant has to raise the issues that (s)he wants to be reviewed by the appellate court in his/her appeal. Generally, attorneys are not allowed to raise new issues and offer new evidence in their appeals. Rather, their complaints are limited to errors that occurred before or during the trial. In cases involving money damages, the defendant may also just appeal the jury's award.

If there is no appeal, the judgment on the verdict takes legal effect. In case the defendant is still unwilling to pay, the plaintiff will have to **enforce the judgment**. The process whereby an official (sheriff, US marshall etc) is directed by an appropriate judicial writ (**writ of execution**) to seize and sell as much of a debtor's nonexempt property as is necessary to satisfy a court's monetary judgment is referred to as **execution**. This can be achieved through placing a lien (garnishment) against the defendant's salary or through

X. Case Flow

seizing his/her property. An order to execute the judgment may command the sheriff to take possession of the defendant's property and sell it at auction to satisfy the judgment. If there is reasonable concern that the defendant might dispose of some of his property, the plaintiff can request an **attachment** preventing him from any such disposition.

In the criminal context, the defendant may also appeal the ruling to a higher court, which only examines the record of the lower court's proceedings to determine if errors occurred that justify a new trial, resentencing or a complete discharge of the defendant. Just as in the civil appellate court, the criminal appellate court **never conducts a new trial**. The prosecution may appeal the sentence but it has no right to go on appeal after an acquittal.

> **SIMPLY**
>
> While criminal and civil pre-trial activities differ considerably from each other, the basic courtroom procedure is the same in both – civil and criminal – trials: After **jury selection** and **opening statements**, the so-called "case-in-chief", which is the evidentiary section of the trial, follows, whereby the plaintiff / prosecution start with the presentation of their case. Once the plaintiff / prosecution rest, the defense may present her case. In **presenting their cases** both sides call their witnesses and for each witness direct- and cross-examination is performed. Once the defense rests, the plaintiff / prosecution will start their **rebuttal**, the purpose of which is to comment on evidence used by the defense. The defense may then have a **surrebuttal**, to further argue points (with reference to the plaintiff's rebuttal). This can go on back and forth until both sides are satisfied. Once both sides have finished, **closing arguments (summations)** begin. After that, the judge will give closing instructions to the jury on how to proceed in the jury room.

Discuss

Which stages of a criminal lawsuit are comparable to civil case proceedings?

Which criminal proceedings do not occur in a civil lawsuit?

When is somebody arrested and how?

What does "booking" mean?

What is the purpose of setting bail?

What happens during the suspect's first court appearance?

What happens in a preliminary hearing?

Explain the "probable cause" legal standard!

What happens if the case is resolved through a plea bargain and why?

What does it mean to be "arraigned in open court"?

What is the main function of pre-trial discovery?

Which tools of discovery do you know?

What is a pre-trial conference?

What is the purpose of an opening statement / closing argument?

X. Case Flow

Explain the typical trial process!

What is a "runaway jury"?

Try to list and explain the motions mentioned in the text!

Concepts

admissions of fact

the defendant admits the truth of some of the factual allegations in the plaintiff's complaint (see: stipulation).

arbitration

various state statutes provide that civil cases, where the amount in controversy is less than a specific amount, must first be heard in an arbitration proceeding (see page 136). For this purpose an attorney is appointed by the court to hear the case and make a decision. Arbitration hearings are much simpler than a trial and can be heard much quicker. If either party is dissatisfied with the arbitration award, they can ask for a trial conducted by the court.

arraignment

after the indictment or information is filed, the defendant is "arraigned," which means (s)he is brought before the trial court and is informed of the charges and the pleas (s)he may enter.

(US) Attorney General (AG)

head of the US department of justice; (s)he is concerned with legal affairs in which the government has an interest and is considered to be the chief lawyer of the US government.

bench warrant

warrant issued by the judge when a defendant fails to appear for a scheduled court appearance.

to bind over (the defendant for trial)

(1) to put under a bond (bail) to do something (as to show up for trial) under court authority; (2) to hold a criminal defendant in jail until the trial starts; (2) to transfer (a case or defendant) to another forum after preliminary hear (grand jury indictment).

bond

here: written guarantee or pledge which is purchased by an individual (called a "bondsman") as security to guarantee some form of performance including showing up in court ("bail bond").

booking a suspect

logging his/her name into an arrest book or computer.

capital offense

crime which is punishable by the death penalty; the term indicates the defendant's risk of "losing his/her head".

cause of action

the basis of a lawsuit founded on legal grounds and alleged facts which, if proven, constitute all the legal elements that are required by statute. In a tort suit, to have a cause of action, the plaintiff must claim that the defendant acted negligently, intentionally wrong (or failed to perform) and that there was a connection between the defendant's actions and the damages (s)he suffered. In many lawsuits, several causes of action are stated separately, such as fraud, breach of contract, and debt.

citation

(1) a notice / order to appear in court; (2) the act of referring to (citing) a statute, precedent-setting case or legal textbook; (3) the name of the case, including the volume number, the reporter and the page number.

complaint, answer, replication, rejoinder

formal civil pleadings which are exchanged between the parties after the initiation of a written lawsuit before the trial.

counterclaim

a claim for relief filed by the defendant in response to the plaintiff's complaint, arguing eg that it is actually the plaintiff who owes money or should be ordered to pay damages.

default judgment (also: judgment by default)

if a civil defendant does not respond to a complaint within the time set by law the plaintiff (suer) can request an entry of default (failure) which gives him/her the right to get a default judgment. If the complaint was for a specific amount of money or the amount due is easy to calculate the court will enter a default judgment.

demurrer

a specific motion to dismiss claiming that the plaintiff's complaint fails to state a cause of action. Ruling on this motion, the judge must assume that all of the plaintiff's allegations are true and must then ask (under this assumption) whether the law permits the plaintiff to prevail over the defendant. If that is the case he has to dismiss or overrule the demurrer.

denials of fact

the defendant explicitly disagrees with the plaintiff's factual allegations in the complaint.

deposition

an oral (pre-trial) interview of a party or a witness under oath with the presence of a court reporter. If a party decides to depose a witness (s)he must inform the other party giving him/her the opportunity to be present when the depo(sition) is taken and to cross-examine the witness. The person being deposed is known as the "deponent".

detention
suspects who have been arrested and booked are put in a lockup or detention cell until taken to court for a hearing, usually for no more than 72 hours, either because they could not make bail or because they were found to be too dangerous to be released.

discharge of bond
a court order to release bond, usually once the case is disposed.

diversion
in criminal procedure, a system for giving a chance for a first-time criminal defendant in minor crimes to perform community service, make restitution for damages, obtain treatment for alcohol or drug problems and/or counseling for anti-social or mentally unstable conduct. If the defendant cooperates and the diversion results in progress, the charges eventually may be dismissed. Usually diversion is not granted after a second offense.

first appearance
an accused's first court hearing, usually 24 hours after his/her arrest.

"Gerstein" hearing
the term Gerstein hearing stems from *Gerstein v. Pugh 420 U.S. 103 (1975)*, where the Supreme Court ruled that, following a warrantless arrest, the 4th Amendment requires that a prompt judicial determination of probable cause be made as a pre-condition to any extended restraint of the arrestee's liberty.

indictment
in criminal law, a formal document containing the criminal charges against a defendant, which is issued by a grand jury (after a grand jury hearing) on request of the prosecution. It is required for federal prosecutions involving felony charges. In about half the US states prosecutors are allowed to issue informations (see below).

information
criminal complaint, followed by a preliminary hearing held by a lower court judge or other magistrate, which contains the criminal charges against a defendant and is issued by a prosecuting officer. It serves the same function as an indictment presented by the grand jury. About half the US states allow prosecutors to issue informations; the rest require an indictment.

interrogatories
a list of written questions sent to the opposing party during pre-trial discovery, which the other party has to answer in writing and under oath.

investigation

the gathering of evidence by the police and the prosecution in order to prove that the accused committed the crime.

judgment on the pleadings

judgment that is based exclusively on the pleadings (complaint, answer, reply, rejoinder) and without consideration of any evidence. After the exchange of the pleadings, the party asking for such a judgment claims that no material issue of fact exists. It is therefore similar to a demurrer (see page 114), except that a demurrer only refers to the complaint.

leading

short for "leading the witness;" it occurs when (during a trial or deposition) the attorney asks questions in a form in which (s)he already suggests the expected answer. Leading is only allowed in cross-examination.

lineup

a law enforcement method used during police investitation to assist a witness or victim in identifying a suspect. Initially the suspect is included in a line of people, including non-criminals and others; then a law enforcement official asks each person in the lineup to speak and turn to profile, while the witness and/or the victim study each of them in order to identify the suspect as the offender.

marshal

law enforcement officer (acting in state and federal courts), who serves official documents and occasionally assists in police matters (e.g by keeping order in the courtroom, making arrests or participating in court-ordered police activities).

"Miranda" warning

requirement (also called "Miranda rule") set by the US Supreme Court in *Miranda v. Arizona* (1966) that prior to any interrogation of an arrested suspect, (s)he must be told that (s)he has the right to remain silent, the right to be represented by counsel and the right to be told that anything (s)he says can be used in court against him/her. These rights are known as Miranda rights.

motion for a summary judgment

one of the parties may make such a motion if the judge can resolve the legal dispute by applying the law to the facts the parties agree are true.

motion in limine

Latin for: "at the threshold"; a motion made before the start of a trial, requesting the judge to rule that certain evidence may or may not be introduced to the jury during trial. If a question is to be decided *in limine*, it will be for the judge to decide. Usually it is used to shield the jury from possibly inadmissible and harmful evidence.

X. Case Flow

motion to dismiss

claims that some procedural problem bars the lawsuit: eg lack of jurisdiction or violation of the statute of limitations. Motions to dismiss are typically filed shortly after the filing of a complaint for the purpose of attempting an early resolution of a case without further expenses.

nolo contendere / no contest

the accused admits the facts, but is unwilling to plead "guilty". In doing so, (s)he neither admits nor denies the charges but lets them stand as they are.

order to compel compliance

court decision ordering a party to cooperate with the other party, eg by delivering papers etc.

parole

a conditional release of a prisoner from a correctional facility who has served part of the term/sentence to which (s)he was sentenced.

physical /mental examinations

tool used during pre-trial discovery; a party is required to submit such an examination (by a doctor of the other party's choice) if so ordered by the court.

plea

in criminal law, the response by an accused to each criminal charge. The rules of criminal procedure in federal- and most state courts permit a defendant to enter a plea of guilty, not guilty, or *nolo contendere*, which means "I do not wish to contest it".

prayer (for relief)

the specific request for damages or relief at the end of a civil complaint. A typical prayer for relief asks for a monetary award as well as compensation for attorney's fees and the costs of the lawsuit. The prayer is an important element of the complaint, since it gives the judge an idea of what is sought and may become the basis of his judgment if the defendant fails to file an answer.

preliminary hearing

also called "preliminary examination"; a hearing conducted in states that have abolished grand jury hearings and which has to be held within a certain time-period (usually two weeks) after an arrestee's initial court appearance. The purpose of the hearing is to determine if there is substantial evidence ("probable cause") to try the defendant.

presentment

a report to a court by a grand jury, made on its own initiative (without a request or presentation of evidence by the prosecution) that a crime has been committed.

pre-trial discovery

process of gathering evidence before the trial begins. Tools of discovery are depositions, interrogatories, requests for admission, requests for the production of documents and physical or mental examinations.

prima facie [pry-mah fay-shah]

Latin for: "at first look," or "on its face"; referring to a lawsuit or criminal prosecution in which the evidence before trial is sufficient to prove the case unless there is substantial contradictory evidence presented at trial. A *prima facie* case presented to a grand jury by the prosecution typically results in an indictment.

probable cause

reasonable belief (*here:* that a crime was committed and that the named person committed the crime). According to the 4th Amendment, probable cause has to exist prior to an arrest, search or seizure.

probation

here: a chance to remain free given to a person convicted of a crime instead of being sent to jail or prison subject to specific court-ordered terms (such as good behavior) and the supervision of a probation officer. "Repeat offenders" are normally not eligible for probation and a violation of probation terms will usually result in the person being sent to jail for the normal term (see: revocation).

proxy

someone who is explicidly authorized to represent somebody else; the term also stands for the written authority given to someone to act or vote in someone's place.

rebuttal

evidence introduced to disprove, challenge or contradict the opposition's evidence.

(re)direct / (re)cross examination

each party calls his/her witnesses (which are considered to be friendly to the party who called him/her) to the witness stand where (s)he responds to the lawyer's questions on direct examination. After that, the witness has to respond to the questions asked by the opposing party's attorney, which is called cross-examination. Since the witness was called to testify by the opposing party, the witness is considered to be hostile to the lawyer conducting cross-examination. Generally, cross-examination is limited to questions concerning matters brought up during direct examination. After cross-examination the plaintiff's lawyer may again question the witness (this is called redirect examination) and this may be followed by recross examination.

X. Case Flow

requests for admission

a "do-you-admit"-question addressed to the opposing party during discovery in order to shorten the trial process. If the other party admits the truth of the specific statement asked, it is no longer a factual issue at trial.

request for the production of documents

formal request addressed to the opposing party during discovery demanding to hand over certain document information. If the opposing party has a good reason for not wanting to release specfic pieces of information (eg because they contain trade secrets), it may turn to the court to request a protective order, which the court may or may not grant.

revocation

a decision to withdraw probation, parole or privileges in a particular case.

service of process

delivery of the summons and the complaint to the defendant to notify him/her that a lawsuit has been filed against him/her and that (s)he needs to react in a certain way.

speedy trial

in the US, the right to a speedy trial refers to a specific right of a criminal defendant (who has either been arrested, indicted, or formally accused of having committed a federal crime) established by the 6th Amendment of the US Constitution. It exists to ensure that an individual who has been charged with a federal crime does not have to wait in jail for an unreasonably long period of time before his/her trial. It also applies to criminal proceedings in many states, whereby the length of time varies.

standing mute

when the defendant, upon his arraignment, refuses to answer any questions (s)he is said to stand mute. If the defendant refuses to make a plea after being informed about the criminal charges the case usually proceeds to trial.

status conference

a pre-trial meeting of the attorneys with the judge which is required under Federal Rules of Procedure. In many states the purpose of the status conference is to lay out the progress of the case, set a timeline for discovery matters and decide the date of the trial. Court rules usually require the filing of a status conference statement prior to the conference.

statute of limitations

a law which sets the maximum period which one can wait before filing a lawsuit, depending on the type of case or claim. The periods vary by state. If the lawsuit or claim is not filed before the statutory deadline, the right to sue or make a claim is forever barred.

stipulation

an agreement between the attorneys, usually on a factual issue (admission) or a procedural matter. Some stipulations are oral, but the courts often require that the stipulation be put in writing, signed and filed with the court.

subpoena

originally spelled: *subpena*; a document issued by the court (usually the court clerk) which must be served personally on the party being summoned and which contains a court order (eg for a witness) to appear at a particular time and place to testify and/or produce certain documents. Failure to appear as required by the subpoena can be punished as contempt of court if the absence was intentional or without cause.

summary judgment

if there is no dispute as to material facts or if only a question of law is involved, the case is decided by the judge without conducting a trial.

summation / closing argument

the final argument of an attorney at the end of a trial in which (s)he attempts to convince the judge and/or jury of the virtues of his/her client's case.

summons

a notice summoning a defendant to appear in court or asking a person to report to court as a witness or a juror (jury summons).

surrebuttal [sər-(r)i- ˈbə-tl]

a plaintiff's reply to a defendant's rebuttal.

"three strikes, you're out"

a law enacted in California in 1994 in response to a tragic murder case. The law imposed a life sentence for almost any crime, no matter how minor, if the defendant had two prior convictions for crimes defined as serious or violent by the California Penal Code. In 2012 voters enacted the Three Strikes Reform Act ("Proposition 36") which eliminated life sentences for non-serious, non-violent crimes and established a procedure for inmates sentenced to life in prison for minor third strike crimes to petition in court for a reduced sentence.

waiver

a voluntary decision by a person to eliminate a legal procedure to which (s)he has a right.

witness conference

a discussion among the victim, witness(es) and the prosecutor to prepare for trial.

X. Case Flow

Vocabulary

admitted facts	außer Streit gestellter Sachverhalt
arraignment	*here:* Anklageverlesung
arrestee	Festgenommene(r)
arrest warrant	Haftbefehl
attachment	Pfändung
auction	Versteigerung
bail	Kaution
cash substitute	Bargeldersatz
to compel	zwingen, nötigen
to confiscate property	*here:* Gegenstände, Besitzstücke wegnehmen, konfiszieren
continuance	Vertagung, Unterbrechung
correctional facility	Justizvollzugsanstalt
correctional officer (CO)	Justizvollzugsbeamter
counterclaim	Widerklage, Gegenforderung, Gegenanspruch
court order	Beschluss
criminal complaint	Anklageschrift, Strafantrag, *also:* Strafanzeige
criminal record	Strafregisterauskunft
demurrer	*here:* Rechtseinwand der mangelnden Schlüssigkeit
device, tool	Gerät, Vorrichtung, Mittel
to discharge	entlassen, absetzen, verabschieden, freisprechen
to elapse	verstreichen, vergehen
eligibility	Auswahl, Eignung, Berechtigung
enforcement	Vollstreckung, Vollzug, Durchsetzung, *also:* Zwang
execution	Pfändung, Vollziehung, *also:* Hinrichtung
expert witness	Sachverständiger
fact in dispute	strittige Tatsache(nbehauptung)
fingerprint	Fingerabdruck
to fingerprint and photograph sb	jemanden erkennungsdienstlich behandeln
to flee	fliehen, flüchten
to frisk	*here:* abtasten
garnishment	Pfändung / Beschlagnahme einer Forderung
holding cell	Zelle
identification tools	Erkennungs-, Identifikationsmittel
imprisonement for contempt, coercive detention	Beugehaft
injunction	gerichtliche Verfügung
interrogator	*here:* Befrager
lay persons / lay assessors	Laien, Laienrichter
(lay) witness	Zeuge

lenient	mild, glimpflich
lien	Pfandrecht, Zurückbehaltungsrecht
medical malpractice case	Arzthaftungsprozess
motion to dismiss	Antrag auf Klageabweisung
motion to suppress (evidence)	Antrag auf Unterdrückung von Beweismitteln
moving party	Antragsteller
nonexempt (assets)	*here*: in die Konkursmasse fallend(es Vermögen)
non-moving party	Antragsgegner
overburdened	überlastet
overcrowded	überfüllt
parole	vorzeitige Haftentlassung
pending case	anhängiges / schwebendes Verfahren
performance	Leistung, Erfüllung, Durchsetzung
to perform a record search	eine Strafregisterauskunft einholen
plea	*here*: Antwort des Angeklagten
preventive detention	Sicherheitsverwahrung
probation	Bewährung
probation officer	Bewährungshelfer
rebuttal	Widerlegung
recognizance	Anerkenntnis, Anerkennungsverpflichtung
record search	*here*: Einholung einer Strafregisterauskunft
recourse	Zuflucht, Rechtsweg
release	*here*: Freilassung
to release on bail	auf Kaution freilassen
search	*here*: Personen-/Haus-)Durchsuchung
search warrant	Hausdurchsuchungsbefehl
to seize	*here*: beschlagnahmen
sequence	Abfolge, Reihenfolge, Ablauf
set	*here*: bestimmt, festgesetzt
to set forth	darlegen
settlement negotiations	Vergleichsgespräche
speedy trial	schnelles Verfahren
to stand mute	die Antwort verweigern; *here*: die vorgeworfene Straftat weder abstreiten noch zugeben / eingestehen
to stem from	sich ableiten von, herrühren, abstammen von
submission	*here*: Unterwerfung
substitute	Ersatz, Vertreter
tangible / intangible assets	bewegliches / unbewegliches Vermögen
to testify	(als Zeuge/Partei) aussagen
threshold	Schwelle, Abgrenzung

X. Case Flow

to try a case	einen Fall verhandeln
to try somebody	jemanden vor Gericht stellen
uncontested facts	unstrittiger Sachverhalt
uncontroversial, indisputable uncontentious, undisputed	unstrittig
wiretapping	Abhören

XI. Mutual Legal Assistance

Mutual Legal Assistance is becoming increasingly important in all fields of law. It seeks to **improve the effectiveness of national and international judicial cooperation** and to regularize and facilitate its procedures.

Letters Rogatory

In the absent of a specific treaty obligation such as the **Hague Evidence Convention** or a **Mutual Legal Assistance Treaty** (MLAT), the execution of a request for judicial assistance by a foreign court is based on **comity** between nations. Consular conventions facilitate international judicial assistance since they normally include provisions authorizing the **transmission of letters rogatory** through **diplomatic channels** through which requests may be made. If such a consular channel is created a letter rogatory has to be transmitted via this channel and not directly between the applicable courts, which can make the whole process fairly slow. Hence, in the 20th century there have been various **international treaties** in regard to **service of process** and the **taking of evidence**.

The creation of the **Hague Conference on Private International Law** (an intergovernmental organization) in 1893 resulted in numerous international conventions such as the Civil Procedure Convention, signed in 1905 at the Hague, which is actually one of the earliest conventions simplifying the exchange of letters rogatory. The **Hague Service Convention**, ratified in 1965, enables designated authorities in each of the signatory states to **transmit documents for service** to each other, bypassing the diplomatic route. The **Hague Evidence Convention**, which was ratified in 1970, formalized the procedures for the taking of evidence. Since 3 April 2007, the European Community has been a participant of the Hague Conference on Private International Law.

For situations exclusively among member states of the European Union, EU legislation supersedes the Hague Conventions.

For countries not signatory to any convention, the letter rogatory, which is sometimes also called "letter of request," is still used in civil and criminal as well as in administrative matters. It is a **formal request from a court** in one country to the judicial authorities of another country requesting legal assistance. In the absence of a treaty obligation, the requested country is not compelled to execute the request. If the request is executed, though, the foreign authority executes it **in accordance with its own laws**, despite the fact that the procedural laws of the requested country may differ substantially from the rules applied in the requesting state. In obtaining evidence, for example, in most cases a foreign attorney will not be permitted to participate in the local proceeding. If such an attorney wants to put forth additional questions to a witness (s)he has to be represented

XI. Mutual Legal Assistance

by an attorney that passed the local bar exam. Furthermore, not all foreign countries utilize the services of court reporters providing verbatim transcripts. Instead, in most European courts the presiding judge dictates his recollection of the witness's responses.

A letter rogatory usually includes the following elements:

- a brief outline of the case, including the identification of the parties and the nature of the claim as well as the relief sought;
- the type of case (civil, criminal, administrative);
- the nature of the assistance required (service of process, production of evidence, summoning a person to give testimony) and a list of documents or other evidence to be produced and/or a list of questions to be asked;
- name, address and other identifiers of the person or entity to be served or from whom evidence is to be compelled;
- a statement expressing the willingness to reimburse the judicial authorities of the receiving state for costs incurred in executing the requesting court's letter rogatory.

Letters rogatory are usually addressed "to *the appropriate Judicial Authority of (name of Country)*" and must be issued **under the seal of the court and the signature of the judge**. Some countries even require further verifying elements.

▶ **SAMPLE REQUEST FOR INTERNATIONAL JUDICIAL ASSISTANCE**

http://travel.state.gov/law/judicial/judicial_683.html#sample
name of the court requesting judicial assistance
docket number
name of plaintiff v. name of defendant

Letter Rogatory

(Name of the requesting court) presents its compliments to the appropriate judicial authority of *(name of receiving state)*, and requests international judicial assistance to *(obtain evidence / effect service of process)* to be used in a *(civil, criminal, administrative)* proceeding before this court in the above captioned matter. A *(trial/hearing)* on this matter is scheduled at present for *(date)* in *(city, state, country)*.

This court requests the assistance described herein as necessary in the interests of justice. The assistance required is that the appropriate judicial authority of *(name of receiving state)*

  compel the appearance of the below named individuals to give evidence/produce documents
  and / or effect service of process upon the below named individuals:
  - names of witnesses / persons to be served
  - nationality of witnesses / persons to be served
  - address of witnesses / persons to be served
  - description of documents or other evidence to be produced

FACTS

The facts of the case pending before the requesting court should be stated briefly, including a list of those laws of the sending state which govern the matter pending before the court in the receiving state.

XI. Mutual Legal Assistance

QUESTIONS

If the request is for evidence, the questions for the witnesses should be listed. Any special rights of witnesses pursuant to the laws of the requesting state should also be stated as well as any special methods or procedures to be followed. Also, a request for notification of time and place for examination of witnesses/documents before the court in the receiving state should be included.

RECIPROCITY

The requesting court should include a statement expressing a willingness to provide similar assistance to judicial authorities of the receiving state.

REIMBURSEMENT FOR COSTS

The requesting court should include a statement expressing a willingness to reimburse the judicial authorities of the receiving state for costs incurred in executing the requesting court's letter rogatory.

typed name and signature of the requesting judge

name, city and state of the requesting court

date and seal of court

SIMPLY

A letter rogatory is a formal request from a court to a foreign authority for some type of judicial assistance. The most common remedies sought by such letters are **service of process** and **taking of evidence.** If there is no consular convention in force between the requesting and a requested state, letters rogatory are received and executed by foreign authorities on the basis of comity.

Mutual Legal Assistance in Criminal Matters

Due to the **principle of sovereignty** a foreign judicial authority may not order a bank in Austria to freeze a foreign deceiver's account and hand over the relevant banking documents as evidence. The instrument of international mutual assistance in criminal matters seeks to overcome the obstacles that borders present to authorities that prosecute criminals by helping states to cooperate in the fight against international criminality. Mutual Legal Assistance Treaties (**MLATs**) establish the procedures for countries to assist each other in criminal investigations. They create a routine channel for obtaining legal assistance and in doing so significantly facilitate the **exchange of information and evidence.**

An MLAT creates a **contractual obligation** between the partners (countries) that have signed the treaty to render to each other assistance in criminal matters in accordance with the terms of the treaty. These terms include the designation of a **central authority** for **direct communication** (usually its justice department) by each treaty partner. If a treaty partner's prosecuting authority intends to investigate a specific criminal case abroad, it may use an **MLAT request** asking the central judicial authority of the country concerned to handle the case on behalf of the requesting treaty partner. This procedure is generally faster and more reliable than the handling of letters rogatory. The requested state will give assistance by **executing** on its territory **the official acts requested** and by **forwarding the results** to the requesting state through the channel created by the treaty. Pursuant to a request under an MLAT, the requested authorities may eg locate persons,

XI. Mutual Legal Assistance

provide service of process, execute searches and seizures of property, arrange for the appearance of witnesses, secure extraditions, transfer accused persons or supply relevant information. The remedies offered by the treaties are usually only available to the prosecuting authorities whereas the defense is obligated to proceed with the methods of obtaining evidence in criminal matters under the laws of the host country, which usually involve letters rogatory.

A general condition for granting mutual assistance usually is the existence of formal **criminal procedures in the requesting state**. If there is no MLAT with the requesting state, requested authorities often still grant the request formulated in a letter rogatory if the requesting state guarantees **reciprocity**, which means that future requests made in return by the requested state will be treated equally by the requesting state.

Another fundamental principle of judicial cooperation is the so called **principle of dual criminality** which, broadly spoken, means that the conduct in question must constitute an offense both in the requesting and in the requested country. Since coercive measures may be ordered in the execution of a mutual assistance request and witnesses may be summoned to appear with a **warning of compulsion** on the event of non-appearance, governments usually consider whether their prospective treaty partner respects the **rule of law**, before concluding an MLAT treaty. Otherwise they might end up having to provide assistance to criminal prosecutions in countries failing to respect fundamental legal principles.

The scope of assistance and the necessary **contents** of a particular request are defined in the underlying MLAT. Because such treaties are negotiated separately between the individual contract partners, the specific provisions of one treaty are not universally applicable. As a general rule, a treaty request includes the information that has to be provided in a letter rogatory (see above), key components being the principal need for the evidence or information sought, the subject matter and the nature of the investigation or proceeding. Depending on the assistance sought, any available information which may aid the request, such as the personal data of a person whose testimony is sought or from whom documents of evidence are requested should be provided as well. To the extent necessary the request also contains a description of the particular procedure to be followed such as, for instance, whether sworn testimony or statements are required.

> **SIMPLY**
>
> Mutual Legal Assistance Treaties (MLATs) are agreements between foreign countries for the purpose of enhancing the effectiveness of criminal law enforcement. MLATs seek to improve international judicial cooperation in criminal matters and to regularize and facilitate criminal procedures by creating formal channels for obtaining legal assistance. This assistance may range from examining and identifying people, places and things to providing assistance with the immobilization of the instruments of criminal activity.

Extradition and Rendition

Extradition is commonly requested by prosecuting authorities for criminal suspects for whom a warrant has been issued. Such a demand (from a state's prosecuting authority) for the surrender of a person initiates so called **extradition proceedings**. These proceedings are not part of the legal process (the trial) to determine an accused's guilt or innocence of the crime. Their sole purpose is to surrender him from one jurisdiction to another. Extradition proceedings take place in the **asylum state** (the state receiving the demand), where, first of all, the **merit** of the demanding state's charge against the accused is considered.

International extradition exists only by authority of an **international treaty** establishing a right or obligation to surrender an alleged criminal to a foreign state. Thus, extradition demands can only be made if there is a treaty with the nation providing an **extradition clause**. These days, most countries have signed **bilateral extradition treaties** with other countries. These treaties usually require that a country seeking extradition be able to show that the event in question qualifies as a crime in both countries. In addition the relevant crime has to be sufficiently serious and the case against the extradited person must be supported by adequate evidence. Furthermore, the fugitive should expect a fair trial in the recipient country. There is no single country in the world that has an extradition treaty with all other countries. The US lack extradition treaties with over fifty nations, including China and North Korea. Absent a treaty, no government has the right to demand or the duty to deliver a fugitive. But even when an extradition treaty exists, the treaty partners may place **restrictions** on the duty to surrender a person. For example, many foreign asylum nations refuse to extradite a fugitive to the US unless they are assured that the death penalty will not be used if the surrendered person is found guilty. The US, on the other hand, – such as many other nations – have a **political offense exception** to extradition, which provides that the US will not extradite to a foreign nation a fugitive accused of certain political crimes.

There are two types of extradition treaties: **dual criminality treaties** and **list treaties**, of which the latter is more common. While list treaties contain a list of crimes for which a suspect will be extradited, dual criminality treaties usually rely on the **principle of reciprocity** by allowing the extradition of a criminal suspect if the threat of punishment the suspect faces for the alleged crime exceeds a certain time of imprisonment in both countries.

The EU and the US signed an **agreement on extradition**, which entered into force on February 1st 2010. The agreement supplements the bilateral extradition treaties between individual EU member states and the US and enhances cooperation in the context of applicable extradition relations. The agreement, which was signed at the EU-US Summit in June 2003, introduces a **sentence threshold**, not a list of offenses. It applies to *any* suspected or attempted offense carrying a prison sentence of one year or more (which is actually a fairly low standard considering that the suspect is being deported to another continent. On the sensitive issue of capital punishment, the EU-US treaty states that extradition to the US can only be granted "on condition that the death penalty shall not be imposed on the person sought" or if this condition cannot be met "on condition that the death penalty – if imposed – shall not be carried out". Article 13 of the EU-US agreement on extradition further provides that the request for extradition *may* be denied if the requesting state does not accept these conditions.

XI. Mutual Legal Assistance

Within the EU, the **European Arrest Warrant** (EAW), which is applicable throughout all EU member states, has replaced lengthy extradition procedures. Once issued, it requires another member state to arrest and transfer a criminal suspect or sentenced person to the issuing state so that the person can be put on trial or complete a detention period. An EAW can only be issued for the purposes of **conducting a criminal prosecution** (not merely an investigation) or enforcing a **custodial sentence**. The warrant applies to cases where a final sentence of imprisonment or a detention order has been imposed for a period of at least four months and for offenses punishable by imprisonment or a detention order for a maximum period of at least one year.

Between political subdivisions on a domestic level, as in the US between the states, extradition is more accurately known as (interstate) **rendition**. Article four, section two, clause two, of the US Constitution, which is referred to as **interstate rendition clause,** reads as follows:

> A Person charged in any State with Treason, Felony or other Crime, who shall flee from Justice and be found in another State, shall on Demand of the executive Authority of the State from which he fled, be delivered up, to be removed to the State having Jurisdiction of the Crime.

For rendition requests within the US, it is the governor of the asylum state who may grant or deny the demand to surrender a fugitive after having received a written demand and after having examined the facts of the charge against the escapee. If the demand is denied, the fugitive can still be brought to trial, but within the asylum state's jurisdiction. The Supreme Court has established certain **exceptions from a state's duty to surrender suspects**. In *Kentucky v. Dennison* (1861), the Supreme Court held that a state cannot petition the federal courts to have another state honor its request for rendition, if the state receiving the request chooses not to do so. In rare cases, usually involving the death penalty, states have **refused or delayed rendition** and decided to allow their own legal proceedings against a suspect to take precedence. In 1987 this precedent was overruled by *Puerto Rico v. Branstad* establishing a federal interest in resolving interstate rendition disputes. However, the right of refusal of rendition was not entirely overturned.

> **SIMPLY**
>
> **Extradition** is the official process through which one sovereign entity surrenders a fugitive (a suspect or a criminal) found on its territory to the authorities of a requesting authority. As between nations, extradition is regulated by treaties. On a domestic level, extradition is more commonly known as (interstate) **rendition**.

Discuss

How do requested states give assistance after receiving MLAT requests?

Explain the scope of the EU-US treaty and the EAW!

What is the difference between extradition and rendition?

XI. Mutual Legal Assistance

Concepts

comity
the principle by which the courts of one jurisdiction may give effect to the laws or decisions of another. Comity is granted out of respect, deference or friendship, rather than obligation. The acceptance or adoption of decisions or laws by a court of another jurisdiction – either foreign or domestic – is therefore based on public policy rather than legal mandate.

dual criminality
in the context of extradition the principle of dual criminality implies that in order for an extradition to take place the conduct alleged must constitute an offense both in the requesting and the requested state.

reciprocity
a relationship between persons, states, or countries whereby favors or privileges granted by one are returned by the other. Reciprocity does not involve a vested right that would exist without it. In regard to lawyers, reciprocity refers to recognizing the license of an attorney from another state without the necessity of taking the local state's bar examination.

rule of law
principle according to which governmental authority is legitimately exercised only in accordance with clearly defined laws and procedures. The principle is intended to be a safeguard against arbitrary governance.

(writ of) habeas corpus
in Common Law countries, habeas corpus (Latin for "you [should] have the body") is the name of a legal action by means of which detainees can seek relief from unlawful imprisonment. A writ of habeas corpus directs a person, usually a prison warden, to produce the prisoner and justify the prisoner's detention. If the prisoner argues successfully that the incarceration is in violation of a constitutional right, the court may order the inmate's release. Habeas corpus relief may also be used to obtain custody of a child or to gain the release of a detained person who is insane, is a drug addict, or has an infectious disease.

Vocabulary

to authenticate	beglaubigen, bestätigen, für echt befinden
coercive measures	zwingende Maßnahmen
comity	Höflichkeit, Einverständnis
to compel evidence	Beweismittel abnötigen, anfordern
compulsion	Zwang
condition	Voraussetzung, Bedingung
contracting state	vertragschließender Staat

XI. Mutual Legal Assistance

convention	Abkommen, Absprache
costs incurred	angefallene Kosten
custodial sentence	Haftstrafe, Freiheitsstrafe
customary	allgemein üblich
deceiver	Betrüger, Schwindler
to deem	erachten, halten für
to demand extradition	Ausweisung verlangen
deportation	Abschiebung, Deportation
designated	vorgesehen, bestimmt, festgelegt
to dictate	diktieren
docket	Geschäftszahl, Registernummer
to execute a request	eine Anfrage ausführen, durchführen, erfüllen
to execute seizures of property	Beschlagnahmung von Besitz / Sachen durchführen
to extradite	ausliefern
extradition	Auslieferung, Ausweisung
extradition clause / provision	Auslieferungsbestimmung
extradition proceedings	Auslieferungsverfahren
extradition request, request for extradition	Auslieferungsantrag
extradition treaty	Auslieferungsabkommen, Auslieferungsvertrag
to forfeit	verwirken, verlustig gehen
to freeze an account	ein Konto einfrieren, sperren
immobilization	Ruhigstellung, Einfrierung, Immobilisierung
in accordance with	entsprechend, gemäß
joinder	Klageverbindung, Klagebeitritt, Intervention
joinder of parties	Streitgenossenschaft, Nebenintervention
libel / slander / defamation	Verleumdung, Beleidigung, üble Nachrede
libel suit / libel action / action for slander	Ehrenbeleidigungsklage
to locate persons	Personen ausfindig machen
merits	Verdienste
mutual	gegenseitig, wechselseitig, einvernehmlich
non-extradition clause	Auslieferungsverbot
to obtain evidence	Beweismittel erlangen, erwirken, bekommen
to preserve documents	Dokumente / Unterlagen (auf)bewahren
principal need	wesentliches Erfordernis, Bedürfnis
to produce documents	Dokumente vorweisen, vorzeigen
to provide service of process, to serve (documents)	Zustellungen vornehmen
to put forth	hervorbringen
reciprocity	Gegenseitigkeit, Wechselseitigkeit
recollection	Erinnerung
to reproduce	*here:* wiedergeben, reproduzieren, kopieren

respective	besonders, jeweilig, einschlägig
rule of law	Rechtsstaatlichkeit, Rechtsgrundsatz
safeguard	Schutzmaßnahme, Absicherung
to secure the extraditions of	die Auslieferung von ... sicherstellen
service of process	Zustellung
subject of investigation	Gegenstand der Untersuchung / Recherche
to supply records	Unterlagen beschaffen, zur Verfügung stellen
to surrender oneself to sb	sich jm ausliefern
threshold agreement	Indexklausel
transmission	*here:* Übermittlung, Übertragung
to uphold	halten, aufrecht erhalten
via / through consular (diplomatic) channels	*here:* im Konsulatsweg, diplomatischen Weg
warning of compulsion	Androhung der zwangsweisen Durchsetzung
writ	Schriftstück, Urkunde, Erlass

XII. Alternative Dispute Resolution

General

Alternative dispute resolution (short ADR) is a catchall term that describes a number of methods used to **resolve disputes out of court**, including negotiation, conciliation, early neutral evaluation, mediation and the many types of arbitration. ADR methods tend to be faster, less formalistic, cheaper and often less adversarial than a trial in court. Due to rising costs of litigation and increasing time delays in court litigation many states have begun experimenting with ADR programs. Some of these programs are voluntary, others are mandatory. Today, the two most well known alternatives to litigation are **arbitration and mediation.**

Arbitration

Arbitration is a **consensual process** which means that parties only arbitrate when they have agreed to do so. Such agreements are either signed before the dispute arises or after it has arisen. An agreement providing that in case a dispute should arise it will be resolved by arbitration is referred to as **arbitration clause.** Such clauses are often contained in contracts.

The UNCITRAL Arbitration Rules (adopted by UNCITRAL in 1976, revised in 2010) provide a comprehensive set of procedural rules upon which parties may agree for the conduct of arbitral proceedings. They include provisions dealing with, amongst others, multiple parties arbitration and joinder, liability and a procedure to object to experts appointed by the arbitral tribunal. A number of features aim to enhance **procedural efficiency**, including revised procedures for the replacement of an arbitrator, the requirement for **reasonableness of costs** and a review mechanism regarding the costs of arbitration. They also include more detailed provisions on **interim measures**.

Most disputes that involve private rights between two parties can be resolved using arbitration. The subject matter of some disputes is – by its nature – not capable of arbitration, though. Matters relating to crimes, status and family law are generally not considered to be arbitrable. In some disputes, parts of claims may be arbitrable and other parts not.

Parties do not only seek to resolve their disputes through arbitration because it is usually faster and cheaper than litigation in court, but also by a number of other reasons, which are perceived as **potential advantages**: If, for example, the subject matter of the dispute is highly technical, they can appoint an arbitrator with an appropriate degree of **expertise**. Also, the arbitral process usually enjoys a greater degree of flexibility than the courts. Besides, through international treaties and conventions arbitration awards are

easier to enforce abroad than court judgments. By 2013, 149 nations had adopted the UNCITRAL (United Nations Commission on International Trade Law) *Convention on the Recognition and Enforcement of Foreign Arbitral Awards ("New York Convention" 1958)*. In Austria and Germany this convention entered into force in 1961. Last but not least, arbitral proceedings and an arbitral awards are generally **private** as opposed to trials and court opinions. However, since arbitrators are generally unable to order interlocutory measures against a party, it is easier for the losing party to take steps to avoid enforcement of an award, eg by relocating assets offshore.

All in all one could say that arbitration is a simplified version of a trial that involves no discovery and uses simplified rules of evidence. Arbitrators are either appointed by the parties *ad hoc* or they are members of institutional **arbitration tribunals** which are permanent professional bodies providing arbitration services, such as the *ICC International Court or Arbitration* in Paris or the *International Arbitral Centre of the Austrian Federal Economic Chamber* in Vienna (VIAC). Permanent tribunals tend to have their own rules and procedures and tend to be much more formal. They also tend to be more expensive and – for procedural reasons – slower.

There are various forms or types of arbitration, the most common of which is known as **binding arbitration.** Binding arbitration is the submission of a dispute to one or more impartial persons for a final decision known as an "award." These awards are made in writing and are binding on the parties involved. The arbitrator's power to impose a decision may be limited by agreement such as in a so called "**Hi/Lo** (high-low) **arbitration**" where the parties agree in advance to a maximum and minimum binding award.

Nonbinding arbitration, on the other hand, is a type of arbitration where the arbitrator makes a determination of the rights of the parties to the dispute, but this determination is not binding upon them and **no enforceable arbitration award** is issued. The "award" is in effect an **advisory opinion** of the arbitrator's view of the respective merits of the parties' cases. Nonbinding arbitration is often used in connection with attempts to **reach a negotiated settlement.** The role of an arbitrator in nonbinding arbitration is, on the surface, similar to that of a mediator in mediation. However, the principal distinction is that, while a mediator will try to help the parties find a middle ground to compromise at, the **arbitrator remains totally removed from the settlement process** and will only give his/her personal determination of the issue. Subsequent to a nonbinding arbitration the parties remain free to pursue their claims either through the courts or by way of a binding arbitration, although in practice a settlement is the most common outcome. The award and reasoning in a nonbinding arbitration are almost invariably inadmissible in any subsequent court action or in an arbitration tribunal.

On the global level, **international arbitration** is most commonly used for the resolution of commercial disputes, particularly in the context of **international commercial transactions.** International arbitration is an established method for resolving disputes between parties to international commercial agreements. As with arbitration in general, it relies on the parties' decision to submit their dispute to private adjudication usually by including an arbitration clause in their contract. The practice of international arbitration has developed so as to allow parties from different legal backgrounds to resolve their disputes without the formalities of their underlying legal systems. The International Court of Arbitration in Paris (short: *ICC Court*) has been serving this purpose since 1923.

In the US, title 9 of the US Code establishes federal law supporting arbitration. There are also numerous state laws on ADR, since most US states have adopted the 1956 version of the *Uniform Arbitration Act* (revised in 2000) as state law. Therefore, arbitration agreements and decisions of the arbiter may be **enforceable** under state and federal law.

Mediation

Mediation is another form of dispute resolution serving as an alternative to the traditional litigation process. One could say that mediation is an attempt to settle a legal dispute through active participation of a third party (a so called **mediator**) who works to find points of agreement and make those in conflict agree on a fair result. This impartial third party **facilitates communication and negotiation** and promotes **voluntary decision making** by the parties to the dispute themselves. This process can be effective for resolving disputes **prior to arbitration or litigation**. The decision to mediate is completely voluntary. Mediation gives the parties the opportunity to discuss the issues, clear up misunderstandings, determine the underlying interests or concerns, find areas of agreement and, ultimately, to incorporate those areas of agreements into their resolution. The mediation process is strictly confidential.

A mediator does not resolve the issue him/herself or impose a decision on the parties. Instead, the mediator helps the parties to agree on a **mutually acceptable resolution**. Mediators are specifically trained in the conduct of negotiations that bring opposing parties together. Some professional mediators or lawyers practice mediation for substantial fees, but the costs are usually still far lower than those involved with fighting the matter out in court, plus, a mediator may achieve an early settlement and in doing so bring the parties' anxieties to an early end.

Mediation is used for a **wide range of case types** ranging from neighbor- and family disputes to contracts as well as cases involving monetary damages. It has even become a significant method for resolving disputes between investors and their stock brokers. Very common mediation cases are domestic relations disputes such as **divorce, child custody and visitation issues**. In such cases mediation is actually frequently ordered by the judge. However, mediation does not always result in a settlement.

> **SIMPLY**
> Alternative Dispute Resolution ("ADR") refers to any means of settling disputes outside of the courtroom. **Arbitration** is a noncourt procedure for resolving disputes using one or more neutral third parties, called arbitrator(s) or arbitration panel. Arbitration uses rules of evidence and procedure that are less formal than those followed in court, which usually lead to a faster and less expensive resolution. There are various types of arbitration that are commonly in use: binding (mandatory) arbitration is similar to a court proceeding in that the arbitrator has the power to impose a decision, although this is sometimes limited by agreement. In nonbinding arbitration, the arbitrator can recommend – but not impose – a decision. **Mediation**, on the other hand, is a dispute resolution method designed to help parties resolve their dispute themselves. In mediation, a neutral third party (the mediator) meets with both sides to help them

XII. Alternative Dispute Resolution

find a mutually satisfactory solution. Unlike a judge or an arbitrator conducting a binding arbitration, the mediator has no power to impose a solution. No formal rules of evidence or procedure control mediation; the mediator and the parties usually agree on their own informal ways to proceed.

Discuss

Which alternatives to court litigation are mentioned in the text?

Which reasons are considered as potential advantages of arbitration as opposed to court proceedings?

Which matters are considered to be non-arbitrable and why? Explain the difference between binding and non-binding arbitration!

In which contexts is international arbitration most commonly used?

Explain the differences between arbitration and mediation!

Concepts

(arbitration) award

here: the decision of an arbitrator, an arbitration board (panel) or any non-judicial arbiter which brings an end to the controversy. Arbitration tribunals have a range of remedies that can form a part of the award, whereby the typical arbitration award is the implementation of damages against a party. Arbitration awards are usually easier to enforce abroad than court judgments.

conciliation

here: general term for the process of adjusting or settling disputes in a friendly manner through extrajudicial means. Conciliation means bringing two opposing sides together to reach a compromise in an attempt to avoid taking a case to trial. In the US conciliation is used in labor disputes before arbitration and may also take place in several areas of the law.

hi/lo (high-low) arbitration

form of binding arbitration where the arbitrator only has a limited power to impose a decision, because the parties have already agreed in advance to a maximum and minimum award.

Vocabulary

adjudication	Entscheidung, Urteil, Zuerkennung
advisory opinion	gutachterliche / fachmännische Stellungnahme
arbitrable	schlichtbar, schiedsrichterlich
arbitral	schiedsgerichtlich
arbitral agreement	Schiedsabrede
arbitral jurisdiction	Schiedsgerichtsbarkeit

XII. Alternative Dispute Resolution

arbitral court, arbitration tribunal	Schiedsgericht
arbitral panel decision	Schiedsspruch
arbitration (procedure) arbitral procedure, process	Schiedsverfahren
arbitration clause	Schiedsklausel, Schlichtungsklausel
arbitrator	Schiedsrichter, Schlichter, Richter am Schiedsgericht
binding	verbindlich
binding arbitration	bindendes Schiedsverfahren, bindende Schlichtung
catchall term / phrase	(unbestimmter / vager) Sammelbegriff
compromise	Übereinkunft, gütliche Einigung
to compromise	*here:* durch einen Kompromiss regeln
conciliation	Schilchtung, Versöhnung, Einigung
confidential	vertraulich
enforceable	durchsetzbar, erzwingbar, vollstreckbar, vollziehbar
extrajudicial	außergerichtlich
to impose a decision	*here:* eine Entscheidung durchsetzen
interim measures	einstweilige Maßnahmen
invariably	grundsätzlich, ständig, ausnahmslos
joinder (of parties)	Klagebeitritt, (Neben)Intervention, Streitgenossenschaft
to mediate	vermitteln
mediator	Mediator, Schlichter, "Mittelsmann"
negotiated settlement	ausgehandelte, außergerichtliche Vereinbarung
non-arbitrable	nicht zu schlichten, nicht schiedsfähig
to pursue a claim	einen Anspruch geltend machen
reasonableness	Angemessenheit, Tragbarkeit, Vernüftigkeit,
resolution	*here:* Lösung
visitation issues	*here:* Besuchsrechtsangelegenheiten

XIII. Selected Issues

Property Law

The law governing the various forms of ownership in **real and personal property**, is referred to as property law. In civil law systems, there is a distinction between **movable and immovable property**, whereby movable property roughly corresponds to personal property and immovable property corresponds to real estate or real property and related rights and obligations. For the most part, states have exclusive jurisdiction over the land (real property) within their borders. Within the real property classification, there are further divisions, the most important of which are **freehold estates**, **leasehold estates**, and **concurrent estates**. Freehold estates are assets in which an individual has ownership for an indefinite period of time. Leasehold is real estate which is the subject of a lease. The term is commonly used to describe expansions on real property when the improvements are built on land owned by one party which is leased for a long term (such as 99 years) to the owner of the building. Concurrent estates exist when property is owned or possessed by two or more individuals simultaneously.

Personal property can again be divided into two major categories: **tangible and intangible property**, whereby the term tangible property encompasses such items as merchandise or jewelry and intangible property includes rights such as bonds, patents, stock and copyrights.

Family Law

Family law is an area of the law dealing with **family-related issues** and **domestic relationships** including (but not limited to) marriage, divorce, spousal abuse, child custody and visitation, alimony, and child support, as well as child abuse issues and adoption. Nowadays family law has grown beyond the boundaries of these traditional family matters and new areas of law have been created dealing with the legal rights of persons who have not been legally married. Still, one major aspect of family law addresses the issue of divorce and its legal consequences.

In both the US and Europe divorce law has changed considerably over time and is still a highly conflicted area of law. In the nineteenth century the concept of **consensual divorce** was not known. Back then, in order to obtain a divorce one party to the marriage had to prove that the other had committed a wrong of such weight that the marriage must be ended. Today, having a **no-fault divorce** enables spouses to dissolve their marriage without having to prove **fault** or **marital misconduct** on the part of the other. To obtain such a divorce a spouse must merely assert incompatibility or irreconcilable differences and show that the marriage has permanently broken down.

The problem of divorce encompasses the topic of **child custody**. During a marriage all custodial rights are exercised by both parents. These rights include the decisionmaking power over all aspects of upbringing and education, as long as the parental decisions and conduct stay within **dependency laws**. Upon divorce, that power used to go solely to the one parent obtaining custody, whereas the other (**noncustodial**) **parent** was only given a **child visitation right**. Naturally, this made the court's custody decision upon divorce a significant and farreaching one. In recent years, the concept of **joint custody** has emerged: Under joint custody, the decisionmaking power over a child's upbringing remains with both parents and physical custody goes to one or the other or is shared. However, in practice exercising joint custody only works if both parents are reasonable. If they play out remaining animosities and confuse the child with conflicting instructions or if they are simply unwilling to agree on basic issues involving the child's welfare they might harm the child. Nowadays, judges generally fashion two doctrines governing child custody: the **"best-interests-of-the-child" doctrine**, focusing on the needs of the child and the **"tender years" doctrine**, giving mothers a presumptive right to their young children.

Another problem arising along with divorce is the issue of **division of marital property**. This issue has also undergone a significant change since the 1970s. Courts now consider both the monetary and nonmonetary contributions of both spouses as is the case when one spouse works and the other partner stays home to raise the kids. In distributing marital assets and setting alimony and child support, the homestayer's contributions are a significant factor, although the spouses often disagree as to their valuation. Furthermore, courts no longer look at alimony as a longterm remedy. Alimony is now often awarded for a fixed term, so as to enable a divorced spouse to acquire education or training before entering the workforce.

Equity

In Common Law systems the name equity refers to a part of law that resolves disputes between persons by resorting to **principles of conscience, fairness and justness**. The concept of equity typically comes into play when none of the parties to the dispute has done anything against the law, but their rights or claims are still in conflict. Hence, equity has to be distinguished form both "statutory law" (the law enacted through legislation) and "case law" (the principles set forth in judicial opinions). Courts of equity (also called **chancery courts**) arose in England in the 14th century in response to the increasingly strict rules of proof and other courts' of law requirements. Equity provided remedies not available under the strict writ system. Often, these remedies involved something other than damages, such as specific performance of contractual obligations, **restitution of goods** wrongfully acquired or the correction of false or misleading documents. Equity courts gradually established their own precedents and legal doctrines until in England the two systems were united in 1873. Most US jurisdictions have also combined their courts of equity, with the courts of law into a single system. Today, modern courts apply both legal and equitable principles and offer both **legal and equitable relief.**

Contract Law

A contract is an agreement or promise that is enforced or recognised by the law. In civil law systems, contracts are considered to be part of the general law of obligations.

Basically, contract law addresses four sets of issues:

- When and how is a contract formed?
- When may a party escape obligations of a contract (such as a contract formed under duress or because of a misrepresentation)?
- What is the meaning and effect to be given to the terms of a contract?
- What is the remedy to be given for breach of a contract?

Contractual liability (as opposed to liability in tort – see below) reflects the constitutive function of a contract and arises when a party to a contract fails to act according to his/her contractual obligations, for instance because he does not render the expected performance.

Tort Law

The law of obligations (in civil law systems) is traditionally divided into contractual obligations, which are voluntarily undertaken and owed to a specific person or persons, and obligations in tort, which are based on the **wrongful infliction of harm** to certain protected interests, primarily imposed by the law and typically owed to a wider class of persons. A **breach of** such a **non-contractual duty** that is owed to groups of society or to the public as a whole is (in civil law countries) referred to as **delict**. The equivalent legal concept in Common Law systems is **tort**. Torts include all negligence cases as well as intentional wrongs which result in a harm for which the law provides a remedy. Therefore, tort law is one of the major areas of law (along with contract, real property and criminal law). Some intentional torts may also be crimes, such as fraud, assault or wrongful death, which result in a criminal lawsuit and at the same time form the basis of a **tort suit** with the injured party privately suing for damages. Hence, unlike criminal prosecutions, which are brought by the government, tort actions are brought by private (injured) citizens. Remedies for tortious acts include **money damages** and/or court orders compelling or forbidding a particular conduct (injunctions).

The law of torts serves several objectives: It primarily seeks to **compensate** victims for injuries suffered by the culpable action or omission of others. It also intends to **shift the expenditure of such injuries** to the person(s) who are legally responsible for inflicting them and seeks to infringe careless and risky behavior in the future. In doing so, tort law endeavors to vindicate legal rights and interests that have been diminished. A tort plaintiff generally has to establish three elements in his action: (1) that the defendant was under a **legal duty** to act in a particular fashion, (2) that the defendant breached this duty by failing to behave according to this duty and (3) that he (the plaintiff) **suffered an injury or loss as a direct result of the defendant's** behavior.

XIII. Selected Issues

Corporate Law

A corporation is a legal entity formed with governmental approval to act as an artificial person to carry on business (or other activities). In most legal systems, corporations are officially treated as (legal) persons that have standing to sue and be sued separate from its stockholders. The legal-person-status of corporations gives the business perpetual life, since the death of an official or a stockholder does not alter the corporation's structure. Accordingly, corporations are also seperate **taxable entities** and thus have a "double tax" problem, since both **corporate profits** and **shareholder dividends** are taxed. The legal independence of a corporation prevents shareholders from being personally liable for **corporate debts** and makes ownership in the company (shares) easily transferable. In the US, the power to promulgate laws relating to the creation, organization and dissolution of corporations (corporate law) rests with the states. However, many state corporate laws follow the *US Model Business Corporation Act* and oblige corporations to issue articles of incorporation in order to document their creation and to provide provisions regarding the management of their internal affairs. Most state corporation statutes also operate under the assumption that each corporation will **adopt bylaws** to define the rights and obligations of persons of authority and groups within its internal structure. In 1933 the US Congress passed the *Securities Act*, which regulates how **corporate securities** are issued and sold. Federal securities law also governs requirements of **fiduciary conduct** (such as requiring corporations to make full disclosures to shareholders and investors) making it a significant component of US Federal corporations' law.

Discuss

What are the differences between real property and personal property? Explain the difference between freehold and leasehold!

Which examples of intangible property can you think of?

Which societal problems are addressed by family law?

Explain the differences between a classical and a no-fault (consensual) divorce!

Which rights does child custody include?

What is your opinion on joint custody?

What is the guiding principle with regard to the division of marital property in your legal system?

Explain the following terms in your own words:
    * spousal / child abuse * child custody * child visitation * alimony
    * child support awards * wrongful infliction of harm * contractual liability

What is the purpose of tort law?

Which elements constitute a cause of action in a tort lawsuit?

What is equitable relief?

Explain the distinguishing characteristics of a corporation!

Concepts

abandoned property

property to which the owner has intentionally relinquished all rights.

accession of property

takes place when the personal property of one owner is physically integrated with the property of another so that it becomes a constituent part of it, losing its own separate identity. Accession can make the personal property of one owner become substantially more valuable chattel as a result of the work of another person.

alimony (spousal support)

payment to support an ex-spouse (or a spouse while a divorce is pending) ordered by the court.

bona fide

from Latin "good faith" – signifying honesty; if a party claims title as bona fide purchaser or holder, it indicates innocence or lack of knowledge of any fact that would cast doubt on the right to hold title (see below).

bona fide purchaser (BFP)

an individual who has bought property for value with no notice of any defects in the seller's title.

child custody

the court's determination of who should have physical and/or legal control and responsibility for a minor (child). Child custody can be decided by a local court in a divorce, or when one (or both) parent(s) is (are) unfit, absent, dead, in prison or dangerous to the child's well-being. In such cases custody can be awarded to a grandparent or other relative, a foster parent or an orphanage or other organization or institution. While a divorce is pending the court may grant temporary custody to one of the parents and require further investigation before making a final ruling.

child support

court-ordered funds to be paid by one parent to the custodial parent of a minor child after divorce (dissolution) or separation of the child's parents. Usually the sum that has to be paid depends on the income of both parents, the number of children, the expenses of the custodial parent and any special needs of the child. Often the amount is determined by a chart which considers all these figures. It may also include health plan coverage, school tuition or other expenses, and may be reduced during periods of extended visitation such as summer vacations. Child support generally continues until the child is emancipated (no longer lives with either parent), or, in some cases, for an extended period such as college attendance.

XIII. Selected Issues

confusion of property

occurs when personal property of several different owners is commingled so that it cannot be separated and returned to its rightful owner although retaining its original characteristics. Any fungible (interchangeable) goods, such as grain or produce, can be the subject of confusion.

consideration

a vital element in the US law of contracts: consideration is a benefit which must be bargained for between the parties; it is the essential reason for a party entering into a contract. Consideration must be of value (at least to the parties) and is exchanged for the performance or promise of performance by the other party.

copyright

the exclusive right of a creator or author of a literary or artistic property (such as a book or musical composition) to print, copy, sell, license, distribute, transform to another medium, translate, record or perform or otherwise use (or not use) and to give it to another by will. Copyrights typically cover works of art such as literature, sculptural, musical, audiovisual and/or dramatic works, periodicals, photographs, prints & labels, movies as well as computer programs, compilations of works and derivative works.

declaratory relief

a judge's determination (also called a "declaratory judgment") of the parties' rights under a contract or a statute often requested (prayed for) in a lawsuit over a contract.

estoppel

an obstruction precluding an individual from asserting a fact or a right or preventing him/her from denying a fact. Such a hindrance (impediment) is usually due to a person's conduct, statements, admissions or failure to act in an identical legal case.

fixture

a movable item that was originally personal property but has become attached to and associated with real property and therefore is considered a part of it. Due to the doctrine of accession, personal property can become real property through its transformation into a fixture.

future interest

a right to receive (real or personal) property some time in the future, either upon a particular date or upon the occurrence of an event. Typical examples are getting title upon marriage or the death of a person.

heir

a person who is entitled to receive a share of the decedent's property via the rules of inheritance in the jurisdiction where the decedent died or owned property at the time of his death.

innuendo

from Latin: *innuere* ("to nod toward"); in law it means "an indirect hint"; in the context of a lawsuit the term stands for defamation (libel or slander). The person suing usually claims that the comments made by the defendant were nasty (defamatory).

intangible property

also known as incorporeal property; something that represents value but is not an actual, tangible object.

intellectual property

a term often used to refer generically to property rights created through intellectual and/or discovery efforts of a creator that are generally protectable under patent, trademark, copyright and/or trade secret law.

lease

a written rental agreement for an extended period of time.

mislaid property

property, which an owner intentionally places somewhere with the idea that he will eventually be able to find it again but subsequently forgets where it has been placed. According to US property law, lost or mislaid property continues to be owned by the person who lost or mislaid it. However, when finding a lost good, the finder is entitled to possession against everyone with the exception of the true owner.

patent

an exclusive right to the benefits of an invention or improvement for a specific period of time, on the basis that it was not previously known or described in a publication, that it is "non-obvious" and useful. There are various types of patents.

possession

a property interest under which an individual – to the exclusion of all others – is able to exercise power over something. It is a basic property right that entitles the possessor to continue peaceful possession against everyone else except someone with a superior right.

promissory estoppel

also called "equitable estoppel;" it is false statement that is treated as a promise by a court when the listener had relied on what was told to him/her to his/her disadvantage. Consequently, the maker of the statement is precluded from denying it and this legal inability to deny it makes the false statement an enforceable promise.

(real, personal) property

anything that is owned by a person or entity. Property is divided into two types: "real property," which is any interest in land, real estate or the improvements on it, and "personal property" (sometimes called "personalty"), which is everything else.

tangible property

physical articles (things) as distinguished from "incorporeal" assets such as rights, patents, copyrights and franchises. Commonly, tangible property is named "personalty."

tenancy

the right to occupy real property permanently, for a time which may terminate upon a certain event, for a specific term, for a series of periods until cancelled (such as month-to-month) or at will ("tenancy at will"), which may be terminated at any time.

tenancy at sufferance

a "hold-over" tenancy after a lease has expired but before the landlord has demanded that the tenant quit (vacate) the premises. During a tenancy at sufferance the tenant is bound by the terms of the lease (including payment of rent) which existed before it expired.

trademark

a distinctive design, picture, emblem, logo or wording (or combination) affixed to goods for sale to identify the manufacturer as the source of the product. Words that merely name the maker (but without particular lettering) or a generic name for the product are not trademarks.

trade name

a name of a business or one of its products which – by use of the name and public reputation – identifies the product as that of the business. A trade name belongs to the first business to use it, and the identification and reputation give it value and the right to protect the trade name against its use by others.

unlawful detainer

keeping possession of real property without a right, such as after a lease has expired, after being served with a notice to quit (vacate, leave) for non-payment of rent or other breach of lease, or being a "squatter" on the property. Such possession entitles the owner to file a lawsuit for "unlawful detainer," asking for possession by court order, unpaid rent and damages.

writ

a written order of a judge requiring specific action by the person or entity to whom the writ is directed.

Vocabulary

to adopt bylaws	Statuten festlegen, übernehmen
adoption	Adoption
aggregate	adj.: (ins)gesamt
to aggregate	angliedern, (an)häufen, (an)sammeln

alimony	Ehegattenunterhalt
breach of a non-contractual duty	Verletzung einer außervertraglichen Pflicht
bylaw(s)	Statut(en)
chattel	bewegliche Sache
child abuse	Kindesmisshandlung
child support	Kindesunterhalt
child visiation right	Besuchsrecht
consensual divorce	einvernehmliche Scheidung
contracting party, party to a contract / an agreement	Vertragspartei
contractual obligation	vertragliche Verpflichtung
corporate dept	Unternehmensschulden
corporate profit	Unternehmensgewinn
corporation	Gesellschaft, Körperschaft
corporation aggregate	jur. Person, Körperschaft
co-venturing	Mitbeteiligung, gemeinsame Risikobeteiligung
dependency law	*here:* Pflegschaftsrecht
decedent	Verstorbener, Erblasser
derivative	*here:* abgeleitet, sekundär
descent	*here:* Geburt, Abstammung, Vererbung
diminish	verringern, schmälern
to dissolve a marriage	eine Ehe scheiden
dividend	Gewinnanteil, Dividende
duration	Dauer, Laufzeit, Zeitdauer
equitable relief	billigkeitsrechtlicher Rechtsbehelf
estoppel	prozesshindernde Einrede, rechtshemmender Einwand
to evict	zwangsräumen, gewaltsam vertreiben
expenditure	Kosten, Aufwendung, Aufwand
fiduciary	Treuhänder
fungible, interchangeable	austauschbar, ersetzbar
heir	Erbe
hindrance, impediment	Behinderung, Hindernis, Hemmnis
incompatibility	Unverträglichkeit
to incorporate	integrieren, umfassen, mit einbeziehen
incorporeal	immateriell, unkörperlich
indefinite	unbefristet, unbegrenzt, *also:* ungenau
to inflict	zufügen
inheritable	vererbbar
inheritance	Erbe, Erbschaft, Vererbung
injured party	geschädigte Partei, Geschädigte(r)
innuendo	versteckte (Andeutung)
irreconcilable	unvereinbar, unversöhnlich, unverträglich

XIII. Selected Issues

joint custody	gemeinsames Sorgerecht, gemeinsame Obsorge
justness	Billigkeit, Gerechtigkeit
to last	bestehen bleiben, fortdauern
misconduct	Fehlverhalten, Verfehlung
misrepresentation	irrtümliche, ungenaue Darstellung
no-fault divorce	verschuldensunabhängige Scheidung
non-custodial	*here:* nicht obsorgeberechtigt
to occur	eintreten, stattfinden, vorfallen
orphanage	Waisenhaus
personalty	unbewegliches Vermögen
to promulgate	verkünden, öffentlich bekanntgeben
restitution of goods	Rückgabe von Gütern
security	*here:* Wertpapier
share	Aktie, Anteil, Beteiligung
shareholder	Gesellschafter, Teilhaber, Aktionär
squatter	Hausbesetzer, illegaler Siedler
stock	*here:* Gesellschaftskapital, Grundkapital
(in)tangible	*here:* (un)körperlich
taxable	steuerpflichtig, zu versteuern
tortious act	unerlaubte Handlung
trademark	Marke, Schutzmarke
under duress	unter Zwang
to vacate a building	ein Gebäude räumen
to vacate a contract	einen Vertrag für nichtig erklären
venturing	wagend, riskierend
venturing enterprise	spekulatives Unternehmen
vindicate	rechtfertigen, verteidigen

Crimes

A crime is committed when someone **breaks the law.** Some are crimes **against property** and others are crimes **against persons,** or more specifically against bodily integrity, personal freedom, sexual selfdetermination, personal status, marriage, the family or life. There are crimes against the national defense, crimes endangering the external security of a country (such as treason), crimes against foreign states, against constitutional organs, against the environment, against competition, crimes dangerous to the public, crimes relating to religion and philosophy of life and criminal violations of the realm of personal privacy and confidentiality. Some crime definitions are short and simple, such as the definition of murder as the "willful (non-negligent) killing of one human being by another". Most kinds of wrongdoing are much more difficult to define, such as "significant **racketeering** activities" which are chargeable under the US *Racketeer Influenced and Corrupt Organizations (RICO) Statute.*

Furthermore, most criminal concepts are used in **various contexts** with **different meanings,** so when translating them it is indispensable to take the underlying context situation into consideration. The term abuse, for instance, is generally used to describe harm caused by one person against another. Abuse may be a crime itself (as in "child sexual abuse") or it may not be a crime (as in "verbal abuse").

The term "criminal enterprise" is defined by the FBI as a group of individuals with an identified hierarchy, or comparable structure, engaged in significant criminal activity. It is often used synonymously with the concept of **organized crime**, referring to both the organizations engaging in multiple criminal activities and to their extensive supporting networks. However, various federal criminal statutes specifically define the elements of an enterprise that need to be proven in order to convict groups of individuals under those individual statutes. So even within the US the **elements of what seems to be the same crime sometimes vary** with the state laws or the individual statutes containing them. Needless to say that most US federal and/or state crimes are not exactly identical to their German or Austrian counterparts.

Sometimes the effort of a **word-by-word translation of legal concepts** by non-lawyers is **misleading**, such as the translation of the German/Austrian crime of "Verleumdung" to "defamation", since in US law, defamation is nearly always a tort and not a criminal action. Typically, the elements of a cause of action for defamation include a false and defamatory statement concerning another, the unprivileged publication of the statement to a third party, if the defamatory matter is of public concern, fault amounting at least to negligence on the part of the publisher and damage to the plaintiff. Generally speaking, in US law defamation is the issuance of a false statement about another person, which causes that person to suffer harm and appears in two forms: slander, involving the making of oral / spoken defamatory statements, and libel, involving the making of defamatory statements in a printed or fixed medium, such as a magazine or newspaper. The German and Austrian penal codes contain two crimes with comparable causes of action: "*Üble Nachrede*" and "*Verleumdung*". These two criminal forms of defamation differ in seriousness, but both can be either permanent or impermanent, in speech or in writing. They also include insult, for which only two people are needed, and a form of assault, whereby the problem with the English term "assault" is that the English reader may not realize its connection to the non-physical term "insult". Thus, it is not correct to translate and to legally distinguish these crimes, specified in the Austrian and German penal codes, by just using the English terms libel and slander. An **exact legal translation** of all the crimes included in continental European criminal codes would certainly be a **challenge** even for a legal professional who is acquainted with the underlying legal systems. Still, in the German Federal Ministry of Justice's translation of the German Criminal Code "*Üble Nachrede*" is translated as "malicious gossip" and "*Verleumdung*" as "defamation" (see: http://www. iuscomp.org/gla/statutes/StGB.htm).

The following **attempted German translations** of criminal actions should be looked at from this viewpoint:

XIII. Selected Issues

Vocabulary

abduction	Verschleppung
abuse	Übergriff, Missbrauch, Beleidigung
acceptance of a benefit	Vorteilsannahme
accessory after the fact	Begünstigung
alien smuggling	Menschenhandel
arson	Brandstiftung
assault and battery	Angriff / Übergriff
bankruptcy	Bankrott
breach of attachment, breach of seals	Verstrickungsbruch, Siegelbruch
breach of official custody	Verwahrungsbruch
breach of trust	Untreue
burglary	Einbruch
capital investment fraud	Kapitalanlagebetrug
casting false suspicion	falsche Verdächtigung
causing a danger of fire	Herbeiführen einer Brandgefahr
concealment of unlawfully acquired assets	Verschleierung unrechtmäßig erlangter Vermögenswerte
counterfeiting of money, money forging	Geldfälschung
credit fraud	Kreditbetrug
crimes of insolvency	Insolvenzstraftaten
defamation	Verleumdung
deprivation of liberty	Freiheitsberaubung
domestic violence	häusliche Gewalt
embezzlement	Veruntreuung, Unterschlagung
extorsion	Erpressung
falsification of documents	Urkundenfälschung
feigning a crime	Vortäuschen einer Straftat
forgery (of documents)	(Urkunden)Fälschung
fraud	Betrug
genocide	Völkermord
grievous bodily harm	schwere / gefährliche Körperverletzung
homicide, (first degree) murder	Mord
hostage taking	Geiselnahme
illegal gambling, unauthorized organization of a game of chance	unerlaubte Veranstaltung eines Glücksspiels
illicit drug trafficking	unerlaubter Drogenhandel
industrial/economic espionage	Industrie- / Wirtschaftsspionage
kidnapping	Menschenraub
malicious gossip	üble Nachrede
manslaughter, second degree murder	Totschlag

misuse of check and credit cards	Missbrauch von Scheck- und Kreditkarten
misuse of identification papers	Missbrauch von Ausweispapieren
money laundering	Geldwäsche
negligent manslaughter	fahrlässige Tötung
obscenity	Unzüchtigkeit
obstruction of justice	Behinderung der Justiz
obstruction of punishment	Strafvereitelung
offering a bribe	Bestechung
organized crime, racketeering	organisiertes Verbrechen
perjury	Meineid
physical injury / bodily injury / bodily harm	Körperverletzung
pimping	Zuhälterei
preferential treatment of a creditor / debtor	Gläubiger- / Schuldnerbegünstigung
prostitution	Prostitution
rape	Vergewaltigung
receiving stolen property	Hehlerei
robbery	Raub
subsidy fraud	Subventionsbetrug
suppression of documents	Urkundenunterdrückung
tax evasion	Steuerhinterziehung
theft	Diebstahl
threat	Drohung
trespass, home invasion	Hausfriedensbruch
unauthorized use of a vehicle	unbefugter Gebrauch eines Fahrzeuges
ursupation of office	Amtsanmaßung
wire fraud, mail fraud	Telekommunikationsbetrug

Elements of Crimes

concurrence, contemporaneity, simultaneity

legal terms referring to the apparent need to prove the simultaneous occurrence of both *actus reus* ("guilty action") and *mens rea* ("guilty mind," see below) to constitute a crime. Generally, if the *actus reus* does not coincide in point of time with the *mens rea* then no crime has been committed.

corporate liability

in the criminal context, corporate liability is an aspect of criminal vicarious liability and determines the extent to which a corporation (as a fictitious person) can be liable for the acts and omissions of the natural persons it employs. This is distinguishable from the situation in which the wording of a statutory offence specifically attaches liability to the corporation as the principal or joint principal with a human agent.

criminal negligence

one of the three general classes of mens rea, also defined as: careless, inattentive, neglectful or willfully blind.

ignorantia juris non excusat

or: *ignorantia legis neminem excusat* (Latin for "ignorance of the law is no excuse") is a public policy holding that a person who is unaware of a law may not escape liability for violating that law merely because (s)he was unaware of its content.

mens rea

Latin term used in criminal law for "guilty mind;" the standard common law test of criminal liability is usually expressed in the Latin phrase, *actus non facit reum nisi mens sit rea*, which means that an act does not make a person legally **liable** unless the mind is legally blameworthy. Therefore, in jurisdictions with due process, there must be an actus reus accompanied by some level of mens rea to constitute the crime with which the defendant is charged (concurrence). In civil law, however, it is not always necessary to prove a subjective mental element to establish liability, say for breach of contract or in strict liability tort cases. There are three general classes of mens rea: intention, recklessness (sometimes termed willful blindness – which may have a different interpretation in the US) and criminal negligence.

strict liability

in the criminal context, strict liability is liability where mens rea does not have to be proven in relation to one or more elements comprising the actus reus (Latin for "guilty act") although intention, recklessness or knowledge may be required in relation to other elements of the offence. The liability is said to be strict because defendants will be convicted even though they were genuinely ignorant of one or more factors that made their acts or omissions criminal.

willful blindness

legal term used to describe a situation, in which an individual seeks to avoid civil or criminal liability for a wrongful act by intentionally putting himself in a position where he is unaware of facts which would render him liable. Such a defense is rarely successful since courts argue that the defendant should have known about the consequences and therefore acted recklessly by failing to consider them. If the court holds that there was willful blindness on the defendant's part, these arguments do not constitute a defense to a claim of contributory infringement.

Exercise

Try to define the elements mentioned above in your own words! Find equivalent or similar concepts/ terms in your legal system!

Read the following definitions of criminal acts by the FBI's Uniform Crime Reporting (UCR) Program and focus on the individual elements of each crime in order to distinguish it from the equivalent concept / statute in your country's penal code:

FEDERAL CRIMINAL ACTS

Murder and non-negligent manslaughter: The willful (non-negligent) killing of one human being by another.

Negligent Manslaughter: The killing of another person through gross negligence.

Sex Offenses, Forcible: Any sexual act directed against another person, forcibly and/or against that person's will; or, not forcibly or against the person's will where the victim is incapable of giving consent.

Sex Offenses, Nonforcible: Unlawful, nonforcible sexual intercourse.

Armed Robbery: The taking, or attempting to take anything of value from the care, custody, or control of a person or persons by force or threat of force or violence and/or by putting the victim in fear.

Arson: Any willful or malicious burning or attempt to burn, with or without intent to defraud, a dwelling house, public building, motor vehicle or aircraft, personal property of another, etc.

Assault, Aggravated: An unlawful attack by one person upon another for the purpose of inflicting severe or aggravated bodily injury. This type of assault is usually accompanied by the use of a weapon or by means likely to produce death or great bodily harm.

Assault, Non-aggravated: Assaults and attempted assaults where no weapon is used and that do not result in serious or aggravated injury to the victim.

Burglary (Breaking or Entering): The unlawful entry into a building or other structure with the intent to commit a felony or a theft. Forced entry is not a required element of the offense; it may be accomplished via an unlocked door or window, so long as the entry is unlawful (constituting a trespass). Included are attempts to commit burglary where force is employed, or where a perpetrator is frightened off while entering an unlocked door or climbing through an open window.

Larceny-Theft: The unlawful taking, carrying, leading or riding away of property from the possession or constructive possessions of another. Examples of offenses in this classification include pocket-picking and purse snatching (where no more force is employed than that necessary to take the property).

Motor Vehicle Theft: Theft or attempted theft of a motor vehicle.

Hate Crimes: Any of the above-listed offenses and other crimes involving bodily injury to any person in which the victim is intentionally selected because of the actual or perceived race, gender, religion, sexual orientation, ethnicity or disability of the victim.

Liquor Law Violations: Violations of laws or ordinances prohibiting the manufacture, sale, purchase, transportation, possession or use of alcoholic beverages (does not include "driving under the influence" or drunkenness).

Drug Abuse Violations: Violations of laws prohibiting production, distribution and/or use of certain controlled substances and the equipment or devices utilized in their preparation and/or use.

Weapons Possessions: Violations of laws or ordinances prohibiting the manufacture, sale, purchase, transportation, possession, concealment, or use of firearms, cutting instruments, explosives, incendiary devices, or other deadly weapons.

Concepts

aggravating circumstances

facts tending to increase the severity of an offense.

conspiracy

when people work together by agreement to commit an illegal act.

deferred prosecution

a person charged with a criminal offense does not enter a plea because the prosecution of the charge is withheld for a period of time, during which the accused is placed under supervision of the Probation Department; if he makes a satisfactory adjustment, the original charges filed against him are dismissed.

mitigation of circumstances

facts tending to lessen the severity of an offense.

victim impact statement

the judge permits the victims to deliver personal statements, sometimes in open court, describing the physical, emotional, financial and social impact of the crime on their lives and families.

white-collar crime

the term generally encompasses a variety of nonviolent crimes usually committed in commercial situations for financial gain. Many of these crimes are difficult to prosecute because the offenders are often very sophisticated criminals who successfully attempt to conceal their activities through a series of complex transactions. The most common white-collar crimes include: tax evasion, insider trading, money laundering, embezzlement, bribery, kickbacks, counterfeiting, antitrust violations, trade secret theft, public corruption, environmental law violations and various kinds of fraud, such as credit card fraud, phone and telemarketing fraud, bankruptcy fraud, healthcare fraud, insurance fraud, mail fraud, government fraud, financial fraud, securities fraud, economic espionage as well as computer and internet fraud. Corporations may also be subject to sanctions for these types of offenses.

Asset Forfeiture

Asset forteiture is an integral part of federal criminal law enforcement in the US. Particularly in the context of white-collar crimes asset forfeiture enables law enforcement agents and prosecutors to **take the profit out of a crime**. There is certainly an element of simple justice in ensuring that a wrongdoer is deprived of the fruits of his illegal acts. But there is also an element of **general deterrence**, since a putative offender's incentive to engage in economic criminal actions is diminished if he has to be afraid of not retaining any profits. White-collar criminals typically spend their spoils on expensive homes, airplanes, electronic goods and other toys that everyone else wishes he had the resources to acquire. Taking a criminal's toys away, as law enforcement agents typically put it, sends a signal to the community and **makes funds available for restitution to the victims**. In white-collar cases one major ambition of law enforcement is the restoration of forfeited property to victims, and much time and effort is expended in such cases to ensure that the wrongdoer's assets are preserved while the trial is pending, so that they remain available until the litigation is over.

Another reason why asset forfeiture is considered to be an important feature of criminal law enforcement is that sometimes **tools of the crime have to be removed from circula-**

tion so that they cannot be used again by the wrongdoer after his release. Therefore, guns, cars with concealed compartments that are used for drug smuggling or electronic devices used in child pornography, counterfeiting or identification fraud cases are usually **seized and forfeitured**. In this sense, asset forfeiture is a form of incapacitation. Finally, asset forfeiture constitutes a form of punishment. Depriving a wrongdoer of the facilities of an expensive lifestyle or the items (s)he used to commit his/her criminal act(s) is certainly a form of **retribution** enacted by the criminal justice system.

There are two types of forfeiture actions: criminal and civil. The **criminal forfeiture** action is referred to as an *in personam* action, meaning that the action is against the person and that – upon conviction – the punitive effect of forfeiture can be used **against the convicted offender**. **Civil forfeiture** is also referred to as *in rem* forfeiture, indicating that the action is against **property**. The two actions differ in many ways, including the burden of proof necessary to forfeit the property.

The most powerful civil forfeiture statute in the US is 18 USC § 981. It authorizes the forfeiture of the proceeds of over 200 different state and federal crimes including, **fraud, bribery, emezzlement, gambling, arson, extortion, obscenity and state drug trafficking**. In addition, there are various broader state forfeiture statutes for drug offenses authorizing law enforcement agencies to not only confiscate the drug proceeds themselves but also the (real or personal) property used to commit or to faciliate the commission of the drug offense. One of the broadest forfeiture statutes is the one permitting the forfeiture of all the property involved in a money laundering offense. If, for example, someone launders the proceeds of a criminal act by commingling the money with clean money from another source or hides it by investing it in land, then all of the property involved in the offense and not just the proceeds that were being laundered can be forfeitured.

Discuss

Try do define asset forfeiture in your own words! What are the goals of asset forfeiture? Which types of property can be forfeitured? What happens to property seized for forfeiture?

Concepts

asset purchases with bulk cash

money laundering method, whereby money launderers purchase high value or luxury items such as cars, boats and jewelry; they usually use these items but distance themselves by having them registered or purchased in an associate's name.

civil (in rem) forfeiture

the loss of property due to a violation of law. Unlike criminal forfeiture, civil forfeiture proceeds against the property, not the person. Under US federal law (18 USC § 981) the government can seize property based solely upon probable cause that the property was used unlawfully.

co-mingling of funds

term for taking over or investing illicit funds in businesses that customarily handle a high cash transaction volume in order to mix the illicit proceeds with those of the legitimate business. Criminals may also purchase businesses that commonly receive cash payments (such as restaurants, bars, night clubs, hotels, currency exchange shops, and vending machine companies) in oder to insert criminal funds as false revenue mixed with the income that would not otherwise be sufficient to sustain a legitimate business.

contraband

goods whose importation, exportation or possession is prohibited by law (eg in time of war, materials carried aboard a vessel that could aid a belligerent in the process of the war, such as arms, weapons or munitions).

criminal (in personam) forfeiture

a punitive (in personam) action by the government against the offender. Criminal forfeiture statutes authorize the forfeiture of property of a person convicted of having violated a federal law for which there is a forfeiture sanction. If that is the case criminal forfeiture is part of the sentence following the conviction of the criminal. Criminal forfeiture is only possible if the property belongs to the convicted defendant, who must be alive and not a fugitive.

electronic funds transfer / telegraphic transfer / wire transfer

sending funds electronically from one city or country to another to avoid the need to physically transport the currency; this way of transferring funds is not in and of itself a crime, but it can be used as a money laundering method to commit a crime.

facilitating property

property which is used to commit or facilitate an offense, any property that makes the crime easier to commit or harder to detect.

money laundering

process whereby criminals conceal illicit funds by converting them into seemingly legitimate income. While the term refers to the monetary proceeds of all criminal activity, it is most often associated with the financial activities of drug traffickers who seek to launder large amounts of cash generated from the sale of narcotics. The principal objective of money laundering is to convert cash into some other form of asset in order to conceal its illegal origins. A person committing the crime of money laundering is also referred to as "launderer".

"Ponzi" scheme

named after Charles Ponzi, a man with a remarkable criminal career in the early 20th century, the term is used to describe an investment swindle in which high profits are promised from fictitious sources and are given the impression that a legitimate profit-making business or investment opportunity exists, whereby the payments made to investors arise from the proceeds of a later investment rather than from profits of the underlying business venture so that early investors are paid off with funds raised from later ones. Ponzi schemes (often called "pyramid schemes/arrangements") progress geometrically until they reach a point where the operators cannot find enough recruits (victims) to continue the payout.

proceeds

property acquired by unlawful activity or property traced to property acquired by unlawful activity.

refining

illegal money laundering method that involves the exchange of small denomination bills for larger ones and can be carried out by an individual who converts the bills at a number of different banks in order to not raise suspicion.

smurfing/ structuring

banking terms used to describe the splitting of a large financial transaction into multiple smaller transactions. This is done to evade scrutiny by regulators or law enforcement. Typically, each of these smaller transactions is below a specific limit, above which financial institutions must file a report with a government due to recordkeeping requirements imposed by regulations. Criminal enterprises often send different couriers to make these transactions, and those couriers are known as "smurfs" in this context.

(temporary) restraining order (TRO)

a temporary order of a court to keep conditions as they are (like not selling marital property) until there is a hearing, where both parties are given the opportunity to take part. Restraining orders are also issued in cases in which spousal abuse or stalking has occurred (or is feared) in an attempt to ensure the victim's safety. These orders typically direct one person not to do something, such as make contact with another person or remove a child from the state.

value tampering

occurs when money launderers look for property owners who agree to sell their property, on paper, at a price below its actual value and then accept the difference of the purchase price "under the table". After holding the property for a period of time, the launderer then sells it for its true value.

Vocabulary

to accomplish	ausführen, vollenden
to acquire	sich bemächtigen, in Besitz nehmen
adherence	*here*: Einhaltung (adherence to schedules)
to adhere to deadlines	Termine einhalten
to aid and abet a criminal	einem Täter Beihilfe leisten, einen Täter begünstigen
attempted transaction	versuchte Abwicklung / Transaktion

XIII. Selected Issues

business transaction	Geschäftsabschluss
claimant	Anspruchsteller, Antragsteller
commingling	Vermischung; zusammenmischend
commission	*here:* Provision, Vergütung
to conceal	kaschieren, verbergen, verhehlen
confiscation	Einziehung
to contemplate	in Erwägung ziehen, betrachten, nachdenken
conveyance	Beförderung, Übertragung, Übermittlung
custody	Gewahrsame, Verwahrung
denomination	*here:* Nennwert
to depreciate	an Wert verlieren, abwerten, mindern
to deprive sb of sth	jm eine Sache vorenthalten, jm einer Sache berauben
to derive from	ableiten von, herleiten (aus, von)
to disclose	offen legen, offenbaren, mitteilen
to facilitate an offense	eine Straftat erleichtern, unterstützen, ermöglichen
forfeiture	Verfall, Verlust
fugitive	flüchtig, Flüchtling
funds	Geldmittel
fungible	austauschbar, vertretbar
gambling offenses	verbotene (Glücks)Spiele
general deterrence	Generalprävention
hardship	Not, Mühsal
illicit	unerlaubt, verboten, ungesetzlich
incapacitation	Unfähigmachung, Untauglichkeit
law-abiding citizens	gesetzestreue Bürger
law enforcement	Rechtsdurchsetzung
misconduct	Fehlverhalten, Verfehlung
money transmitting	Geldweitergabe / -übertragung
obligation to disclose, duty to give notive	Anzeigepflicht, Offenbarungspflicht
ordinance	Anordnung, Verordnung
particularity requirement	Spezifikationserfordernis
to recover property	Besitz / Vermögen zurückerlangen, wiederbekommen
restitution	Rückerstattung, Zurückzahlung, Wiederherstellung
retraceable	zurückverfolgbar
retroactive	rückwirkend
to seize	*here:* beschlagnahmen
spoils	*here:* Beute
to transfer money to an account	Geld auf ein Konto überweisen
vicarious liability	Haftung für fremdes Verschulden
to withhold	vorenthalten, zurückhalten
wrongdoer	Missetäter

Index Concepts

Accession of property 143
accreditation 69
administrative law 6
admission of evidence 21
admissions of fact 114
affidavit 84
affirmative action 54
aggravating circumstances 153
alimony (spousal support) 143
alternate juror 101
alumnus, alumna, almuni 69
ambulance chaser 84
amicus curiae brief 54
appellate brief 54
approaching the bench 25
arbitration 114
arraignment 114
array 101
arrest warrant 12
asset purchases with bulk cash 155
Attorney General 114
(arbitration) award 137

Bachelor's degree 69
Bakke 54
bar 25
bar review course 69
bench 25
bench trial 25
bench warrant 114
beyond a reasonable doubt 12
BigLaw 84
to bind over (the defendant for trial) 114
Bluebook ("A Uniform System of Citation") 44
bona fide 143
bona fide purchaser (BFP) 143
bond 114
booking a suspect 114
branches of government 2
brief 69

Capital case 101
capital offense 115
case brief 54
case law 2
case method 70
case syllabus 70
casebook 70
cause of action 115
censure 84
cert. denied 36
certiorari 36
(criminal) charge 12
child custody 143
child support 143
citation 44, 115
civil (in rem) forfeiture 155
civil law 2
Civil Rights movement 55
class action 55
clear and convincing evidence 13
code 2
college / university 70
co-mingling of funds 156
comity 131
Common Law 3
(civil) complaint 13
(criminal) complaint 12
complaint, answer, replication, rejoinder 115
compromise verdict 101
conciliation 137
concurring opinion 44
confusion of property 144
consideration 144
Conspiracy 153
consumer protection law 6
contempt of court 102
contraband 156
copyright 144
(in house) counsel / corporate attorney 84
count 13
counterclaim 115

Index Concepts

Court of Equity 3
criminal (in personam) forfeiture 156

Deadlock 102
declaratory relief 144
default judgment (also judgment by default) 115
deferred prosecution 154
deliberation 21
(juvenile) delinquency case 36
demurrer 115
denials of fact 115
dependency case 36
deposition 115
detention 116
dictum (plural dicta, obiter dicta) 55
(re)direct / cross examination (re)119
directed verdict 102
disbarment 85
discharge of bond 116
dissenting opinion, dissent 44
diversion 116
double jeopardy 12
dual criminality 131
due process of law 6

Education records 55
electronic funds transfer / telegraphic transfer / wire transfer 156
employment law 6
en banc 36
estoppel 144
expert testimony 21
externship 70

Facilitating property 156
Federal Rules of Evidence (FRE) 21
felony 12
first appearance 116
fixture 144
fraternity / sorority 70
freshman / sophomore / junior / senior (students) 70
future interest 144

"**G**erstein" hearing 116
GPA 71
grade 70
guardian 36

Hearsay 21
hearsay rule 21
heir 144
hi/lo arbitration 137
holding 55
hung jury 102

Impanel(l)ing 102
impeachment 85
indictment 116
indigent party 13
information 116
innuendo 145
inquisitorial system 21
intangible property 145
intellectual property 145
interrogatories 116
investigation 117
ivy league law school 71

J.D. 71
judgment on the pleadings 117
judiciary 3
jurisdiction 36
jury commission(er) 102
jury consultant, jury consulting team 102
jury tampering 102
juvenile court 36

King of torts 85

Law Review 44, 71
leading 117
lease 145
legal aid organization / agency 14
legal clinics 71
legal methodology 3
Legal Periodical 45
legislative act 3
legislative enactment / legislation 3
liability insurance 13
lifetime tenure 85
lineup 117
litigation 14
litigation team/ trial unit 85
LL.M. 71
LSAT 71

M&A – mergers and acquisitions 85
major 71

marshal 117
matter of law/ question of law/ issue of law 37
minor 71
"Miranda" warning 117
misdemeanor 12
mislaid property 145
mistrial 103
mitigation of circumstances 154
money laundering 156
moot court 72
motion 37
motion for a summary judgment 117
motion in limine 117
motion to dismiss 118

Nolo contendere / no contest 118

Objection 21
on retainer 85
one shot client 86
order to compel compliance 118

Pain and suffering 13
parole 118
patent 145
paternity suit 37
petition 37
petition for (a) writ of certiorari 37
physical /mental examinations 118
physical evidence 22
plea 118
plea bargaining 13
pleadings 37
polling the jury 103
"Ponzi" scheme 156
possession 145
prayer (for relief) 118
precedent 3
preliminary hearing 118
preliminary injunction 14
preponderance 14
presentment 118
pre-trial discovery 119
prima facie 14, 119
pro bono 14
pro se (representation) 14
probable cause 119
probate 37
probation 119

(legal) procedure 6
proceeds 157
promissory estoppel 145
(real, personal) property 145
provision (of law) 3
proxy 119
punitive damages 13

Quotation 45

Ratio decidendi, ratio 55
rebuttal / rebuttar 119
reciprocity 131
record 38
recusal 86
refining 157
rehearing en banc (short reh'g en banc) 45
relief 14
reporter 45
(law) reports 44
request for the production of documents 120
requests for admission 120
(temporary) restraining order (TRO) 157
revocation 120
rule of law 131

Salaried attorney 86
selective incorporation doctrine 14
senior status 38
service of process 120
small-claims courts 38
smurfing/ structuring 157
Socratic method 72
solo attorney, solo practitioner 86
special verdict 103
speedy trial 120
standing mute 120
stare decisis 3
status conference 120
statute 3
statute of limitations 120
stipulation 121
subpoena 121
summary judgment 121
summation 121
summer/ first year/ senior associate 86
summons 121
supermajority 103
surrebuttal / surrebutter 121

Index Concepts

Tangible property 146
temporary (interlocutory) injunction 15
tenancy 146
tenancy at sufferance 146
"three strikes, you're out" 121
trade name 146
trademark 146
trial de novo 38

Undergraduate/ graduate education 72
unlawful detainer 146

Value tampering 157
venire 103
venireperson 103
verdict 103
victim impact statement 154

Waiver 121
Wall Street lawyer 86
white-collar crime 154
witness conference 121
writ 146
writ of certiorari 38
(writ of) habeas corpus 131

Vocabulary

abbreviation	Abkürzung(szeichen), Verkürzung
abduction	Verschleppung
to abet	beitragen
to abolish	abschaffen
abuse of authority	Amtsmissbrauch, Autoritätsmissbrauch
acceptance of a benefit	Vorteilsannahme
accessory	Gehilfe, Mittäter
to accomplish	ausführen, vollenden
in accordance with	entsprechend, gemäß
to accredit	zulassen, akkreditieren, anerkennen
accused	beschuldigt, Beschuldigter
acknowledgment	Bestätigung, Anerkennung, Quittierung
to acquire	sich bemächtigen, in Besitz nehmen
to acquit	freisprechen
acquittal	Freispruch
to adhere to deadlines	Termine einhalten
adherence	*here:* Einhaltung (adherence to schedules)
to adjudicate	(gerichtlich) entscheiden, urteilen, zuerkennen
adjudication	Entscheidung, Urteil, Zuerkennung
administrative law	Verwaltungsrecht
admissible	zulässig
to admit evidence	Beweise zulassen
admitted facts	außer Streit gestellter Sachverhalt
to be admitted to the bar	zur Anwaltsprüfung zugelassen werden
to adopt bylaws	Statuten, Satzungsbestimmungen festlegen, übernehmen
adoption	Adoption
advance training	Fortbildung
advancement	Vorwärtskommen, Beförderung, (beruflicher) Aufstieg
advisory opinion	gutachterliche / fachmännische Stellungnahme
affidavit	eidesstattliche Erklärung
affiliated	angegliedert, angeschlossen
affiliated group (of companies)	Konzern
to affirm	bestätigen, bejahen, *also:* behaupten

Vocabulary

to afford	*here:* sich leisten können
aggregate	adj. (ins)gesamt
to aggregate	angliedern, (an)häufen, (an)sammeln
aid	Förderung, Unterstützung
to aid and abet a criminal	einem Täter Beihilfe leisten, einen Täter begünstigen
albeit	obgleich, obschon, wenn auch
alien smuggling, human trafficking	Menschenhandel, Menschenschmuggel
alimony	(Ehegatten)Unterhalt(szahlungen), Alimente
allegation / contention	(Parteien)Vorbringen, Behauptung
to allege	vorbringen, behaupten
allocation of earnings	Erfolgszurechnung, Gewinnverteilung
alternate	Ersatz-, alternativ
amount in controversy	Streitwert
appeal	Berufung
appellant	Berufungswerber, Rechtsmittelführer, Rechtsmittelkläger
appellate	die Berufung betreffend, Berufungsappellate
appellate court, court of appeals	Rechtsmittelgericht, Rechtsmittelinstanz
appellee	Berufungsgegner, Rechtsmittelgegner/-beklagter
applicable experience	*here:* einschlägige Berufserfahrung
applicant	Bewerber, Antragsteller; *also:* Beschwerdeführer
to appoint	ernennen, berufen, bestellen
to appoint a judge	einen Richter ernennen
appointment of counsel	Bestellung eines Vertreters / Anwaltes
apprentice	Lehrling, Auszubildende ('Azubi')
apprenticeship	Lehre, Lehrverhältnis
approach	Annäherung, Ansatz, Methode
to approach the bench	sich der Richterbank nähern
to be apt to do sth	dazu neigen; geneigt sein etwas zu tun
arbiter	Schlichter, Vermittler, Schiedsmann
arbitrable	schlichtbar, schiedsrichterlich
arbitral agreement	Schiedsabrede
arbitral court, arbitration tribunal	Schiedsgericht
arbitral jurisdiction	Schiedsgerichtsbarkeit
arbitral panel decision	Schiedsspruch
arbitration (procedure), arbitral procedure / process	Schiedsverfahren
arbitration clause	Schiedsklausel, Schlichtungsklausel
arbitrator	Schiedsrichter, Schlichter, Richter am Schiedsgericht
to arraign	anklagen, Anklage erheben
to arraign somebody for something	jemanden wegen etw vor Gericht bringen
arrest warrant	Haftbefehl

arson	Brandstiftung
article	Paragraph
assault and battery	Angriff / Übergriff
assessment	Beurteilung, Einschätzung, Bewertung
associated with	verbunden mit, einhergehend mit
attachable earnings	pfändbare Bezüge
attachment	Pfändung
attachment of earnings	Lohnpfändung
attempted transaction	versuchte Abwicklung / Transaktion
to attest	attestieren, beglaubigen, bescheinigen
attorney	Rechtsanwalt
attrition rate	Schwundquote
auction	Versteigerung
to authenticate	beurkunden, legalisieren, bescheinigen
authentication	Echtheitsprüfung, Beglaubigung, Beurkundung
automobile registration	Automobilzulassung
avoidance	Vermeidung, Meiden
(to) award	zuerkennen, zusprechen; Zuspruch
to award damages	Schadenersatz zusprechen
Bachelor's degree	Bakkalaureus, niedrigster akadem. Grad
bail	Kaution
bailiff	Gerichtsdiener, Gerichtsvollzieher, Verwalter
bankruptcy	Bankrott
bankruptcy court	Insolvenzgericht(sabteilung)
bankruptcy law	Insolvenzrecht
bar	*here:* Balken/Barren (im Gerichtssaal)
(local) bar association	(örtliche) Rechtsanwaltskammer
the Bar	*here:* Anwaltschaft
bargain	Abmachung, *also:* (gutes) Geschäft, Schnäppchen
barred from	ausgeschlossen von
bench	Gerichtsbank; *also:* Richter
to be on the Bench	Richter sein
benchmark	Bezugspunkt, Richtgröße, Vergleichspunkt
benchmark score	Richtwert (Punktezahl)
bias	Neigung, Vorliebe
binding	verbindlich
binding arbitration	bindendes Schiedsverfahren, bindende Schlichtung
binding precedent	bindender Präzedenzfall
(military) boot camp	Ausbildungslager
boot camp training	*here:* Grundausbildung
bracket	(eckige) Klammer

Vocabulary

breach of a non-contractual duty	Verletzung einer außervertraglichen Pflicht
breach of attachment, breach of seals	Verstrickungsbruch, Siegelbruch
breach of contract; to breach a contract	Vertragsbruch; gegen eine vertragliche Verpflichtung verstoßen
breach of official custody	Verwahrungsbruch
breach of trust	Untreue
bribery	Bestechung
brief	Kurzdarstellung, Abriss; adj.: knapp, kurz
to brief	jm einweisen, instruieren
brief-case	Aktentasche
burden of proof	Beweislast
burglary	Einbruch
business transaction	Geschäftsabschluss
bylaw(s)	Statut(en), Satzungsbestimmungen
to bypass	umgehen
canon law	kanonisches Recht
capital contribution	finanzieller Beitrag
capital investment fraud	Kapitalanlagebetrug
on a case-by-case basis	im Einzelfall
(a) case on appeal	Fall beim Berufungsgericht
case report / opinion	schriftliche Urteilsausfertigung
cash substitute	Bargeldersatz
to cast suspicion (up)on	verdächtig machen, Misstrauen wecken
cause of action	Klagegrund
causing a danger of fire	eine Brandgefahr herbeiführen
(writ of) certiorari	Anordnung zur Vorlage der Akten an ein höheres Gericht
to chair a panel	*here:* den Vorsitz (eines) Rechtsmittelsenates führen
to challenge evidence	die Beweisführung anfechten
chamber	Richterzimmer, Kammer
charge	*here:* Beschuldigung, Belastung, Anklage
to charge (with)	beschuldigen, anschuldigen, belasten, bezichtigen
to charge somebody (with)	jemanden unter Anklage stellen, anklagen, anschuldigen
to charge	*also:* in Rechnung stellen
chattel	bewegliche Sache
chief justice	vorsitzende Richter
child abuse	Kindesmisshandlung
child custody	Obsorge, Sorgerecht (für Kinder)
child visitation right	Besuchsrecht
circulation	Umlauf
citation	Zitierung, Zitat, Fundstelle; *also:* Vorladung

city ordinance	Stadtverordnung
civil action / civil complaint /civil (law)suit	Klagsschrift, zivilrechtliche Klage
civil law	Zivilrecht
civil law remedy	zivilrechtliche(r) Rechtsbehelf / Sanktion
civil procedure	Zivilprozessrecht
claim	Forderung, Anspruch, Behauptung
to claim	geltend machen, fordern, verlangen
claimant	Anspruchsteller, Antragsteller
clinical course	praxisbezogener Kurs
to close a contract	einen Vertrag abschließen
to cluster	anhäufen, gruppieren
to coach a witness	einen Zeugen vorbereiten (auf die Verhandlung)
code of evidence	Gesetz, das die Zulässigkeit von Beweisen regelt
codification	Kodifizierung
coercion	Zwang, Nötigung
coercive measures	zwingende Maßnahmen
comity	Höflichkeit, Einverständnis
commercial law	Handelsrecht
commingling	Vermischung; zusammenmischend
commission	*here:* Provision, Vergütung
to commit a crime	eine Straftat begehen
to compel	zwingen, nötigen
to compel evidence	Beweismittel abnötigen, anfordern
compelling	zwingend
compelling interest	zwingendes Interesse
compensation	Wiedergutmachung
compensatory damages	Schadenersatz, Entschädigungszahlungen
competition law	Wettbewerbsrecht
to compile	zusammentragen, zusammenstellen
completion	Beendigung, Abschluss
compliance (with)	Befolgung, Einhaltung (von); *also:* Zustimmung
to comprise, contain, to include, to consist of	bestehen aus
compromise	Übereinkunft, gütliche Einigung
to compromise	*here:* durch einen Kompromiss regeln
compulsion	Zwang
compulsory	verpflichtend; bindend
to conceal	kaschieren, verbergen, verhehlen
concealment of unlawfully acquired assets	Verschleierung unrechtmäßig erlangter Vermögenswerte
to concur	übereinstimmen, beipflichten
condition	Voraussetzung, Bedingung

Vocabulary

conduct	Führung, Leitung, Verwaltung
to conduct a trial / noun: conduct	einen Prozess führen / leiten
confession	Geständnis
confidential	vertraulich
to confirm	bestätigen, bekräftigen, zusagen
to confiscate property	*here:* Gegenstände, Besitzstücke wegnehmen, -konfiszieren
confiscation	Einziehung
conflict of interests	Interessenkollision
conflict of laws	Kollisionsrecht
to confound	vereiteln, verwischen, verwirren
conjecture	Vermutung, Mutmaßung
conjunctive	verbindend
conscientious	gewissenhaft
consent	Einwilligung, Zustimmung, Erlaubnis
to constitute	zusammensetzen, bilden
constitutional law	Verfassungsrecht
via / through consular (diplomatic) channels	*here:* im Konsulatsweg / diplomatischen Weg
consumer protection	Konsumentenschutz
to contemplate	in Erwägung ziehen, betrachten, nachdenken
contempt of court	Missachtung gerichtlicher Anweisungen, Nichterscheinen vor Gericht
to contest	anfechten, bestreiten, bekämpfen
continuance	Vertagung, Unterbrechung
contracting party, party to a contract / an agreement	Vertragspartei
contracting state	vertragschließender Staat
contract law	Vertragsrecht
contractual obligation	vertragliche Verpflichtung
to convene, to assemble	zusammentreffen, versammeln
convention	Abkommen, Absprache
to convert	umwandeln, transformieren
conveyance	Beförderung, Übertragung, Übermittlung
to convict /conviction	verurteilen / Verurteilung
corporate dept	Unternehmensschulden
corporate law, corporation law	Gesellschaftsrecht
corporate profit	Unternehmensgewinn
corporate tax	Körperschaftsteuer
corporation	Gesellschaft, Körperschaft
corporation management	Unternehmensführung
correctional facility	Justizvollzugsanstalt
correctional officer (CO)	Justizvollzugsbeamter

costs incurred	angefallene Kosten
counsel	Vertreter, *here:* Rechtsfreund, Anwalt
(legal) counsel	(rechtl.) Vertreter
counterclaim	Widerklage, Gegenforderung, Gegenanspruch
counterfeiting of money, money forging	Geldfälschung
court clerk	nichtrichterlicher Gerichtsbediensteter
court file	Gerichtsakte
court opinion	schriftliche Urteilsausfertigung
court order	Beschluss
court reporter	Schriftführer(in)
co-venturing	Mitbeteiligung, gemeinsame Risikobeteiligung
coveted	begehrt
credit fraud	Kreditbetrug
creditworthy debtors	kreditwürdige Schuldner
creed	(Glaubens)Bekenntnis, Credo, Überzeugung
crimes of insolvency	Insolvenzstraftaten
criminal complaint	Anklageschrift, Strafantrag, *also:* Strafanzeige
criminal defendant	Angeklagter, Beschuldigter
criminal law	Strafrecht
criminal procedure	Strafprozessrecht
criminal record	Strafregisterauskunft
critic	Kritiker, Bewerter
cross examination	Kreuzverhör
curriculum	Lehrplan, Studienplan
custodial sentence	Haftstrafe, Freiheitsstrafe
custody	Gewahrsam, Verwahrung
customary	allgemein üblich
damage / harm / loss	Nachteil, Schaden
damage mitigation	Schadensbegrenzung, Schadensminderung(spflicht)
death knell	Totenglocke
death penalty	Todesstrafe
deceased person	verstorbene Person
decedent	Verstorbener, Erblasser
deceiver	Betrüger, Schwindler
decisive	ausschlaggebend, maßgebend, entscheidend
decline	Verfall, Untergang, Rückgang
decree	Beschluss / Urteil (des Equity-Gerichtes); *also:* Verfügung
deductible	abzugsfähig, absetzbar
to deem	erachten, halten für
defamation	Verleumdung

Vocabulary

default judgment, judgment by default	Versäumnisurteil
defendant	Beklagter (*also:* Angeklagter)
to defray	(Kosten) tragen, bestreiten
to delineate	beschreiben, darstellen, skizzieren
to demand extradition	Ausweisung verlangen
demanding	anspruchsvoll
demurrer	*here:* Rechtseinwand der mangelnden Schlüssigkeit
denial	Leugnung, Verweigerung
denomination	*here:* Nennwert
dependency laws	*here:* Pflegschaftsrecht
deportation	Abschiebung, Deportation
depreciate	an Wert verlieren, abwerten, mindern
deprivation of liberty	Freiheitsberaubung
to deprive sb of sth	jm eine Sache vorenthalten, jm einer Sache berauben
deputy	(Stell)Vertreter, Bevollmächtigter
derisive	spöttisch, höhnisch
derivative	*here:* abgeleitet, sekundär
to derive from	ableiten von, herlauten (aus, von)
descent	*here:* Geburt, Abstammung, Vererbung
designated	vorgesehen, bestimmt, festgelegt
detention	Festnahme, Arrest
to deter (sb from doing sth)	abhalten, abschrecken
determined by	ermittelt durch
deterrence	Abschreckung
(to the) detriment (of)	(zum) Nachteil, Schaden (von)
device, tool	Gerät, Vorrichtung, Mittel
to dictate	diktieren
diligence	Sorgfalt, Fleiß, Eifer, Gewissenhaftigkeit
diligent	genau, sorgfältig, fleißig
to dilute	verdünnen
direct examination	direkte Befragung
discernible	erkennbar, wahrnehmbar
to discharge	entlassen, absetzen, verabschieden, freisprechen
to disclose	offenlegen, offenbaren, mitteilen
discretion, discretionary	Ermessen
discretionary review	im Ermessen des Rechtmittelgerichts liegende Überprüfung der Entscheidung (der untergeordneten Instanz)
to dismiss a case / lawsuit	eine Klage zurückweisen oder abweisen
to dismiss an appeal	eine Berufung zurückweisen, verwerfen
dismissed	*here:* entlassen
to be dismissed for misbehavior in office	wegen schweren Verfehlungen entlassen werden

to dispose of sth	erledigen, regeln; *also:* loswerden
disposition	*here:* Anordnung, Verfügung
disregard (of rules)	Nichtbeachtung (von Regeln)
to disregard	missachten, nicht beachten
dissatisfied party	unzufriedene Partei
dissolution	Auflösung
distinctive	charakteristisch, bezeichnend
to distinguish	unterscheiden, auseinanderhalten
diversity	Vielfalt, Unterschiedlichkeit, Diversität
dividend	Gewinnanteil, Dividende
docket	Geschäftszahl, Registernummer
documentary evidence	dokumentarische Beweisführung
domestic relations court, family court	Familiengericht
domestic violence	häusliche Gewalt
double jeopardy	Doppelbestrafung
to draft jurors	*here:* Geschworene einberufen
due diligence, due care	Sorgfaltspflicht
due process of law	faires / ordentliches Verfahren, Rechtsstaatsprinzip
DUI (driving under the influence)	Alkohol am Steuer
duration	Dauer, Laufzeit, Zeitdauer
DWI (driving while intoxicated)	unter Drogeneinfluss am Steuer
earshot	Hörweite
edition	Auflage, Ausgabe
egregious	ungeheuerlich, unerhört, entsetzlich
elaborate	ausgearbeitet, durchdacht, aufwändig
to elapse	verstreichen, vergehen
elder law	Altenrecht
to elevate	anheben, hervorheben, erhöhen
eligibility	Auswahl, Eignung
elite law school	Eliteuni
elitism	Elitismus
to embarrass	beschämen, in Verlegenheit bringen, verlegen machen
embezzlement	Veruntreuung, Unterschlagung
employment law	Arbeitsrecht
to be empowered to hear a case	berechtigt sein, einen Fall zu hören bzw. zu behandeln
to enact	verfügen, verordnen, Gesetzeskraft geben
to enact a law, to pass a law	ein Gesetz erlassen, verordnen
to encompass	umfassen; *also:* umgeben, umschließen
enforceable	durchsetzbar, erzwingbar, vollstreckbar, vollziehbar
to engage in	beschäftigt sein mit
to enjoin sb from doing sth	jm untersagen etwas zu tun

Vocabulary

to ensure	absichern, garantieren, sicherstellen
to be entitled (to have)	Anspruch auf etw haben
entity	Gebilde, Organisation, Einheit
entrenched	etabliert, fest verwurzelt
environmental law	Umweltrecht
environmental legislation	Umweltgesetzgebung, Umweltgesetze
equitable	billig, billigkeitsgerichtlich
equivalent	Äquivalent, Gegenwert, Gegenstück
to be equivalent to	gleichwertig sein mit
error of law	Rechtsfehler, Rechtsirrtum
to establish a precedent	einen Präzedenzfall schaffen
EU law	Europarecht
to evaluate	einschätzen, beurteilen, evaluieren
to evict	zwangsräumen, gewaltsam vertreiben
evidence	Beweis(mittel)
to evolve	herausbilden, entwickeln
ex officio [ex oh-fish-ee-oh] (Latin for: „from the office")	in der österr. Rechtssprache: Amtswegigkeit
examination board	Prüfungskommission
excuse	*here:* Hinderungsgrund, Befreiung
to execute a request	eine Anfrage ausführen, durchführen, erfüllen
to execute seizures of property	Beschlagnahmung von Besitz / Sachen durchführen
execution	Pfändung, Vollziehung, *also:* Hinrichtung
executive order	Durchführungsverordnung
exempt	ausgenommen, befreit
to exempt	befreien, freistellen
to exercise control	Kontrolle ausüben
to exert pressure	Druck ausüben
to expedite sth	etwas vorantreiben, beschleunigen
expense	Aufwendung, Ausgabe, Kosten
expertise	Fachwissen, Sachkenntnis, Gutachten
expert witness	Sachverständiger
extensively	ausgiebig, flächendeckend
extortion	Erpressung
to extradite	ausliefern
extradition	Auslieferung, Ausweisung
extradition clause / provision	Auslieferungsbestimmung
extradition proceedings	Auslieferungsverfahren
extradition request, request for extradition	Auslieferungsantrag
extradition treaty	Auslieferungsabkommen, Auslieferungsvertrag
extrajudicial	außergerichtlich

to facilitate an offense	eine Straftat erleichtern, unterstützen, ermöglichen
fact in dispute	strittige Tatsache
facts (of a case)	Sachverhalt, Tatsachenfeststellungen
failure to pay child support	Verletzung der Unterhaltspflicht
false confession	falsches Geständnis
falsification of documents	Urkundenfälschung
family law	Familienrecht
fancy	schick, raffiniert, hochtrabend
to feign a crime	eine Straftat vortäuschen
fellow panelists	*here:* Senatskollegen
fellowship / scholarship / grant	Stipendium
felony	Verbrechen
fiduciary	Treuhänder
field of interest	Interessensgebiet
file	*here:* Akte, Aktenmappe
to file an appeal	Berufung einlegen, in Berufung gehen
to find the facts	*here:* den Sachverhalt feststellen
fine	Geldstrafe, Geldbuße
fingerprint	Fingerabdruck
to fingerprint and photograph sb	jemanden erkennungsdienstlich behandeln
to flee	fliehen, flüchten
to follow a precedent	einem Präzedenzfall folgen
forensic	gerichtsmedizinisch, forensisch
forensic expert	Spurensicherungsexperte
forensic medicine	Gerichtsmedizin
foreperson	gewählter Sprecher der Jury
to forfeit	verwirken, verlustig gehen, einbüßen
forgery (of documents)	(Urkunden)Fälschung
formatting	Formatierung, Formatieren
to foster (certain skills)	fördern
fraud	Betrug
free-lance	freiberuflich
free legal assistance	kostenlose rechtliche Unterstützung
to freeze an account	ein Konto einfrieren, sperren
to frisk	*here:* abtasten
fugitive	flüchtig, Flüchtling
funds	Geldmittel
fungible, interchangeable	austauschbar, ersetzbar
to further	fördern, voranbringen
gambling offenses	verbotene (Glücks)Spiele
garnishment	Beschlagnahme einer Forderung

Vocabulary

to gather	(an)sammeln, erfassen
general deterrence	Generalprävention
genocide	Völkermord
to govern	regulieren, steuern, leiten
governance	Kontrolle, Herrschaft, Gewalt
at government expense	auf Staatskosten
grade	Note
(law school)graduation	Abschluss (des rechtswiss. Studiums)
to grant admission	Zulassung gewähren
grievous bodily harm	schwere / gefährliche Körperverletzung
guarantee	Bürgschaft, Garantie
guardianship (court)	Sachwalterschaft(-sgericht)
guilty plea	Schuldeingeständnis des Angeklagten
hardship	harte Umstände, Not, Mühsal
hazy	unscharf, undeutlich, verschwommen, vage, unklar
hearsay	Hörensagen
to hedge	absichern, sich schützen
heir	Erbe
high-grossing	umsatzstark
hindrance, impediment	Behinderung, Hindernis, Hemmnis
holding cell	Zelle
home (equity) loan	Hypothek auf Wohnhaus
homicide, (first degree) murder	Mord
hostage taking	Geiselnahme
humanities	Humanwissenschaften, Geisteswissenschaften
identification tools	Erkennungs-, Identifikationsmittel
illegal gambling, unauthorized organization of a game of chance	unerlaubte Veranstaltung eines Glücksspiels
illicit	unerlaubt, verboten, ungesetzlich
illicit drug trafficking	unerlaubter Suchtstoffverkehr
immobilization	Ruhigstellung, Einfrierung, Immobilisierung
impact	(Aus)Wirkung, Aufprall
to impanel (a jury)	(eine Jury) zusammenstellen
impartiality	Objektivität, Unbefangenheit, Unparteilichkeit
to impeach	anklagen (wegen eines Amtsvergehens), *also:* anzweifeln
impeachment	Anklage wegen Amtsmissbrauchs, Amtsenthebungsverfahren
implementation	Durchführung, Umsetzung
to impose a decision	*here:* eine Entscheidung durchsetzen
impoverished	dürftig, arm, verarmt

imprisonement for contempt, coercive detention	Beugehaft
improper	ungebührlich, unpassend, ungeeignet
impropriety	Fehlverhalten, Ungehörigkeit
inadmissible	unzulässig
incapacitation	Unfähigmachung, Untauglichkeit
to incarcerate / incarceration	einkerkern / Einkerkerung
to incline	tendieren, neigen
incompatibility	Unverträglichkeit
incompetence	Unfähigkeit, Inkompetenz
inconvenience	Unannehmlichkeit, Unbequemlichkeit
to incorporate	integrieren, umfassen, mit einbeziehen
incorporation	Angliederung, Aufnahme
indefinite	unbefristet, unbegrenzt, *also:* ungenau
to indict	von der Grand Jury (siehe Seite 91) in den Anklagestand versetzt werden
indictment	Anklageschrift / Anklage durch die Grand Jury
indigent	bedürftig, mittellos, notleidend
indispensable	unverzichtbar, unumgänglich, notwendig
industrial / economic espionage	Industrie- / Wirtschaftsspionage
infamous crime	niederträchtige Straftat, Schandtat
to infer from	ableiten
to inflict	zufügen
inheritable	vererbbar
inheritance	Erbe, Erbschaft, Vererbung
inheritance law	Erbrecht
injunction	gerichtliche Verfügung
injured party	geschädigte Partei, Geschädigte(r)
inmate	(Gefängnis)Insasse, Häftling
innuendo	versteckte Andeutung, Anspielung
inquiry	Nachforschung, Ermittlung, Untersuchung, Befragung
insolvency, bancruptcy	Insolvenz
instruction of the jury	Belehrung der Geschworenen
to insulate	isolieren
interdisciplinary	fächerübergreifend, interdisziplinär
to interrogate	befragen, vernehmen, verhören
interrogation	Befragung
interrogator	*here:* Befrager
intimidating	einschüchternd
to invalidate	annullieren, entkräften, unwirksam machen
invariably	grundsätzlich, ständig, ausnahmslos

Vocabulary

investigate	ermitteln
investigative judge	Untersuchungsrichter, Ermittlungsrichter
to invoke	sich berufen auf, anführen, zitieren
irreconcilable	unvereinbar, unversöhnlich, unverträglich
jail / prison	Gefängnis
jeopardy	Gefahr
joinder	Klageverbindung, Klagebeitritt, Intervention
joinder (of parties)	Klagebeitritt, (Neben)Intervention, Streitgenossenschaft
joint custody	gemeinsames Sorgerecht, gemeinsame Obsorge
joint-degree program	Doppelstudium
judicial discretion	richterliches Ermessen,
judiciary	Justiz, Richterschaft
jurisdiction	Zuständigkeit, Gerichtsbakreit, auch: Rechtsprechung
jurisprudence	Rechtswissenschaft, Jurisprudenz, Rechtslehre
juror	Geschworener
juror identification badge	Namensschild der Geschworenen
jury	Geschworene(nbank)
jury summons	Geschworenenladung
justice of the peace	Friedensrichter
justness	Billigkeit, Gerechtigkeit
juvenile court	Jugendgericht
kidnapping	Menschenraub
labor court	Arbeitsgericht
labor law	Arbeitsrecht
landlord / tenant	Bestandgeber / Bestandnehmer
landmark	Grenzstein, Meilenstein, Wahrzeichen
landmark decision	bahnbrechende Entscheidung
to last	bestehen bleiben, fortdauern
latitude	Freiraum, Spielraum
law-abiding citizens	gesetzestreue Bürger
law class	Lehrveranstaltung, Vorlesung
law dispute	Rechtsstreit
law enforcement	Rechtsdurchsetzung
law of contracts	Vertragsrecht
law of obligation	Schuldrecht
law of torts / tort law	Deliktsrecht, Recht der unerlaubten Handlung
law school admission	Zulassung zum rechtswiss. Studium
law school applicant	Bewerber für das Studium der Rechtswiss.
lawsuit	Rechtsstreit, Prozess, *also:* (An)Klage
lawyer	Jurist

lawyer referral service	here: Anwalts-Empfehlungsdienst
lay judge	Laienrichter, Schöffe
lay persons / lay assessors	Laien, Laienrichter
to lay/put emphasis on sth	etwas betonen
layer	Ebene, Schicht
leading	Suggestivfrage
lecture, course taught in the confrontational manner	Vorlesung
legal costs (expense/s) insurance	Rechtsschutzversicherung
legal counsel / representative	Rechtsbeistand, Rechtsberater, rechtlicher Vertreter
legal dispute, lawsuit	Rechtsstreit
legal division, legal department	Rechtsabteilung
legal ethics	Rechtsethik
legal procedure	Gerichtsverfahren
legislative enactment	Gesetzgebung
lenient	mild, glimpflich
liability insurance	Haftpflichtversicherung
liaison	Angelegenheit, Verbindung
libel, slander, defamation	Verleumdung, Beleidigung, üble Nachrede
libel suit, libel action, action for slander	Ehrenbeleidigungsklage
liberal arts, humanities	Geisteswissenschaften
licensed	lizenziert, zugelassen, zugesagt
lien	Zurückbehaltungsrecht, Pfandrecht
limited / general jurisdiction	spezielle, generelle Zuständigkeit
lingering	nachklingend, zurückbleibend, verweilend
litigation	Prozess, Gerichtsverfahren
litigation team	Verhandlungsteam
litigator, trial attorney	Prozessanwalt
to live off campus	abseits des Campus wohnen
loan, credit	Kredit
loan repayment assistance	Kreditrückzahlungshilfe
to locate persons	Personen ausfindig machen
to lodge	here: deponieren ("to lodge a challenge"), also: wohnen
lofty	stolz, erhaben, hochmütig
lucrative	lohnend, rentabel, lukrativ
major	here: Studiengang, Hauptfach
malicious	mutwillig, böswillig, niederträchtig
malicious gossip	üble Nachrede
manslaughter, second degree murder	Totschlag
to mediate	vermitteln
mediator	Mediator, Schlichter, „Mittelsmann"

Vocabulary

medical examiner	Gerichtsmediziner
medical malpractice case	Arzthaftungsprozess
mental disability	geistige Behinderung
merciless	unbarmherzig
merit	Verdienst, Wert, Verdienstlichkeit
misconduct	Fehlverhalten, Verfehlung
misdemeanor	Vergehen
misrepresentation	irrtümliche, ungenaue Darstellung
mistake in venue	fehlende örtliche Zuständigkeit
misuse	Missbrauch, Zweckentfremdung
misuse of check and credit cards	Missbrauch von Scheck- und Kreditkarten
misuse of identification papers	Missbrauch von Ausweispapieren
mock court / moot court	*here:* Scheingericht
mock trial	Scheinprozess, Probeverfahren
to modify (a judgment)	(eine gerichtliche Entscheidung) abändern, modifizieren
monetary award	Geldersatz
money laundering	Geldwäsche
money transmitting	Geldweitergabe /-übertragung
moot	Streit; adj.: strittig
mortgage	Hypothek, Pfand, Belastung
motion	*here:* Antrag
motion to dismiss	Antrag auf Klageabweisung
moving party	Antragsteller
multiple	mehrfach, vielfach, multipel
mutual	gegenseitig, wechselseitig, einvernehmlich
narrowly tailored	*here:* eng ausgelegt
nationalization	Nationalisierung
negligence	Fahrlässigkeit
negligent manslaughter	fahrlässige Tötung
negotiated settlement	ausgehandelte außergerichtliche Vereinbarung
negotiation	Verhandlung
no-fault divorce	verschuldensunabhängige Scheidung
nominal	symbolisch, äußerst gering
nominal fee	Anerkennungsgebühr
non-arbitrable	nicht zu schlichten, nicht schiedsfähig
non-compliance	Nichterfüllung, Nichtübereinstimmung, Diskrepanz
non-custodial	*here:* nicht obsorgeberechtigt
nonexempt (assets)	*here:* in die Konkursmasse fallend(es Vermögen)
non-moving party	Antragsgegner
notable	beachtenswert, bemerkenswert

notary public / civil law notary	Notar(in) (im Common- / civil-law-System)
notary seal	Siegel des Notars
notary trust account	Treuhandkonto, Notar-Anderkonto
notation	Vermerk, Bezeichnung
notice	*here*: Bekanntmachung, Aushang
notion	Gedanke, Idee, Vorstellung
numeral	Zahl(zeichen, symbol), Ziffer
oath	Eid, Schwur
objection!	*here*: Einspruch!
obligation to disclose, duty to give notice	Anzeigepflicht, Offenbarungspflicht
obligation to pay child support	Unterhaltspflicht
to be obliged to do sth	verpflichtet sein etw zu tun
obscenity	Unzüchtigkeit
obstruction of justice	Behinderung der Justiz
obstruction of punishment	Strafvereitelung
to obtain evidence	Beweismittel erlangen, erwirken, bekommen
to occur	eintreten, stattfinden, vorfallen
offender	Gesetzesbrecher
offering a bribe	Bestechung
to omit	unterlassen, auslassen, weglassen
onerous	beschwerlich, mühsam
ordinance	Anordnung, Verordnung
organized crime, racketeering	organisiertes Verbrechen
original jurisdiction	originäre Zuständigkeit
orphanage	Waisenhaus
outcome	Ergebnis, Folge, Auswirkung
to outlaw	verbieten
overburdened	überlastet
overcrowded	überfüllt
overhead	*here*: Fixkosten
to overrule an objection	den Einspruch abweisen
to overrule a precedent	einen Präzedenfall außer Kraft setzen, aufheben
pain and suffering	Schmerzen(s)geld
paralegal	juristische Hilfskraft
parenthesis	(runde) Klammer
parole	vorzeitige Haftentlassung
particularity requirement	Spezifikationserfordernis
party	*here*: Partei
to pass / enact a law	ein Gesetz erlassen
to pass / meet muster	Anforderungen genügen
to pass the bar (exam)	die Anwaltsprüfung schaffen

Vocabulary

paternity suit	Vaterschaftsprozess, Vaterschaftsklage
peer	Gleichrangiger, adj.: seinesgleichen
peer pressure	Gruppendruck
penal law	Strafrecht
pending	*here:* vorbehaltlich, anstehend
pending case	anhängiges / schwebendes Verfahren
penultimate	vorletzte(r)
to perform	leisten, etw tun, vollbringen
performance	*here:* Erfüllung einer Verpflichtung
to perform a record search	eine Strafregisterauskunft einholen
to perform near the top of a class	bei den besten eines Jahrgangs sein, als eine(r) der besten eines Jahrgangs abschneiden
perjury	Meineid
to persist	beharren, fortdauern
personality	unbewegliches Vermögen
to pertain	betreffen, gehören, gelten, zutreffen
petty offense, petty crime	Bagatelldelikt, Kleinkriminalität
physical exhibit	Beweisstück
physical injury / bodily injury / bodily harm	Körperverletzung
pimping	Zuhälterei
to place emphasis on sth	etwas betonen, hervorheben
plaintiff	Kläger
plea	*here:* „Antwort" des Angeklagten auf die Anklage
plea agreement, plea deal	„Deal" im Strafverfahren
pleading	Plädoyer, Schriftsatz, Verteidigungsschrift
(preliminary)pleadings	*here:* (prozessvorbereitende) Schriftsätze
to poll	abfragen, befragen
pool of potential jurors	Ansammlung der potenziellen Geschworenen
population stratum	Bevölkerungsschicht
post-trial	nach dem Prozess
precedent (case)	Präzedenzfall
preconceived	vorgefasst
predetermined	vorherbestimmt, vorher festgelegt
predominant	vorwiegend, vorherrschend, überlegen
to predominate	vorwiegen, vorherrschen
preferential treatment of a creditor / debtor	Gläubiger- / Schuldnerbegünstigung
prejudice	Vorurteil, Befangenheit
prejudiced	befangen, voreingenommen
preliminary	Vorarbeit, vorbereitende Maßnahme; vorbereitende Tätigkeit
preponderance	Übergewicht, Überwiegen

to preserve documents	Dokumente / Unterlagen (auf)bewahren
to preside	den Vorsitz führen, leiten
presiding judge	vorsitzender Richter
to press charges	gegen jm Anzeige erstatten / Anklage erheben
prestigious	angesehen, prestigeträchtig, renommiert
presumption of innocence	Unschuldsvermutung
pre-trial	vorprozessual
preventive detention	Sicherheitsverwahrung
principal need	wesentliches Erfordernis, Bedürfnis
prisoner	Gefangener, Häftling
private law	Privatrecht
privilege	Sonderrecht, Begünstigung
probate court	Verlassenschaftsgericht
probation	Bewährung
probationary	zur/auf Probe
probation officer	Bewährungshelfer
procedural mistake / error	Verfahrensfehler
to proceed	fortfahren, weitermachen
proceeding	Verfahren, (Prozess)Verlauf, Vorgehen
to produce documents	Dokumente vorweisen, vorzeigen
professionalism	Professionalität, fachliche Qualifikation
profitable	ertragreich, gewinnbringend, profitabel
to promote	(be)fördern, unterstützen, voranbringen
to promulgate	verkünden, öffentlich bekanntgeben
proof of identity	Identitätsnachweis, Legitimation
property law	Sachenrecht
proponent	Befürworter, Verfechter, Vertreter
prosecutor	Staatsanwalt
prostitution	Prostitution
to provide service of process, to serve (documents)	Zustellungen vornehmen
provision	*here:* Klausel
publication	Veröffentlichung, Publikation
public defender	staatl. finanzierter Verfahrenshelfer im Strafverfahren
public international law	Völkerrecht
public law	öffentliches Recht
publishing company	Verlag(shaus, gesellschaft)
punishment / penalty / sentence	Strafe
punitive damages	Strafschadenersatz
to pursue a claim	einen Anspruch geltend machen
to pursue an academic career	eine akademische Laufbahn verfolgen

Vocabulary

to pursue an offender	einen Gesetzesbrecher verfolgen
to put forth	hervorbringen
putative defendant	vermutlicher, mutmaßlicher Beschuldigter
(fixed) quota system	(festes) Quoten-, Kontingentierungssystem
radio scanner	*here:* Funkscanner
railing	Geländer, Barriere
random selection	Zufallsauswahl
rank	Ebene, Rang, Stufe
ranking	reihend, Rangordnung
to rank law school candidates	Bewerber nach Qualifikationen reihen
rape	Vergewaltigung
real estate law	Immobilienrecht
realm	Bereich, Gebiet
reasonable	plausibel, vernünftig, verständlich
rebuttal	Widerlegung
to receive	erhalten, bekommen, empfangen
receiving stolen property	Hehlerei
reciprocity	Gegenseitigkeit, Wechselseitigkeit
recognizance	Anerkenntnis, Anerkennungsverpflichtung
recollection	Erinnerung
recommendation	Empfehlung, Vorschlag
record search	*here:* Einholung einer Strafregisterauskunft
recourse	Zuflucht, Rechtsweg
to recover property	Besitz / Vermögen zurückerlangen, wiederbekommen
to recruit	anwerben
to recuse a judge	einen Richter ablehnen
referee	Schiedsrichter
referral	Empfehlung, Verweis, Überweisung
to refrain from	etwas unterlassen, von etw Abstand nehmen
to refute, to rebut	widerlegen, anfechten, entkräften
to register, to enroll	inskribieren
registration, enrollment	Inskription
to rehabilitate	Ansehen wiederherstellen, sanieren, wieder einstellen
to reimburse	entschädigen, rückerstatten, rückvergüten
reimbursement	Entschädigung, Ersatz, Rückvergütung
to reject an application	eine Bewerbung ablehnen
to release	entlassen, freilassen
to release on bail	auf Kaution freilassen
relevancy	Sachbezogenheit, Erheblichkeit
relevant	bedeutsam, wichtig, relevant
relief	*here:* Rechtsbehelf, Rechtsmittel

reluctant	widerwillig, zögernd
to rely on	sich auf etw stützen, sich auf etw verlassen
to remain silent	schweigen, stumm bleiben
to remand (a case)	eine Rechtssache an die untere Instanz zurückverweisen
remedy	Abhilfe, Rechtsbehelf, Rechtsmittel
to remedy	Schaden / Mangel beheben
to remove	beseitigen
to render / reach a verdict	eine Entscheidung finden, ein Urteil fällen (bezogen auf die Geschworenen)
renowned	renommiert, wohlbekannt, angesehen, namhaft
to repeal	aufheben, widerrufen
report	Bericht
reporter, law reports	*here:* Entscheidungssammlung
to reproduce	*here:* wiedergeben, reproduzieren, kopieren
reputation	Reputation, Ansehen, Ruf
request for extradition	Auslieferungsantrag
to be required to sit a test	eine Prüfung machen müssen
to reside	sich niederlassen
to reside on campus	am Campus wohnen
resignation	Rücktritt
resolution	*here:* Lösung
to resolve	lösen, beseitigen, aufklären
resource	(Einsatz-, Betriebs-, Produktions-)Mittel
respective	besonders, jeweilig, einschlägig
restitution	Rückerstattung, Zurückzahlung, Wiederherstellung
restitution of goods	Rückgabe von Gütern
resume, curriculum vitae	Lebenslauf
to retain (= to hold within, to remain in a place)	behalten, einbehalten, zurückbehalten
retainer	*here:* Anwaltsvorschuss
retention vote	Abstimmung / Wahl über Beibehaltung
retraceable	zurückverfolgbar
retroactive	rückwirkend
revenue	Einkünfte, Einnahmen, Ertrag
reversal of a decision / a verdict	Urteilsaufhebung
to reverse and remand	*here:* eine Entscheidung aufheben und an die untere Instanz zur neuerlichen E zurückverweisen
to review	überprüfen
to reward	belohnen, vergelten
robbery	Raub
rule of law	Rechtsstaatlichkeit, Rechtsgrundsatz

Vocabulary

rules of evidence	Beweisregeln
rumor	Gerücht
safeguard	Schutzmaßnahme, Absicherung
salary	Gehalt, Vergütung
sample	Beispiel
scholar	Wissenschaftler, Gelehrter, Schüler
scope	(Anwendungs)Bereich, Umfang, Reichweite
score	Punktezahl
scruples	Skrupel, Bedenken
scrutiny	genaue Überprüfung, Untersuchung
seal	*here:* Siegel, Stempel; *also:* Verschluss, Dichtung
search	*here:* (Personen- / Haus-)Durchsuchung
search warrant	Hausdurchsuchungsbefehl
second mortgage	zweitrangige Hypothek
to secure the extraditions of	die Auslieferungen von ... sicherstellen
securities law	Wertpapierrecht
security	*here:* Wertpapier
to seize	*here:* beschlagnahmen
selection criteria	Auswahlkriterien
selective	pingelig, selektiv
seminar style course	Seminar
senate, panel	Senat
sequence	Abfolge, Reihenfolge, Ablauf
series	Folge, Reihe, Serie
to serve life term	lebenslang im Dienst stehen
service of process	Zustellung
set	*here:* bestimmt, festgelegt
to set forth	darlegen
settlement	Vergleich
settlement negotiations	Vergleichsgespräche
settlement of estates	Nachlassabwicklung
share	Aktie, Anteil, Beteiligung
shareholder	Gesellschafter, Teilhaber, Aktionär
shorthand	kurzerhand, stichwortartig; Stenografie
to show cause	seine Gründe zeigen, begründen
significant	bedeutsam, erheblich, maßgeblich
silent, mute	stumm, still, sprachlos
social law	Sozialrecht
social sciences	Sozialwissenschaften, Gesellschaftswissenschaften
sociological differences	soziologische Unterschiede
sociology	Soziologie

solo	einzeln, allein
sophomore	Student im zweiten Studienjahr
to sort the wheat from the chaff	Spreu von Weizen trennen
sources of law	Rechtsquellen
speedy trial	schnelles Verfahren
spoils	*here:* Beute
squatter	Hausbesetzer, illegaler Siedler
stalemate (situation)	Pattsituation
to stand mute	die Antwort verweigern; *here:* die vorgeworfene Straftat weder abstreiten noch zugeben / eingestehen
stare decisis	Grundsatz der Bindung an Vorentscheidungen
(assistant) state attorney (ASA), (deputy) district attorney (DDA)	Staatsanwalt (in den US-Bundesstaaten)
to steer	steuern, lenken, führen
to stem from	sich ableiten von, herrühren, abstammen von
stigma	Brandmal, Schandfleck, Stigma
stipend	Gehalt, Bezüge
stock	*here:* Gesellschaftskapital, Grundkapital
stratification	Schichtung, Stratifizierung
stratum, strata	Schicht(en)
to strike (remove) a prospective juror from the panel	einen angehenden Geschworenen erfolgreich ablehnen
subject of investigation	Gegenstand der Untersuchung / Recherche
to be subject to	unterworfen
subjugation	Unterwerfung, Unterjochung
submission	*here:* Unterwerfung
subordination	Unterordnung, Subordnination
to subpoena	unter Strafandrohung vorladen
subsidy fraud	Subventionsbetrug
substitute	Ersatz, Vertreter
to sue	klagen
to suffer a harm / loss	einen Schaden erleiden
to summon	auffordern, bestellen, rufen
to supersede	ersetzen, an Stelle von ... treten
to supply records	Unterlagen beschaffen, zur Verfügung stellen
to be supposed to	vorgesehen sein zu, sollen
suppression of documents	Urkundenunterdrückung
to surpass	übertreffen, übersteigen, überbieten
to surrender oneself to sb	*here:* ausliefern
suspect	Verdächtige(r), vermutliche(r) Täter(in)
to sustain an objection	einem Einspruch stattgeben
to swear in	beeiden

Vocabulary

sympathetic	wohlgesonnen, wohlwollend, mitfühlend
to take the bar exam	zur Anwaltsprüfung antreten
to take the stand	den Zeugenstand betreten
tangible/ intangible assets	bewegliches / unbewegliches Vermögen
to target	anvisieren, abzielen auf, zum Ziel setzen
taxable	steuerpflichtig, zu versteuern
taxation	Steuerwesen
tax evasion	Steuerhinterziehung
tax law	Steuerrecht
tax return	Steuererklärung
to team-teach	gemeinsam / als Team unterrichten
tenure	*here:* Amtszeit, Anstellung
to testify	bezeugen
testimony	Zeugenaussage
theft	Diebstahl
thesis	Diplom-/ Doktorarbeit
threat	Bedrohung
three-tiered hierarchy	dreistufige Hierarchie
threshold	Schwelle, Abgrenzung
tiered	gestaffelt
title	Titel, Rechtsanspruch
tort (claim)	delikt. Schadenersatz(anspruch)
(law of) torts, torts law	Deliktsrecht, Recht der unerlaubten Handlungen
traceable	nachweislich, auffindbar
traffic court	Verkehrsgericht
transaction	Abwicklung, Durchführung, Transaktion
transcript	*here:* Protokoll
transcript (of grades)	*here:* Abschrift der Noten, Zeugnis mit allen Noten
(academic) transcript	*here:* amtliches Zeugnis / Aufstellung aller Einzelnoten
to transfer	umbuchen, umschreiben, anweisen
to transfer money to an account	Geld auf ein Konto überweisen
transmission	*here:* Übermittlung, Übertragung
to tread	betreten, schreiten, auftreten
trespass, home invasion	Hausfriedensbruch
trial	*here:* Gerichtsverhandlung
trial attorney, litigator	Prozessanwalt
trial award	Zuspruch, Zuerkennung, Zahlungsverpflichtung des Beklagten
trial court	Prozessgericht, erstinstanzliches Gericht
trier	Prüfer
trust	Treuhand, Vermögensverwaltung

to try a case	einen Fall verhandeln
to try somebody	jemanden vor Gericht stellen
tuition	Studiengebühr
two-tier(ed)	zweigeteilt, zweigestuft
typeface	Schriftart, Schrift
unanimous	einstimmig
unauthorized use of a vehicle	unbefugter Gebrauch eines Fahrzeuges
uncontested facts	unstrittiger Sachverhalt
uncontroversial, indisputable, uncontentious, undisputed	unstrittig
to undergo	erdulden, durchleben, erfahren
underlying	darunterliegend, zugrundeliegend
under oath	unter Eid
undue influence	unzulässige Beeinflussung
unequivocally	eindeutig, zweifelsfrei
uninhibited	ungehemmt, hemmungslos
unjust enrichment	ungerechtfertigte Bereicherung
unresolved	offen, ungelöst
unresolved issues	ungelöste Fragen
to uphold	halten, aufrecht erhalten
using equitable discretion	nach billigem Ermessen
usurpation of office	Amtsanmaßung
to vacate, to declare void	*here:* (eine Entscheidung) als nichtig aufheben, annullieren
to vacate a building	ein Gebäude räumen
to vacate a contract	einen Vertrag für nichtig erklären
valence	Wertigkeit, Valenz
validity	Aussagekraft, Echtheit, Gültigkeit
venturing	wagend, riskierend
venturing enterprise	spekulatives Unternehmen
verdict	Urteilsspruch der Geschworenen
vicarious liability	Haftung für fremdes Verschulden
victim	Opfer, Betroffene(r), Verunglückte(r)
vindicate	rechtfertigen, verteidigen
to violate / break a law	gegen ein Gesetz verstoßen
visitation issues	*here:* Besuchsrechtsangelegenheiten
to waive a right	auf ein Recht verzichten
warning of compulsion	Androhung der zwangsweisen Durchsetzung
warrant	richterliche Anordnung
to weigh the evidence fairly and objectively	die Beweise objektiv und unvoreingenommen abwägen
will	Testament, letzter Wille

Vocabulary

willful disregard	vorsätzliche Missachtung
wire fraud, mail fraud	Telekommunikationsbetrug
wiretapping	Abhören
withdrawal	*here:* Rückzug, Ausstieg, Rücktritt
to withhold	vorenthalten, zurückhalten
witness (friendly / hostile)	Zeuge (der eigenen / gegnerischen Partei)
(lay) witness	Zeuge
witness stand	Zeugenstand
witness statement	Zeugenerklärung
writ	Schriftstück, Urkunde, Erlass
wrongdoer	Missetäter
zoning regulations	Bauordnungsbestimmungen

Vokabular

(eine gerichtliche Entscheidung) abändern, modifizieren	to modify (a judgment)
Abfolge, Reihenfolge, Ablauf	sequence
abfragen, befragen	to poll
abgeleitet, sekundär	derivative
abhalten, abschrecken	to deter (sb from doing sth)
Abhilfe, Mittel, Rechtsmittel	remedy
Abhören	wiretapping
Abkommen, Absprache	convention
Abkürzung(szeichen), Verkürzung	abbreviation
ablehnen (eine Bewerbung)	to reject (an application)
ableiten	to infer from
ableiten von, herrühren, abstammen	to derive / stem from
Ableitbarkeit	deducibility, derivability
Abmachung, *auch:* (gutes) Geschäft, Schnäppchen	bargain
abschaffen	to abolish
Abschiebung, Deportation	deportation
Abschluss (des rechtswiss. Studiums)	(law school) graduation
abschrecken, abhalten	to deter
Abschreckung	deterrence
Abschrift der Noten, Zeugnis mit allen Noten	transcript (of grades)
absichern, garantieren, sicherstellen	to ensure
absichern, sich schützen	to hedge
Abstimmung / Wahl über Beibehaltung	retention vote
abtasten	to frisk
abweisen, zurückweisen	to dismiss
Abwicklung, Durchführung, Transaktion	transaction
versuchte Abwicklung / Transaktion	attempted transaction
abzugsfähig, absetzbar	deductible
Adoption	adoption
eine akademische Laufbahn verfolgen	to pursue an academic career
Akte, Aktenmappe	file
Aktentasche	brief-case
Aktie, Anteil, Beteiligung	share

Vokabular

Alkohol am Steuer	DUI (driving under the influence)
allgemein üblich	customary
Altenrecht	elder law
Amtsanmaßung	usurpation of office
Amtswegigkeit (in der österr. Rechtssprache)	ex officio [ex oh-fish-ee-oh] (Latin for: "from the office")
Amtszeit, Anstellung	tenure
Androhung der zwangsweisen Durchsetzung	warning of compulsion
Anerkenntnis, Anerkennungsverpflichtung	recognizance
Anerkennungsgebühr	nominal fee
anfechten, bestreiten, bekämpfen	to contest
Anforderungen genügen	to pass / to meet muster
Anfrage ausführen, durchführen, erfüllen	to execute a request
angegliedert, angeschlossen	affiliated
Angeklagter, Beschuldigter	criminal defendant
angesehen, prestigeträchtig, renommiert	prestigious
angliedern, (an)häufen, (an)sammeln	to aggregate
Angliederung, Aufnahme	incorporation
Angriff / Übergriff	assault and battery
anhängiges / schwebendes Verfahren	pending cases
anhäufen, gruppieren	to cluster
anheben, hervorheben, erhöhen	to elevate
Anklage wegen Amtsmissbrauchs, Amtsenthebungsverfahren	impeachment
anklagen (wegen eines Amtsvergehens), *auch:* anzweifeln	to impeach
anklagen, Anklage erheben	to arraign
Anklageschrift, Anklage durch die Grand Jury	indictment
Anklageschrift, Strafantrag; *auch:* Strafanzeige	criminal complaint
Annäherung, Ansatz, Methode	approach
annullieren, entkräften, unwirksam machen	to invalidate
richterliche Anordnung	warrant
Anordnung zur Vorlage der Akten an ein höheres Gericht	(writ of) certiorari
Anordnung, Verfügung	disposition
Anordnung, Verordnung	ordinance
Ansammlung der potenziellen Geschworenen	pool of potential jurors
Ansehen wiederherstellen, sanieren, wieder einstellen	to rehabilitate
Anspielung, versteckte Andeutung	innuendo
Anspruch auf etw haben	to be entitled (to have)
Anspruch geltend machen	to pursue a claim
Anspruchsteller, Antragsteller	claimant

anspruchsvoll	demanding
Antrag	motion
Antrag auf Klageabweisung	motion to dismiss
Antragsgegner	non-moving party
Antragsteller	moving party
Antwort des Angeklagten auf die Anklage	plea
die Antwort verweigern; *hier:* die vorgeworfene Straftat weder abstreiten noch zugeben / eingestehen	to stand mute
anvisieren, abzielen auf, zum Ziel setzen	to target
Anwaltschaft	the Bar
Anwalts-Empfehlungsdienst	lawyer referral service
zur Anwaltsprüfung antreten	to take the bar exam
die Anwaltsprüfung schaffen	to pass the bar (exam)
zur Anwaltsprüfung zugelassen werden	to be admitted to the bar
Anwaltsvorschuss	retainer
anwerben	to recruit
gegen jm Anzeige erstatten / Anklage erheben	to press charges
Anzeigepflicht, Offenbarungspflicht	obligation to disclose, duty to give notice
Äquivalent, Gegenwert, Gegenstück	equivalent
Arbeitsgericht	labor court
Arbeitsrecht	labor law, employment law
Arzthaftungsprozess	medical malpractice case
attestieren, beglaubigen, bescheinigen	to attest
auffordern, bestellen, rufen	to summon
aufheben, widerrufen	to repeal
Auflage, Ausgabe	edition
Auflösung	dissolution
Aufwendung, Ausgabe, Kosten	expense
Ausbildungslager	boot camp military
ausführen, vollenden	to accomplish
ausgearbeitet, durchdacht, aufwändig	elaborate
ausgehandelte (außergerichtliche) Vereinbarung	negotiated settlement
ausgenommen, befreit	exempt
ausgeschlossen von	barred from
ausgiebig, flächendeckend	extensively
ausliefern	to extradite, to surrender
Auslieferung, Ausweisung	extradition
die Auslieferungen von ... sicherstellen	to secure the extradition
Auslieferungsabkommen, Auslieferungsvertrag	extradition treaty
Auslieferungsantrag	extradition request, request for extradition
Auslieferungsbestimmung	extradition clause / provision
Auslieferungsverfahren	extradition proceedings

Vokabular

Aussagekraft, Echtheit, Gültigkeit	validity
(als Zeuge/Partei) aussagen	to testify
ausschlaggebend, maßgebend, entscheidend	decisive
außergerichtlich	extrajudicial
austauschbar, ersetzbar	fungible, interchangeable
Auswahl, Eignung	eligibility
Auswahlkriterien	selection criteria
Ausweisung verlangen	to demand extradition
Automobilzulassung	automobile registration
bahnbrechende Entscheidung	landmark decision
Bakkalaureus, niedrigster akadem. Grad	Bachelor's degree
Balken/Barren (im Gerichtssaal)	bar
Bankrott	bankruptcy
Bargeldersatz	cash substitute
Bauordnungsbestimmungen	zoning regulations
beachtenswert, bemerkenswert	notable
bedeutsam, erheblich, maßgeblich	significant
bedeutsam, wichtig, relevant	relevant
Bedrohung	threat
bedürftig, mittellos, notleidend	indigent
beeiden	to swear in
unzulässige Beeinflussung	undue influence
Beendigung, Abschluss	completion
befangen, voreingenommen	prejudiced
Befolgung, Einhaltung (von); *auch:* Zustimmung	compliance (with)
Beförderung, Übertragung, Übermittlung	conveyance
befragen, vernehmen, verhören	to interrogate
Befrager	interrogator
Befragung	interrogation
direkte Befragung	direct examination
befreien, freistellen	to exempt
Befürworter, Verfechter, Vertreter	proponent
begehrt	coveted
begründen	to show cause
Begünstigung	accessory after the fact
(bei)behalten, einbehalten, zurückbehalten	to retain (= to hold within, to remain in a place)
beharren, fortdauern	to persist
Behinderung der Justiz	obstruction of justice
geistige Behinderung	mental disability
Behinderung, Hindernis, Hemmnis	hindrance, impediment
Beihilfe leisten, einen Täter begünstigen	to aid and abet a criminal

Beispiel	sample
finanzieller Beitrag	capital contribution
beitragen	to abet
Bekanntmachung, Aushang	notice
(Glaubens)Bekenntnis, Credo, Überzeugung	creed
Beklagter (auch: Angeklagter)	defendant
Belehrung der Geschworenen	instruction of the jury
belohnen, vergelten	to reward
sich bemächtigen, in Besitz nehmen	to acquire
berechtigt sein, einen Fall zu behandeln / hören	to be empowered to hear a case
Bereich, Gebiet	realm
(Anwendungs)Bereich, Umfang, Reichweite	scope
ungerechtfertigte Bereicherung	unjust enrichment
Bericht	report
sich berufen auf, anführen, zitieren	to invoke
Berufung	appeal
die Berufung betreffend, Berufungs-	appellate
Berufung einlegen, in Berufung gehen	to file an appeal
eine Berufung zurückweisen, verwerfen	to dismiss an appeal
Berufungsgegner, Rechtsmittelgegner	appellee
Berufungswerber, Rechtsmittelführer	appellant
beschäftigt sein mit	to engage in
beschämen, in Verlegenheit bringen, verlegen machen	to embarrass
Beschlagnahme einer Forderung	garnishment
beschlagnahmen	to seize
Beschlagnahmung von Besitz / Sachen durchführen	to execute seizures of property
Beschluss	court order
Beschluss / Urteil (des Equity-Gerichtes); *auch*: Verfügung	decree
beschreiben, darstellen, skizzieren	to delineate
beschuldigen, anschuldigen, belasten, bezichtigen	to charge (with)
beschuldigt, Beschuldigter	accused
Beschuldigung, Belastung, Anklage	charge
beschwerlich, mühsam	onerous
beseitigen	to remove
Besitz / Vermögen zurückerlangen, wiederbekommen	to recover property
besonders, jeweilig, einschlägig	respective
Bestandgeber / Bestandnehmer	landlord / tenant
bestätigen, bejahen; *auch*: behaupten	to affirm
bestätigen, bekräftigen, zusagen	to confirm
Bestätigung, Anerkennung, Quittierung	acknowledgment

Vokabular

Bestechung	bribery/offering a bribe
bestehen aus	to comprise, contain, to include, to consist of
bestehen bleiben, fortdauern	to last
Bestellung eines Vertreters / Anwaltes	appointment of counsel
bei den besten eines Jahrgangs sein, als eine(r) der besten eines Jahrgangs abschneiden	to perform near the top of a class
bestimmt, festgelegt	set
Besuchsrecht	child visitation right
Besuchsrechtsangelegenheiten	visitation issues
betonen, hervorheben	to lay / put / place emphasis on sth
betreffen, gehören, gelten, zutreffen	to pertain
betreiben	to engage in
betreten, schreiten, auftreten	to tread
Betrug	fraud
Betrüger, Schwindler	deceiver
Beugehaft	imprisonment for contempt, coercive detention
beurkunden, legalisieren, bescheinigen	to authenticate
Beurteilung, Einschätzung, Bewertung	assessment
Beute	spoils
Bevölkerungsschicht	population stratum
Bewährung	probation
Bewährungshelfer	probation officer
bewegliche Sache	chattel
bewegliches / unbewegliches Vermögen	tangible / intangible assets
Beweis(mittel)	evidence
Beweise objektiv und unvoreingenommen abwägen	to weigh the evidence fairly and objectively
Beweise zulassen	to admit evidence
die Beweisführung anfechten	to challenge evidence
dokumentarische Beweisführung	documentary evidence
Beweislast	burden of proof
Beweismittel abnötigen, anfordern	to compel evidence
Beweismittel erlangen, erwirken, bekommen	to obtain evidence
Beweisregeln	rules of evidence
Beweisstück	physical exhibit
Bewerber nach Qualifikationen reihen	to rank law school candidates
Bewerber, Antragsteller; *auch:* Beschwerdeführer	applicant
eine Bewerbung ablehnen	to reject an application
bezeugen	to testify
pfändbare Bezüge	attachable earnings
Bezugspunkt, Richtgröße, Vergleichspunkt	benchmark
billig, billigkeitsgerichtlich	equitable

Billigkeit, Gerechtigkeit	justness
Brandgefahr herbeiführen	causing a danger of fire
Brandmal, Schandfleck, Stigma	stigma
Brandstiftung	arson
gesetzestreue Bürger	law-abiding citizens
Bürgschaft, Garantie	guarantee
abseits des Campus wohnen	to live off campus
am Campus wohnen	to reside on campus
charakteristisch, bezeichnend	distinctive
darlegen	to set forth
irrtümliche, ungenaue Darstellung	misrepresentation
darunterliegend, zugrundeliegend	underlying
Dauer, Laufzeit, Zeitdauer	duration
„Deal" im Strafverfahren	plea agreement, plea deal
delikt. Schadenersatz(anspruch)	tort (claim)
Deliktsrecht, Recht der unerlaubten Handlungen	(law of) torts, torts law
deponieren ("to lodge a claim")	to lodge
Diebstahl	theft
diktieren	to dictate
Diplom- / Doktorarbeit	thesis
Dokumente / Unterlagen (auf)bewahren	to preserve documents
Dokumente vorweisen, vorzeigen	to produce documents
Doppelbestrafung	double jeopardy
Doppelstudium	joint-degree program
unter Drogeneinfluss am Steuer	DWI (driving while intoxicated)
Druck ausüben	to exert pressure
Durchführung, Umsetzung	implementation
Durchführungsverordnung	executive order
durchsetzbar, erzwingbar, vollstreckbar, vollziehbar	enforceable
(Personen- / Haus-)Durchsuchung	search
dürftig, arm, verarmt	impoverished
Ebene, Rang, Stufe	rank
Ebene, Schicht	layer
Echtheitsprüfung, Beglaubigung, Beurkundung	authentication
Ehegattenunterhalt	alimony
Ehrenbeleidigungsklage	libel suit, libel action, action for slander
unter Eid	under oath
Eid, Schwur	oath
eidesstattliche Erklärung	affidavit
Einbruch	burglary
eindeutig, zweifelsfrei	unequivocally

Vokabular

Einhaltung (von Terminen)	adherence (to schedules)
Einheit, Gebilde, Organisation	entity
Einholung einer Strafregisterauskunft	record search
einkerkern / Einkerkerung	to incarcerate / incarceration
Einkünfte, Einnahmen, Ertrag	revenue
einschätzen, beurteilen, evaluieren	to evaluate
einschlägige Berufserfahrung	applicable experience
einschüchternd	intimidating
Einspruch abweisen	to overrule an objection
Einspruch stattgeben	to sustain an objection
Einspruch!	objection!
einstimmig	unanimous
eintreten, stattfinden, vorfallen	to occur
Einwilligung, Zustimmung, Erlaubnis	consent
im Einzelfall	on a case-by-case basis
einzeln, allein	solo
Einziehung	confiscation
Eliteuni	elite law school
Elitismus	elitism
Empfehlung, Verweis, Überweisung	referral
Empfehlung, Vorschlag	recommendation
eng ausgelegt	narrowly tailored
entlassen	dismissed
entlassen, absetzen, verabschieden, freisprechen	to discharge
entlassen, freilassen	to release
entlassen werden wegen schwerer Verfehlungen (im Amt)	to be dismissed for misbehavior in office
entschädigen, rückerstatten, rückvergüten	to reimburse
Entschädigung, Ersatz, Rückvergütung	reimbursement
(gerichtlich) entscheiden, urteilen, zuerkennen	to adjudicate
eine Entscheidung aufheben und an die untere Instanz zur neuerlichen E zurückverweisen	to reverse and remand
eine Entscheidung durchsetzen	to impose a decision
eine Entscheidung finden, ein Urteil fällen (bezogen auf die Geschworenen)	to render / reach a verdict
Entscheidung, Urteil, Zuerkennung	adjudication
Entscheidungssammlung	reporter, law reports
entsprechend, gemäß	in accordance with
erachten, halten für	to deem
Erbe	heir
Erbe, Erbschaft, Vererbung	inheritance
Erbrecht	inheritance law

erdulden, durchleben, erfahren	to undergo
Erfolgszurechnung	allocation of earnings
wesentliches Erfordernis, Bedürfnis	principal need
Erfüllung einer Verpflichtung	performance
Ergebnis, Folge, Auswirkung	outcome
erhalten, bekommen, empfangen	to receive
Erinnerung	recollection
erkennbar, wahrnehmbar	discernible
Erkennungs-, Identifikationsmittel	identification tools
ein Gesetz erlassen	to enact a law, to pass a law
erledigen, regeln; *auch:* loswerden	to dispose of sth
Ermessen	discretion, discretionary
nach billigem Ermessen	using equitable discretion
richterliches Ermessen	judicial discretion
ermitteln	investigate
ermittelt durch	determined by
ernennen, berufen, bestellen	to appoint
ernennen (einen Richter)	to appoint (a judge)
Erpressung	extortion
Ersatz-, alternativ	alternate
Ersatz, Vertreter	substitute
ersetzen, an Stelle von treten	to supersede
ertragreich, gewinnbringend, profitabel	profitable
nachdenken, in Erwägung ziehen, betrachten	to contemplate
etabliert, fest verwurzelt	entrenched
etwas betonen, hervorheben	to place emphasis on sth
Europarecht	EU law
fächerübergreifen, interdisziplinär	interdisciplinary
Fachkenntnis, Kompetenz, Sachverstand	expertise
Fahrlässigkeit	negligence
faires / ordentliches Verfahren, Rechtsstaatsprinzip	due process of law
Fall beim Berufungsgericht	a case on appeal
einen Fall verhandeln	to try a case
falsche Verdächtigung	casting false suspicion
falsches Geständnis	false confession
(Urkunden)Fälschung	forgery (of documents)
Familiengericht	domestic relations court, family court
Familienrecht	family law
Fehlverhalten, Ungehörigkeit	impropriety
Fehlverhalten, Verfehlung	misconduct
Festnahme, Arrest	detention

Vokabular

Fingerabdruck	fingerprint
Fixkosten	overhead
fliehen, flüchten	to flee
flüchtig, Flüchtling	fugitive
Folge, Reihe, Serie	series
fördern (gewisse Begabungen)	to foster (certain skills)
(be)fördern, unterstützen, voranbringen	to promote
fördern, voranbringen	to further
Forderung, Anspruch, Behauptung	claim
Förderung, Unterstützung	aid
Formatierung, Formatieren	formatting
Fortbildung	advance training
fortfahren, weitermachen	to proceed
ungelöste Fragen	unresolved issues
freiberuflich	free-lance
Freiheitsberaubung	deprivation of liberty
Freiraum, Spielraum	latitude
freisprechen	to acquit
Freispruch	acquittal
Friedensrichter	justice of the peace
Führung, Leitung, Verwaltung	conduct
Funkscanner	radio scanner
Geburt, Abstammung, Vererbung	descent
Gedanke, Idee, Vorstellung	notion
Gefahr	jeopardy
Gefangener, Häftling	prisoner
Gefängnis	jail / prison
gegenseitig, wechselseitig, einvernehmlich	mutual
Gegenseitigkeit, Wechselseitigkeit	reciprocity
Gegenstand der Untersuchung / Recherche	subject of investigation
Gegenstände / Besitzstücke wegnehmen, konfiszieren	to confiscate property
Gehalt, Bezüge	stipend
Gehalt, Vergütung	salary
Geiselnahme	hostage taking
Geisteswissenschaften	liberal arts, humanities
Geländer, Barriere	railing
Geld auf ein Konto überweisen	to transfer money to an account
Geldersatz	monetary award
Geldfälschung	counterfeiting of money, money forging
Geldmittel	funds
Geldstrafe, Geldbuße	fine

Geldwäsche	money laundering
Geldweitergabe / -übertragung	money transmitting
geltend machen, fordern, verlangen	to claim
gemeinsam / als Team unterrichten	to team-teach
genau, sorgfältig, fleißig	diligent
geneigt sein etwas zu tun	to be apt to do sth
Generalprävention	general deterrence
Gerät, Vorrichtung, Mittel	device, tool
Gerichtsakte	court file
Gerichtsbank; *auch:* Richter	bench
nichtrichterlicher Gerichtsbediensteter	court clerk
Gerichtsdiener, Gerichtsvollzieher, Verwalter	bailiff
Gerichtsmedizin	forensic medicine, medical examiner
gerichtsmedizinisch, forensisch	forensic
Gerichtsverfahren	legal procedure
Gerichtsverhandlung	trial
Gerücht	rumor
(ins)gesamt	aggregate
geschädigte Partei, Geschädigte(r)	injured party
Geschäftsabschluss	business transaction
Geschäftszahl, Registernummer	docket
Geschworene einberufen	to draft jurors
Geschworene(nbank)	jury
einen angehenden Geschworenen erfolgreich ablehnen	to strike (remove) a prospective juror from the panel
Geschworenenladung	jury summons
Geschworener	juror
Gesellschaft, Körperschaft	corporation
Gesellschafter, Teilhaber, Aktionär	shareholder
Gesellschaftskapital, Grundkapital	stock
Gesellschaftsrecht	corporate law
ein Gesetz erlassen, verordnen	to enact a law, to pass a law
gegen ein Gesetz verstoßen	to violate / break a law
Gesetz, das die Zulässigkeit von Beweisen regelt	code of evidence
Gesetzesbrecher	offender
Gesetzesbrecher verfolgen	to pursue an offender
Gesetzgebung	legislative enactment
gestaffelt	tiered
Geständnis	confession
Gewahrsam, Verwahrung	custody
häusliche Gewalt	domestic violence

Vokabular

Gewinnanteil, Dividende	dividend
gewissenhaft	conscientious
Gläubiger- / Schuldnerbegünstigung	preferential treatment of a creditor / debtor
Gleichrangiger, adj.: seinesgleichen	peer
gleichwertig sein mit	to be equivalent to
von der Grand Jury (siehe Seite 91) in den Anklagestand versetzt werden	to indict
Grenzstein, Meilenstein, Wahrzeichen	landmark
Grundausbildung	boot camp training
Grundsatz der Bindung an Vorentscheidungen	stare decisis
grundsätzlich, ständig, ausnahmslos	invariably
Gruppendruck	peer pressure
Haftbefehl	arrest warrant
vorzeitige Haftentlassung	parole
Haftpflichtversicherung	liability insurance
Haftstrafe, Freiheitsstrafe	custodial sentence
Haftung für fremdes Verschulden	vicarious liability
halten, aufrecht erhalten	to uphold
Handelsrecht	commercial law
Hausbesetzer, illegaler Siedler	squatter
Hausdurchsuchungsbefehl	search warrant
Hausfriedensbruch	trespass, home invasion
Hehlerei	receiving stolen property
herausbilden, entwickeln	to evolve
hervorbringen	to put forth
dreistufige Hierarchie	three-tiered hierarchy
juristische Hilfskraft	paralegal
Hinderungsgrund, Befreiung	excuse
Höflichkeit, Einverständnis	comity
Hörensagen	hearsay
Hörweite	earshot
Humanwissenschaften, Geisteswissenschaften	humanities
Hypothek auf Wohnhaus	home (equity) loan
zweitrangige Hypothek	second mortgage
Hypothek, Pfand, Belastung	mortgage
Identitätsnachweis, Legitimation	proof of identity
Immobilienrecht	real estate law
Indexklausel	threshold agreement
Industrie- / Wirtschaftsspionage	industrial / economic espionage
(Gefängnis)Insasse, Häftling	inmate
inskribieren	to register, to enroll

Inskription	registration, enrollment
Insolvenz	insolvency
Insolvenzgericht(sabteilung)	bancruptcy court
Insolvenzrecht	bankruptcy law
Insolvenzstraftaten	crimes of insolvency
integrieren, umfassen, mit einbeziehen	to incorporate
zwingendes Interesse	compelling interest
Interessenkollision	conflict of interests
Interessensgebiet	field of interest
isolieren	to insulate
jemanden unter Anklage stellen, anklagen, anschuldigen	to charge somebody (with)
jemanden wegen etw vor Gericht bringen	to arraign somebody for something
jm eine Sache vorenthalten, jm einer Sache berauben	to deprive sb of sth
jm einweisen, instruieren	to brief
jm erkennungsdienstlich behandeln	to fingerprint and photograph sb
jm untersagen etwas zu tun	to enjoin sb from doing sth
jm vor Gericht stellen	to try somebody
Jugendgericht	juvenile court
Jurist	lawyer
juristische Lehrveranstaltung / Vorlesung	law class
Justiz, Justizgewalt, Rechtssystem	judiciary
Justizvollzugsanstalt	correctional facility
Justizvollzugsbeamter	correctional officer (CO)
Kanonisches Recht	canon law
Kapitalanlagebetrug	capital investment fraud
Kaution	bail
auf Kaution freilassen	to release on bail
Kindesmisshandlung	child abuse
eine Klage zurückweisen oder abweisen	to dismiss a case / lawsuit
Klagebeitritt, (Neben)Intervention, Streitgenossenschaft	joinder (of parties)
Klagegrund, Klagsgrund	cause of action
klagen	to sue
Kläger	plaintiff
Klageschrift, zivilrechtliche Klage	civil complaint / civil action / civil lawsuit
Klageverbindung, Klagebeitritt, Intervention	joinder
(eckige) Klammer	bracket
(runde) Klammer	parenthesis
Klausel	provision
Kodifizierung	codification
Kollisionsrecht	conflict of laws

Vokabular

einen Kompromiss regeln durch	to compromise
in die Konkursmasse fallend(es Vermögen)	nonexempt (assets)
im Konsulatsweg / diplomatischen Weg	via / through consular (diplomatic) channels
Konsumentenschutz	consumer protection
Konto einfrieren, sperren,	to freeze an account
Kontrolle ausüben	to exercise control
Kontrolle, Herrschaft, Gewalt	governance
Konzern	affiliated group (of companies)
Körperschaftsteuer	corporate tax
Körperverletzung	physical injury / bodily injury / bodily harm
schwere / gefährliche Körperverletzung	grievous bodily harm
angefallene Kosten	costs incurred
Kredit	loan, credit
Kreditbetrug	credit fraud
Kreditrückzahlungshilfe	loan repayment assistance
Kreuzverhör	cross examination
Kritiker, Bewerter	critic
praxisbezogener Kurs	clinical course
Kurzdarstellung, Abriss; adj.: knapp, kurz	brief
kurzerhand, stichwortartig; Stenografie	shorthand
Laien, Laienrichter	lay persons / lay assessors
Laienrichter, Schöffe	lay judge
Law-school-Bewerber	law school applicant
lebenslang im Dienst stehen	to serve life term
Lebenslauf	resume, curriculum vitae
Lehre, Lehrverhältnis	apprenticeship
Lehrling, Auszubildende ('Azubi')	apprentice
Lehrplan, Studienplan	curriculum
Lehrveranstaltung, Vorlesung	law class
sich leisten können	to afford
leisten, etw tun, vollbringen	to perform
Leugnung, Verweigerung	denial
lizenziert, zugelassen, zugesagt	licensed
lohnend, rentabel, lukrativ	lucrative
Lohnpfändung	attachment of earnings
lösen, beseitigen, aufklären	to resolve
Lösung	resolution
zwingende Maßnahmen	coercive measures
Mediator, Schlichter, "Mittelsmann"	mediator
mehrfach, vielfach, multipel	multiple
Meineid	perjury

Menschenhandel	alien smuggling
Menschenraub	kidnapping
mild, glimpflich	lenient
missachten, nicht beachten	to disregard
Missachtung gerichtlicher Anweisungen, Nichterscheinen vor Gericht	contempt of court
vorsätzliche Missachtung	willful disregard
Missbrauch von Ausweispapieren	misuse of identification papers
Missbrauch von Scheck- und Kreditkarten	misuse of check and credit cards
Missbrauch, Zweckentfremdung	misuse
Missetäter	wrongdoer
Mitbeteiligung, gemeinsame Risikobeteiligung	co-venturing
andere Mitglieder des Senats	fellow panelists
Mittäter	accessory, accomplice, co-perpetrator
(Einsatz-, Betriebs-, Produktions-)Mittel	resource
Mord	homicide, (first degree) murder
mutwillig, böswillig, niederträchtig	malicious
Nachforschung, Ermittlung, Untersuchung, Befragung	inquiry
nachklingend, zurückbleibend, verweilend	lingering
Nachlassabwicklung	settlement of estates
üble Nachrede	malicious gossip
Nachteil, Schaden	damage / harm / loss
(zum) Nachteil, Schaden (von)	(to the) detriment (of)
nachweislich, auffindbar	traceable
Namensschild der Geschworenen	juror identification badge
Nationalisierung	nationalization
Neigung, Vorliebe	bias
Nennwert	denomination
nicht obsorgeberechtigt	non-custodial
nicht zu schlichten	non-arbitrable
Nichtbeachtung (von Regeln)	disregard (of rules)
Nichterfüllung, Nichtübereinstimmung, Diskrepanz	non-compliance
nichtig erklären (einen Vertrag)	to vacate (a contract)
(eine Entscheidung) als nichtig aufheben, annullieren	to vacate, to declare void
sich niederlassen	to reside
Notar (im Common- / Civil-law-System)	notary public, civil law notary
Notar-Anderkonto	notary trust account
Note	grade
obgleich, obschon, wenn auch	albeit
Objektivität, Unbefangenheit, Unparteilichkeit	impartiality

Vokabular

Obsorge, Sorgerecht (für Kinder)	child custody
offen, ungelöst	unresolved
offenlegen, offenbaren, mitteilen	to disclose
öffentliches Recht	public law
Opfer, Betroffene(r), Verunglückte(r)	victim
Paragraph	article
Partei	party
unzufriedene Partei	dissatisfied party
Pattsituation	stalemate (situation)
verstorbene Person	deceased person
jur. Person, Körperschaft	corporation aggregate
Personen ausfindig machen	to locate persons
pfändbare Bezüge	attachable earnings
Pfändung	attachment
Pfändung / Beschlagnahme einer Forderung	garnishment
Pfändung, Vollziehung, *auch:* Hinrichtung	execution
Pflegschaftsrecht	dependency laws
pingelig, selektiv	selective
Plädoyer, Schriftsatz, Verteidigungsschrift	pleading
plausibel, vernünftig, verständlich	reasonable
einen Präzedenfall außer Kraft setzen, aufheben	to overrule a precedent
Präzedenzfall	precedent (case)
bindender Präzedenzfall	binding precedent
Präzedenzfall einen außer Kraft setzen, aufheben	to overrule a precedent
einem Präzedenzfall folgen	to follow a precedent
einen Präzedenzfall schaffen	to establish a precedent
Privatrecht	private law
zur/auf Probe	probationary
Professionalität, fachliche Qualifikation	professionalism
Prostitution	prostitution
Protokoll	transcript
Provision, Vergütung	commission
Prozess führen / leiten	to conduct a trial / noun: conduct
nach dem Prozess	post-trial
Prozess, Gerichtsverfahren	litigation
Prozessanwalt	litigator, trial attorney
Prozessgericht, erstinstanzliches Gericht	trial court
Prüfer	trier
eine Prüfung machen müssen	to be required to sit a test
Prüfungskommission	examination board
Punktezahl	score

(festes) Quoten-, Kontingentierungssystem	(fixed) quota system
Raub	robbery
räumen, ein Gebäude	to vacate a building
in Rechnung stellen	to charge
kanonisches Recht	canon law
auf ein Recht verzichten	to waive a right
rechtfertigen, verteidigen	vindicate
Rechtsabteilung	legal division, legal department
Rechtsanwalt	attorney
(örtliche) Rechtsanwaltskammer	(local) bar association
Rechtsbehelf, Rechtsmittel	relief
Rechtsbeistand, Rechtsberater, rechtlicher Vertreter	legal counsel / representative
Rechtsdurchsetzung	law enforcement
Rechtseinwand der mangelnden Schlüssigkeit	demurrer
Rechtsethik	legal ethics
Rechtsfehler, Rechtsirrtum	error of law
Rechtsmittelgericht, Rechtsmittelinstanz	appellate court, court of appeals
Rechtsquellen	sources of law
eine Rechtssache an die untere Instanz zurückverweisen	to remand (a case)
Rechtsschutzversicherung	legal costs (expense/s) insurance
Rechtsstaatlichkeit, Rechtsgrundsatz	rule of law
Rechtsstreit, Prozess; *auch:* (An)Klage	law dispute, legal dispute, lawsuit
Rechtswissenschaft, Jurisprudenz, Rechtslehre	jurisprudence
regulieren, steuern, leiten	to govern
reihend, Rangordnung	ranking
renommiert, wohlbekannt, angesehen, namhaft	renowned
Reputation, Ansehen, Ruf	reputation
einen Richter ablehnen	to recuse a judge
einen Richter ernennen	to appoint a judge
Richter sein	to be on the Bench
vorsitzender Richter	chief justice, presiding judge
sich der Richterbank nähern	to approach the bench
Richterzimmer, Kammer	chamber
Richtwert (Punktezahl)	benchmark score
Rückerstattung, Zurückzahlung, Wiederherstellung	restitution
Rückgabe von Gütern	restitution of goods
Rücktritt	resignation
rückwirkend	retroactive
Rückzug, Ausstieg, Rücktritt	withdrawal
Ruhigstellung, Einfrierung, Immobilisierung	immobilization

Vokabular

Sachbezogenheit, Erheblichkeit	relevancy
Sachenrecht	property law
den Sachverhalt feststellen	to find the facts
unstrittiger Sachverhalt	uncontested facts
Sachverhalt, Tatsachenfeststellungen	facts (of a case)
Sachverständiger	expert witness
Sachwalterschaft(-sgericht)	guardianship (court)
(an)sammeln, erfassen	to gather
Schaden / Mangel beheben	to remedy
Schaden erleiden	to suffer a harm / loss
Schaden, Nachteil	damage / harm / loss
Schadenersatz zusprechen	to award damages
Schadenersatz, Entschädigungszahlungen	compensatory damages
Schadenersatzrecht	law of torts / tort law
Schadensbegrenzung, Schadensminderung(spflicht)	damage mitigation
verschuldensunabhängige Scheidung	no-fault divorce
Scheingericht, hypothetisches Gericht	mock court / moot court
Scheinprozess, Probeverfahren	mock trial
Schicht(en)	stratum, strata
Schichtung, Stratifizierung	stratification
schick, raffiniert, hochtrabend	fancy
Schiedsabrede	arbitral agreement
Schiedsgericht	arbitral court, arbitration tribunal
Schiedsgerichtsbarkeit	arbitral jurisdiction
Schiedsklausel, Schlichtungsklausel	arbitration clause
Schiedsrichter	referee
Schiedsrichter, Schlichter, Richter am Schiedsgericht	arbitrator
Schiedsspruch	arbitral panel decision
Schiedsverfahren	arbitration (procedure) arbitral procedure, process
bindendes Schiedsverfahren, bindende Schlichtung	binding arbitration
schlichtbar, schiedsrichterlich	arbitrable
Schlichter, Vermittler, Schiedsmann	arbiter
Schmerzen(s)geld	pain and suffering
Schriftart, Schrift	typeface
Schriftführer(in)	court reporter
(prozessvorbereitende) Schriftsätze	(preliminary) pleadings
Schriftstück, Urkunde, Erlass	writ
Schuldeingeständnis des Angeklagten	guilty plea
kreditwürdige Schuldner	creditworthy debtors
Schuldrecht	law of obligation

Schutzmaßnahme, Absicherung	safeguard
schweigen, stumm bleiben	to remain silent
Schwelle, Abgrenzung	threshold
Schwundquote	attrition rate
Seminar	seminar style course
Senat	senate, panel
Sicherheitsverwahrung	preventive detention
Siegel des Notars	notary seal
Siegel, Stempel; *auch:* Verschluss, Dichtung	seal
Skrupel, Bedenken	scruples
Sonderrecht, Begünstigung	privilege
gemeinsames Sorgerecht, gemeinsame Obsorge	joint custody
Sorgfalt, Fleiß, Eifer, Gewissenhaftigkeit	diligence
Sorgfaltspflicht	due diligence, due care
Sozialrecht	social law
Sozialwissenschaften, Gesellschaftswissenschaften	social sciences
Soziologie	sociology
Spezifikationserfordernis	particularity requirement
verbotene (Glücks)Spiele	gambling offenses
spöttisch, höhnisch	derisively
gewählter Sprecher der Jury	foreperson
Spreu von Weizen trennen	to sort the wheat from the chaff
Spurensicherungsexperte	forensic expert
vertragschließender Staat	contracting state
Staatsanwalt	prosecutor
Staatsanwalt (in den US-Bundesstaaten)	(assistant) state attorney (ASA), (deputy) district attorney (DDA)
auf Staatskosten	at government expense
Stadtverordnung	city ordinance
Statut(en)	bylaw(s)
Statuten festlegen, übernehmen	to adopt bylaws
gutachterliche / fachmännische Stellungnahme	advisory opinion
Steuererklärung	tax return
Steuerhinterziehung	tax evasion
steuern, lenken, führen	to steer
steuerpflichtig, zu versteuern	taxable
Steuerrecht	tax law
Steuerwesen	taxation
Stipendium	fellowship, scholarship, grant
stolz, erhaben, hochmütig	lofty
unter Strafandrohung vorladen	to subpoena

Vokabular

Strafe	punishment / penalty / sentence
Strafprozessrecht	criminal procedure
Strafrecht	criminal law, penal law
Strafregisterauskunft	criminal record
Strafregisterauskunft einholen	to perform a record search
Strafschadenersatz	punitive damages
Straftat begehen	to commit a crime
Straftat erleichtern, unterstützen, ermöglichen	to facilitate an offense
Straftat vortäuschen	feigning a crime
niederträchtige Straftat, Schandtat	infamous crime
Strafvereitelung	obstruction of punishment
außer Streit gestellter Sachverhalt	admitted facts
Streit; adj.: strittig	moot
Streitgenossenschaft, Nebenintervention	joinder of parties
Streitwert	amount in controversy
Student im zweiten Studienjahr	sophomore
Studiengang, Hauptfach	major
Studiengebühr	tuition
stumm, still, sprachlos	silent, mute
sich auf etw stützen, sich auf etw verlassen	to rely on
Subventionsbetrug	subsidy fraud
Suggestivfrage	leading
symbolisch, äußerst gering	nominal
strittige Tatsache	fact in dispute
Telekommunikationsbetrug	wire fraud, mail fraud
tendieren, neigen	to incline
Termine einhalten	to adhere to deadlines
Testament, letzter Wille	will
Todesstrafe	death penalty
Totenglocke	death knell
Totschlag	manslaughter, second degree murder
fahrlässige Tötung	negligent manslaughter
(Kosten) tragen, bestreiten	to defray
Treuhand, Vermögensverwaltung	trust
Treuhänder	fiduciary
Treuhandkonto	notary trust account
Übereinkunft, gütliche Einigung	compromise
übereinstimmen, beipflichten	to concur
überfüllt	overcrowded
Übergewicht, Überwiegen	preponderance
überlastet	overburdened

Übermittlung, Übertragung	transmission
überprüfen	to review
im Ermessen des Rechtmittelgerichts liegende Überprüfung der Entscheidung (der untergeordneten Instanz)	discretionary review
(genaue) Überprüfung, Untersuchung	scrutiny
übertreffen, übersteigen, überbieten	to surpass
umbuchen, umschreiben, anweisen	to transfer
umfassen; *auch:* umgeben, umschließen	to encompass
umgehen	to bypass
Umlauf	circulation
umsatzstark	high-grossing
harte Umstände, Not, Mühsal	hardship
umwandeln, transformieren	to convert
Umweltrecht	environmental law
Unannehmlichkeit, Unbequemlichkeit	inconvenience
unbarmherzig	merciless
unbefristet, unbegrenzt; *auch:* ungenau	indefinite
unbefugter Gebrauch eines Fahrzeuges	unauthorized use of a vehicle
unerlaubt, verboten, ungesetzlich	illicit
unerlaubte Veranstaltung eines Glücksspiels	illegal gambling, unauthorized organization of a Game of chance
unerlaubter Suchtstoffverkehr	illicit drug trafficking
Unfähigkeit, Inkompetenz	incompetence
Unfähigmachung, Untauglichkeit	incapacitation
ungebührlich, unpassend, ungeeignet	improper
ungehemmt, hemmungslos	uninhibited
ungeheuerlich, unerhört, entsetzlich	egregious
unscharf, undeutlich, verschwommen, vage, unklar	hazy
Unschuldsvermutung	presumption of innocence
unstrittig	uncontroversial, indisputable uncontentious, undisputed
(Ehegatten)Unterhalt(szahlungen), Alimente	alimony
Unterhaltspflicht	obligation to pay child support
Verletzung der Unterhaltspflicht	failure to pay child support
Unterlagen beschaffen, zur Verfügung stellen	to supply records
unterlassen, auslassen, weglassen	to omit
unterlassen, von etw Abstand nehmen	to refrain from
spekulatives Unternehmen	venturing enterprise
Unternehmensgewinn	corporate profit
Unternehmensschulden	corporate dept
Unterordnung, Subordnination	subordination

Vokabular

unterscheiden, auseinanderhalten	to distinguish
soziologische Unterschiede	sociological differences
kostenlose rechtliche Unterstützung	free legal assistance
Untersuchungsgegenstand	object of investigation
Untersuchungsrichter, Ermittlungsrichter	investigative judge
Unterwerfung, Unterjochung	subjugation, submission
unterworfen	to be subject to
Untreue	breach of trust
unvereinbar, unversöhnlich, unverträglich	irreconcilable
Unverträglichkeit	incompatibility
unverzichtbar, unumgänglich, notwendig	indispensable
Unzüchtigkeit	obscenity
unzulässig	inadmissible
Urkundenfälschung	falsification of documents
Urkundenunterdrückung	suppression of documents
Urteilsaufhebung	reversal of a decision / a verdict
schriftliche Urteilsausfertigung	case report (opinion), court opinion
Urteilsspruch der Geschworenen	verdict
Vaterschaftsprozess, Vaterschaftsklage	paternity suit
verbergen, kaschieren, verhehlen	to conceal
verbieten	to outlaw
verbindend	conjunctive
verbindlich	binding
Verbindung	liaison
Verbrechen	felony
organisiertes Verbrechen	organized crime, racketeering
verbunden mit, einhergehend mit	associated with
Verdächtige(r), vermutliche(r) Täter(in)	suspect
Verdienst, Leistung	merit
verdünnen	to dilute
vereiteln, verwischen, verwirren	to confound
vererbbar	inheritable
schnelles Verfahren	speedy trial
Verfahren, (Prozess)Verlauf, Vorgehen	proceeding
Verfahrensfehler	procedural mistake / error
staatl. finanzierter Verfahrenshelfer im Strafverfahren	public defender
Verfall, Untergang, Rückgang	decline
Verfassungsrecht	constitutional law
wegen schweren Verfehlungen entlassen werden	to be dismissed for misbehavior in office
verfolgen, einen Gesetzesbrecher	to pursue an offender
verfügen, verordnen, Gesetzeskraft geben	to enact

gerichtliche Verfügung	injunction
Vergehen	misdemeanor
kleines Vergehen, Kleinkriminalität	petty offense, petty crime
Vergewaltigung	rape
Vergleich	settlement
Vergleichsgespräche	settlement negotiations
Verhandlung	negotiation
Verhandlungsteam	litigation team
Verkehrsgericht	traffic court
verkünden, öffentlich bekanntgeben	to promulgate
Verlag(shaus, gesellschaft)	publishing company
Verlassenschaftsgericht	probate court
Verletzung der Unterhaltspflicht	failure to pay child support
Verletzung einer außervertraglichen Pflicht	breach of a non-contractual duty
Verleumdung, Beleidigung, üble Nachrede	libel, slander, defamation
Vermeidung, Meiden	avoidance
Vermerk, Bezeichnung	notation
Vermischung; zusammenmischend	commingling
vermitteln	to mediate
unbewegliches Vermögen	personalty
vermutlicher, mutmaßlicher Beschuldigter	putative defendant
Vermutung, Mutmaßung	conjecture
Veröffentlichung, Publikation	publication
verpflichtend, bindend	compulsory
verpflichtet sein etw zu tun	to be obliged to do sth
Versäumnisurteil	default judgment, judgment by default
Verschleierung unrechtmäßig erlangter Vermögenswerte	concealment of unlawfully acquired assets
Verschleppung	abduction
Versicherungsbetrug	abuse of insurance
Versteigerung	auction
Verstorbener, Erblasser	decedent
verstoßen, gegen ein Gesetz	to violate a law
verstreichen, vergehen	to elapse
Verstrickungsbruch, Siegelbruch	breach of attachment, breach of seals
Vertagung, Unterbrechung	continuance
Vertrag abschließen	to close a contract
Vertrag für nichtig erklären	to vacate a contract
vertragliche Verpflichtung	contractual obligation
Vertragsbruch; gegen eine vertragliche Verpflichtung verstoßen	breach of contract; to breach a contract

Vokabular

Vertragspartei	contracting party, party to a contract / an agreement
Vertragsrecht	law of contracts, contract law
vertraulich	confidential
Vertreter, Rechtsfreund, Anwalt	counsel
(rechtl.) Vertreter	(legal) counsel
(Stell)Vertreter, Bevollmächtigter	deputy
Veruntreuung, Unterschlagung	embezzlement
verurteilen / Verurteilung	to convict /conviction
Verwahrungsbruch	breach of official custody
Verwaltungsrecht	administrative law
verwirken, verlustig gehen, einbüßen	to forfeit
Vielfalt, Unterschiedlichkeit, Diversität	diversity
Völkermord	genocide
Völkerrecht	public international law
etwas vorantreiben, beschleunigen	to expedite sth
Vorarbeit, vorbereitende Maßnahme; vorbereitende Tätigkeit	preliminary
Voraussetzung, Bedingung	condition
vorbehaltlich, anstehend	pending
vorbringen, behaupten	to allege
(Parteien)Vorbringen, Behauptung	allegation / contention
vorenthalten, zurückhalten	to withhold
vorgefasst	preconceived
vorgesehen sein zu, sollen	to be supposed to
vorgesehen, bestimmt, festgelegt	designated
vorherbestimmt, vorher festgelegt	predetermined
Vorlesung	lecture, course taught in the confrontational manner
vorletzte(r)	penultimate
vorprozessual	pre-trial
den Vorsitz (eines) Rechtsmittelsenates führen	to chair a panel
den Vorsitz führen, leiten	to preside
Vorteilsannahme	acceptance of a benefit
Vorurteil, Befangenheit	prejudice
Vorwärtskommen, Beförderung, (beruflicher) Aufstieg	advancement
vorwiegen, vorherrschen	predominate
vorwiegend, vorherrschend, überlegen	predominant
wagend, riskierend	venturing
Waisenhaus	orphanage
an Wert verlieren, abwerten, mindern	depreciate

Wertigkeit, Valenz	valence
Wertpapier	security
Wertpapierrecht	securities law
Wettbewerbsrecht	competition law
Widerklage, Gegenforderung, Gegenanspruch	counterclaim
widerlegen, anfechten, entkräften	to refute, to rebut
Widerlegung	rebuttal
widerwillig, zögernd	reluctant
wiedergeben, reproduzieren, kopieren	to reproduce
Wiedergutmachung	compensation
(Aus)Wirkung, Aufprall	impact
Wissenschaftler, Gelehrter, Schüler	scholar
wohlgesonnen, wohlwollend, mitfühlend	sympathetic
Zahl(zeichen, symbol), Ziffer	numeral
Zelle	holding cell
Zeuge	(lay) witness
Zeuge (der eigenen / gegnerischen Partei)	witness (friendly / hostile)
(einen) Zeugen vorbereiten (auf die Verhandlung)	to coach a witness
Zeugenaussage	testimony
Zeugenstand	witness stand
(den) Zeugenstand betreten	to take the stand
amtliches Zeugnis / Aufstellung aller Einzelnoten	(academic) transcript
Zitierung, Zitat, Fundstelle; *auch:* Vorladung	citation
Zivilprozessrecht	civil procedure
Zivilrecht	civil law
zivilrechtliche(r) Rechtsbehelf / Sanktion	civil law remedy
zuerkennen, zusprechen; Zuspruch	(to) award
Zufallsauswahl	random selection
Zuflucht, Rechtsweg	recourse
zufügen	to inflict
Zuhälterei	pimping
zulassen, akkreditieren, anerkennen	to accredit
zulässig	admissible
Zulassung / Aufnahme zur juristischen Fakultät	law school admission
Zulassung gewähren	to grant admission
Zurückbehaltungsrecht, Pfandrecht	lien
zurückverfolgbar	retraceable
zusammensetzen, bilden	to constitute
zusammentragen, zusammenstellen	to compile, to impanel (a jury)
zusammentreffen, versammeln	to convene, to assemble

Vokabular

Zuspruch, Zuerkennung, Zahlungsverpflichtung des Beklagten	trial award
Zuständigkeit der Rechtsmittelinstanz	jurisdiction
fehlende örtliche Zuständigkeit	mistake in venue
originäre Zuständigkeit	original jurisdiction
spezielle, generelle Zuständigkeit	limited / general jurisdiction
Zuständigkeit, Gerichtsbakreit; *auch:* Rechtsprechung, Jurisdiktion	jurisdiction
Zustellung	service of process
Zustellungen vornehmen	to provide service of process, to serve (documents)
Zwang, Nötigung	coercion, compulsion
zwangsräumen, gewaltsam vertreiben	to evict
zweigeteilt, zweigestuft	two-tier(ed)
zwingen, nötigen	to compel
zwingend	compelling